W9-BFP-087

Setting Up A Linux Intranet Server

Visual Black Book

Hidenori Tsuji   Acrobyte   Takashi Watanabe

 CORIOLIS

The Coriolis Group:

President, CEO
Keith Weiskamp

Publisher
Steve Sayre

Acquisitions Editor
Stephanie Wall

Marketing Specialist
Michele Shoen

Project Editor
Don Eamon

Technical Reviewer
Ivan McDonagh

Production Coordinator
Kim Eoff

Cover Designer
Jody Winkler

Translation By DNA Media
Services Inc:

President, CEO
Steven Forth

Project Manager/Editor
Tim Oftebro

Editing Advisor/Coordinator
Ian McKenzie

Project Manager
Dave Paslawski

Layout Designer
Junko Izumi

Production Coordinator
Marcel Cariou

User Functionality Tester
Slava Tskachenko

Setting Up A Linux Intranet Server Visual Black Book

© 2000 Acrobyte and Impress Corporation
Dekiru Linux Server Kochikuhen
©1999 Acrobyte and Impress Corporation
Original edition published in Japan by Impress Corporation.
All rights reserved.

English Edition Published By The Coriolis Group.
This book may not be duplicated in any way without the express written consent of the publisher, except in the form of brief excerpts or quotations for the purposes of review. The information contained herein is for the personal use of the reader and may not be incorporated in any commercial programs, other books, databases, or any kind of software without written consent of the publisher. Making copies of this book or any portion for any pupose other than your own is a violation of United States copyright laws.

Limits Of Liability And Disclaimer Of Warranty
The author and publisher of this book have used their best efforts in preparing the book and the programs contained in it. These efforts include the development, research, and testing of the theories and programs to determine their effectiveness. The author and publisher make no warranty of any kind, expressed or implied, with regard to these programs or the documentation contained in this book.
The author and publisher shall not be liable in the event of incidental or consequential damages in connection with, or arising out of, the furnishing, performance, or use of the programs, associated instructions, and/or claims of productivity gains.

Trademarks
Trademarked names appear throughout this book. Rather than list the names and entities that own the trademarks or insert a trademark symbol with each mention of the tramarked name, the publisher states that it is using the names for editorial purposes only and to the benefit of the trademark owner, with no intention of infringing upon that tradmark.

The Coriolis Group, LLC
14455 N. Hayden Road Suite 220
Scottsdale, Arizona 85260

480/483-0192
FAX 480/483-0193
http://www.coriolis.com

Library of Congress Cataloging-in-Publication Data
Tsuji, Hidenori, 1973-
     Setting up a Linux Server Visual Black Book/by Hidenori Tsuji and Takashi Watanabe.
     p. cm.
     Includes index.
     ISBN 1-57610-568-7
     1. Linux. 2. Client/server computing. I. Watanabe, Takashi, 1975-. II. Title.
QA76.9.C55 T78   2000
005.4'4769--dc21

                                                                    99-045421
                                                                         CIP

Printed in the United States of America
10   9   8   7   6   5   4   3   2   1

14455 North Hayden Road • Suite 220 • Scottsdale, Arizona 85260

Dear Reader:

The CoriolisOpen™ Press was founded to create a very elite group of books: the ones you keep closest to your machine. Sure, everyone would like to have the Library of Congress at arm's reach, but in the real world, you have to choose the books you rely on every day very carefully.

To win a place for our books on that coveted shelf beside your PC, we guarantee several important qualities in every book we publish. These qualities are:

- *Technical accuracy* - It's no good if it doesn't work. Every CoriolisOpen™ Press book is reviewed by technical experts in the topic field, and is sent through several editing and proofreading passes in order to create the piece of work you now hold in your hands.

- *Innovative editorial design* - We've put years of research and refinement into the ways we present information in our books. Our books' editorial approach is uniquely designed to reflect the way people learn new technologies and search for solutions to technology problems.

- *Practical focus* - We put only pertinent information into our books and avoid any fluff. Every fact included between these two covers must serve the mission of the book as a whole.

- *Accessibility* - The information in a book is worthless unless you can find it quickly when you need it. We put a lot of effort into our indexes, and heavily cross-reference our chapters, to make it easy for you to move right to the information you need.

Here at The Coriolis Group we have been publishing and packaging books, technical journals, and training materials since 1989. We're programmers and authors ourselves, and we take an ongoing active role in defining what we publish and how we publish it. We have put a lot of thought into our books; please write to us at **ctp@coriolis.com** and let us know what you think. We hope that you're happy with the book in your hands, and that in the future, when you reach for software development and networking information, you'll turn to one of our books first.

Keith Weiskamp
President and CEO

Jeff Duntemann
VP and Editorial Director

About The Authors

Hidenori Tsuji
The Linux and Unix operating systems are Hidenori's life; not only in his everyday research, but also in his part-time jobs. Presently pursuing a Ph.D. at Tokyo University researching next-generation high-performance microprocessor architecture, he supports himself with various part-time work, including managing Unix workstations, configuring networks, programming and writing books. He has written books including *Setting Up a Linux Intranet Server* (Impress) and *A Practical guide to Dial-Up Routers* (Softbank Press).
Hidenori Tsuji E-mail: **hide@hide.net**

Acrobyte
Acrobyte's focus is on PC-related books and magazines, but is also involved in various projects, from software development and production of multimedia content right through to installing Unix OS systems and assembling servers for clients. Acrobyte is based in Akihabara in Tokyo. They supervised the translation of *Windows 98 Bible*, *Windows 98 Bible Professional*, *Windows 98 Secrets*, *Windows 98 Registry Blackbook*, and the *Dekiru Windows 98* (all by Impress).
URL: **www.acrobyte.co.jp/**

Takashi Watanabe
Takashi Watanabe started in the computer world by spending half of his time at elementary school writing frustratingly dysfunctional sample programs in FamilyBasic. After toying with N88BASIC and MS-DOS, in 1996 he made the move to Linux. At present, he is a graduate student at Waseda University and uses Linux at home and Solaris and FreeBSD at school. His favorite programming function is getopt_long. His main pastime is playing with the search engine Verno.
Verno: **http://verno.ueda.info.waseda.ac.jp/**
E-mail: **watanabe@hide.net**

Acknowledgments

The Coriolis Group would like to thank the people who made things work at the Scottsdale part of this project: Stephanie Wall, acquisitions editor, whose drive and perseverance got this project off the ground; Don Eamon, project editor; Ivan McDonagh, technical reviewer, who--although in Western Australia-- was instrumental in finessing the accuracy of the text and images; April Eddy, copyeditor; Kim Eoff, production coordinator; and Jody Winkler, cover designer. Coriolis would also like to thank Dan Fiverson (our in-house Linux connection) and Geoff Leach of Impress Group (for quick answers and much help with the fine points raised during all of the project's phases.

DNA Media Services Inc. would like to thank the people who contributed to the translation, localization and production of this book. Tim B. Oftebro, Junko Izumi, Dave Paslawski, JianPing Luo, Marcel Cariou, Masato Ishida, Slava Tkachenko, Ian Mackenzie, Mark Matisoff, Dave Burgess and all the rest of the DNA Media staff.

Contents At A Glance

Table Of Contents

Chapter 4

Chapter 7
Using Linux As A Macintosh File Server

.

Preface

Recently, Linux has been in the spotlight. The reasons for Linux's popularity include dissatisfaction with personal computer environments such as Windows, a desire to explore the concept of open-source software, and the attraction of using a cost-free and easy-to-use operating system.

It is possible, however, to lose your way when attempting to use Linux for the first time. This is one reason why this Unix-like OS has, like the rest of the Unix family, a reputation for being difficult to use. It is true that Linux can be more intimidating than the more familiar and intuitive Windows or Macintosh OSs, but this is often due to a lack of familiarity with Linux. You don't need to be intimidated by Linux if you have some knowledge and proper training. With Linux, a profound world—far different from that of Windows and Macintosh—will open up to you.

When using Linux, it's important to get to know the OS. However, the best shortcut to mastering Linux is to use it with a specific goal in mind. Your overall objective will be to set up an easy-to-use intranet server that will serve both Windows and Macintosh workstations. Your goal, then, is twofold: to understand Linux and to set up a practical intranet server. This book gives you the best of both worlds: true hands-on training with Linux, all in an easy-to-use, visual format, that results in an inexpensive intranet server.

When you finish this book, you'll have a more concrete view of Linux. Because the first step in Linux is intranets, the focus of this book is restricted to this area. This book will use intranets to guide your first steps into the world of Linux.

In conclusion, I would like to thank my friends, who advised me in their capacity as Unix users, and Mr. Kazuhiro Fukuura and other staff members in the Impress editorial department.

The Authors, February 1999

About This Book

This book describes how to build a small-scale *LAN* (local area network) using Linux (Red Hat Linux 6.0) as a server. Linux requires many initial settings before you can use it as a server, and the sequence of the settings you choose is very important. Please check the sections on basic settings and, in particular; be sure to read the following chapters:

• **Chapter 1 Linux Basics**

This chapter introduces the components you will need when you build a server. If you are new to networks, you should read this chapter thoroughly.

• **Chapter 2 Installing Linux**

This chapter describes how to install Linux. It deals with the basics, so look it over carefully.

• **Chapter 3 Mastering The Basic Operations Of Linux**

This chapter explains the basic operations of the Linux OS. Newcomers to Linux should first grasp the basic operations outlined in this chapter.

• **Chapter 4 Registering Linux Users**

This chapter describes the first step in using Linux: registering users.

• **Chapter 5 Using Linux From Windows And Macintosh**

This chapter gives details on connecting to a network. If you want to set up a network, read this chapter.

The remaining chapters are broken down into specific topics, such as connecting Windows and Macintosh and Web and mail settings. To avoid making incorrect settings when you are setting up the Linux intranet server, read all the chapters, in order, from Chapter 1.

How To Use The Command Notation In This Book

Command Notation

Command line operations are described here.

A history of your previous choices is indicated in gray. Use this history to confirm the operation just prior to executing it.

Commands that you must enter are indicated by bold characters. If ⏎ is displayed next to a command, press the Enter key after typing the command.

```
[root@server /root]# cd /usr/local
[root@server local]# cd / ⏎
[root@server /]# _
```

Shows a description of the location from the command prompt. Use this to confirm the current directory and user.

About Red Hat Linux 6

Red Hat Linux 6.0 from Red Hat Software is available in two ways: either on CD-ROM or by download from the Internet. For all exercises in this book, we used the CD version of Red Hat Linux 6. If you purchase the CD-ROM, you will also receive additional open source and commercial software packages for Red Hat Linux. The Linux configuration files are also included on the disk. These files will be necessary as you read through the book. If you want to download the Red Hat Linux distribution from the Internet, you should go to the Red Hat Software home page at **www.redhat.com.** This web page also contains a large amount of documentation and many links to other Linux related web pages. Even if you don't intend to download the distribution, it is recommended that you visit this page on a regular basis.

An alternative download site is MetaLab (which used to be called Sunsite and is still frequently referred to by that name). The MetaLab home page is **http://metalab.unc.edu.** The Red Hat distribution is available from the MetaLab ftp server at **ftp://metalab.unc.edu/pub/Linux/ distributions/redhat/redhat-6.0.** In this directory (folder), you will find additional directories specific to the different platforms for which Red Hat Linux is available. Choose your platform (i386 for the most common Intel 386-, 486-, and Pentium-based computers), and then the welcome message will be displayed, which tells you how to download the distribution. The MetaLab Web site is a huge repository of Linux software and is the home of the Linux Documentation Project. Start from the home page (**http://metalab.unc.edu**) and browse the site.

Before deciding to download the distribution from the Internet, it is worth considering that, depending on the speed of your Internet connection, you may require 12 or more hours of actual downloading time. If you are subject to long-distance, time, and/or download charges or limits, you may find it substantially cheaper to purchase the CD-ROM. Another point to consider is that if you make a mistake during the installation, you may have to start again... from scratch. Do this two or three times, and you'll soon be wishing you had purchased the CD-ROM.

Some of the different Linux distributions are discussed briefly in Chapter 1. The Red Hat Linux distribution has become popular because of its ease of use and the availability of high-quality commercial support (included when you purchase the CD-ROM package). Because of this and its high availability, this is the distribution we have chosen to use in this book.

"Red Hat" is a registered trademark of Red Hat Software, Inc. Used with permission.

About The Windows And Macintosh Software

To access Linux from Windows, you can use the following telnet software:

Windows

Tera Term Pro (by T. Teranishi)
Telnet application for Windows

You can download Tera Term Pro from tucows at **www.tucows.com** or from Softseek at **http://192.41.3.165**.

To access Linux from Macintosh systems, you need a telnet application such as the following:

Macintosh

BetterTelnet V. 2.0fc1
Telnet application for Macintosh

You can download BetterTelnet from **http://www.cstone.net/~rbraun/mac/telnet/**.

Chapter 1
Linux Basics

Before using Linux for the first time, you should understand what Linux is and what it does best. This chapter explains what is required to use Linux and provides the fundamental knowledge necessary to implement a system.

Contents Of This Chapter

What Is Linux?

Linux Basics

Linux is an operating system (OS) like Windows and Mac OS that provides the environment necessary to start up and use a PC. Each OS has its own area of effectiveness and operating characteristics. Windows and Mac OS are designed for *client* (an application that runs on a personal computer or workstation)

functions; Linux provides *server* (a computer or device on a network that manages network resources) functions for the integration of these clients on a network. Linux has built-in stability and a high level of security–both essential qualities for use as a server OS.

Linux Is An OS

Windows and Mac OS are operating systems that provide the environment necessary to start up and use a personal computer. Linux also is an OS like the Windows and Mac operating systems installed in the computers around you. Each operating system has its own area of effectiveness and operating characteristics.

Windows   Mac OS   Linux

Manipulations Differ

In Windows and Mac OS, icons are manipulated to execute operations. In Linux, operations are primarily executed interactively; that is, the commands you enter from the keyboard are displayed on command lines.

Windows   Linux

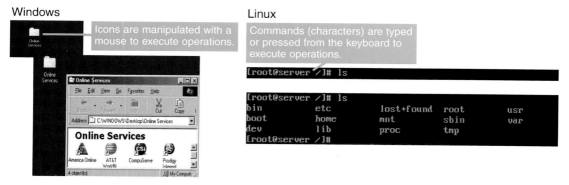

The Best OS For Servers

Windows and Mac OS are designed to execute operations on the particular PC on which they are installed. This type of operating system is called a client OS. A server OS like Linux, however, provides functions that seamlessly link clients through a network and provide functions and resources that are available to all clients.

Server Function

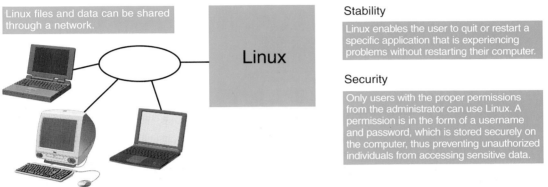

Linux files and data can be shared through a network.

Linux

Stability

Linux enables the user to quit or restart a specific application that is experiencing problems without restarting their computer.

Security

Only users with the proper permissions from the administrator can use Linux. A permission is in the form of a username and password, which is stored securely on the computer, thus preventing unauthorized individuals from accessing sensitive data.

Linux is an OS that can be used by multiple users from multiple clients on a network. In addition to network functions, stability and security (essential for use as a server) are highly effective features of Linux. Linux is best used, therefore, as a server for integrating clients. This book explains the procedures to install Linux as a server OS and to construct a server.

Client OS

Server OS

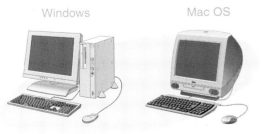

Windows   Mac OS

Linux

Windows and Mac OS are user-friendly OSs for which numerous applications are available commercially. As such, they are best suited for business, hobby, or home use on an individual PC.

Linux provides complete network functions, as well as stability and security. As such, it is best suited for use as a file server or other network server.

What You Can Do With Linux

Server Functions

Setting up a server by installing Linux on a PC means that you can conveniently connect and use multiple computers, previously used as standalone PCs, on a *local area network* (LAN).

Linux also enables you to connect to the Internet to post information and to communicate by email. As a first step in constructing a server, this book explains how to set up a Linux server for an intranet.

Linux Is Best Suited For An Intranet

A small network formed by computers connected by a LAN is called an intranet. You can do the following by using Linux as the intranet server:
• Share data among computers.
• Connect only one printer for use by multiple computers.
• Construct a Web server for transmitting information within the intranet.
• Exchange email within the intranet.

To use Linux for an intranet:
• Connect the PCs and a printer by a network.
• Use Linux as the server.

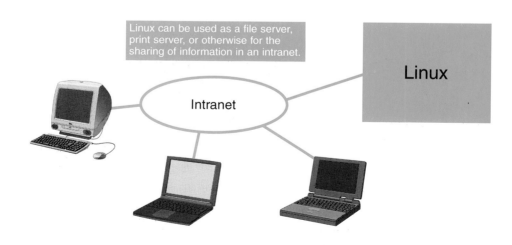

Linux can be used as a file server, print server, or otherwise for the sharing of information in an intranet.

Linux

Intranet

Internet Connection

A Linux server enables an intranet to be connected to the Internet. The following list describes the benefits of this connection:

- PCs on an intranet can access the Internet.
- A Web server can be built to transmit information to the Internet.
- Email can be exchanged inside and outside of the intranet.

To use Linux with the Internet, you must do the following:

- Make the necessary preparations to connect to the Internet. (You must apply for an IP address and so on.)
- Use a leased line or other digital communications network to connect to the Internet.
- Set up Linux for Internet use. (Security considerations are essential.)

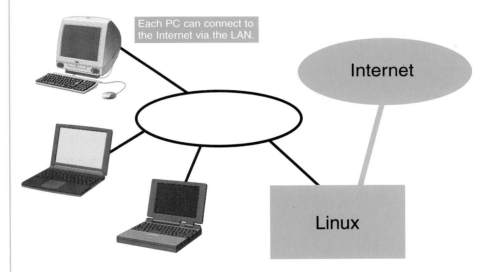

As a first step in using Linux as a server, this book explains how to set up an intranet server.

Objectives Of This Book

- To understand the type of OS that Linux is.
- To understand the basics of using Red Hat Linux 6 to set up a server and to construct an intranet server.

The Varieties Of Linux

Linux Distributions

Linux is the name of a program called a *kernel*. A kernel is the core of an OS and acts as an intermediary between the computer and all programs being run by the OS. The kernel, basic tools, and applications are installed as a compiled set, known as a *distribution*.

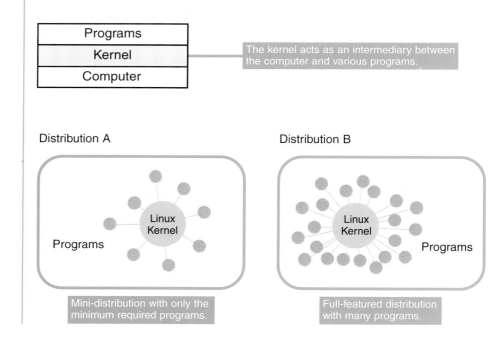

Programs
Kernel
Computer

The kernel acts as an intermediary between the computer and various programs.

Distribution A

Linux Kernel

Programs

Mini-distribution with only the minimum required programs.

Distribution B

Linux Kernel

Programs

Full-featured distribution with many programs.

Available Distributions

Red Hat Linux 6

This distribution was developed by Red Hat Software and is the most widely used distribution. Installation is simple, and many applications for Red Hat Linux are available commercially.

Slackware

This older distribution is structured as a very simple package. It is ideal if you want to do everything, including installation, by yourself.

Debian GNU/Linux

This distribution is packaged with a large selection of programs and is suited for people who have immediate use for a wide variety of applications. The volume of applications, however, may make this distribution too confusing for novice users.

Linux-Mandrake

This new distribution provides ease of use both for home and office users, and it has the usual Linux stability. Mandrake is freely available in many languages, all over the world.

Other Distributions

There are many other distributions including Caldera Open Linux distributed by Caldera, a subsidiary of Novell; MLD, developed by Media Laboratory; SuSE, used mainly in Europe; and LiveLinux, which can be started directly from a CD-ROM.

Linux Distribution Explained In This Book

Red Hat Linux 6
- Is the most widely used distribution.
- Provides support data.
- Can be installed easily.

This book was specifically written to be used in conjunction with Red Hat Linux 6.

Understanding A Network

TCP/IP

Usually, in a network of PC clients and a server, data is transmitted over the network in accordance with the TCP/IP protocol (the most common method). Numbers called IP addresses identify computers and peripheral devices connected to a TCP/IP network. In constructing a TCP/IP network, a range of IP addresses is set, specifying the maximum number of IP addresses to be used therein.

Connecting Personal Computers

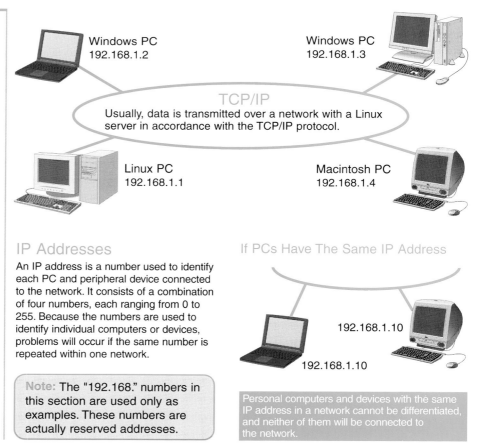

Windows PC
192.168.1.2

Windows PC
192.168.1.3

TCP/IP
Usually, data is transmitted over a network with a Linux server in accordance with the TCP/IP protocol.

Linux PC
192.168.1.1

Macintosh PC
192.168.1.4

IP Addresses

An IP address is a number used to identify each PC and peripheral device connected to the network. It consists of a combination of four numbers, each ranging from 0 to 255. Because the numbers are used to identify individual computers or devices, problems will occur if the same number is repeated within one network.

Note: The "192.168." numbers in this section are used only as examples. These numbers are actually reserved addresses.

If PCs Have The Same IP Address

192.168.1.10

192.168.1.10

Personal computers and devices with the same IP address in a network cannot be differentiated, and neither of them will be connected to the network.

Explaining IP Addresses

In building a TCP/IP network, the range of IP addresses for the network must be determined. For this, determine the maximum number of IP addresses that will be used, then specify the range required to secure this number of addresses. In earlier versions, the maximum number was set as 256 addresses, 65,536 addresses, or 1,677,216 addresses (IPv6, which is already supported by Linux, extends this maximum substantially and will probably be in common usage within the next one to two years). IP addresses for use with an intranet are private addresses for which assigned addresses are limited by class.

10.0.0.0 to 10.255.255.255   Range for using 1,677,216 addresses (Class A)
172.16.0.0 to 172.31.255.255   Range for using 65,536 addresses (Class B)
192.168.0.0 to 192.168.1.255   Range for using 256 addresses (Class C)

This book explains the construction of a simple intranet in which a Linux server and multiple personal computers, printers, and other devices are connected by a LAN. The Class C range of 256 addresses from 192.168.1.0 to 192.168.1.255 was selected.

Use Of IP Addresses

In this book, the IP address 192.168.1.1 is assigned to the Linux server. This is the first number that can be used within the range of IP addresses from 192.168.1.0 to 192.168.1.255.

Range Of IP Addresses Used In This Book

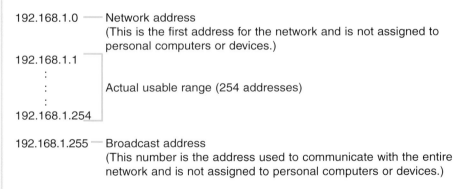

192.168.1.0 ——— Network address
(This is the first address for the network and is not assigned to personal computers or devices.)
192.168.1.1
⋮
⋮   Actual usable range (254 addresses)
⋮
192.168.1.254

192.168.1.255 ——— Broadcast address
(This number is the address used to communicate with the entire network and is not assigned to personal computers or devices.)

A network address and a broadcast address are used to specify the range of addresses used by a network. The broadcast address is the last address of the specified range and is used to communicate a notice to the entire network. Neither the network address nor the broadcast address can be assigned to specific personal computers or devices. For the range of addresses from 192.168.1.0 to 192.168.1.255 as used in this book, 192.168.1.0 is the network address and 192.168.1.255 is the broadcast address.

Network Essentials

Two Ethernet products for constructing a LAN are commonly available: a 10Base Ethernet with a maximum data transfer rate of 10Mbps and a 100Base Ethernet with a maximum data transfer rate of 100Mbps. Either product can be connected by several methods, but the main connections in use are 10Base-T (the most common alternative cable is coaxial, which is 10Base-2), and 100Base-TX, which use cables with jacks similar to the modular telephone jack (known as the RJ-45 connector). Be aware that these connections require different accessories.

Network Cards

There are many network cards produced by different manufacturers, with great differences in price and performance. To use a network with Linux, make sure that you purchase a network card that is compatible with NE2000; that is, the performance of the network card should be equivalent to the specifications of the NE2000 product. Check that "NE2000-compatible" is printed on

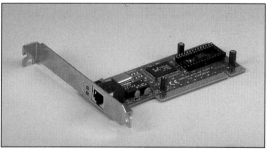

- NE2000-compatible card.
- Card made for PCI slot.

the package or have the sales clerk confirm this for you. Also, NE2000-compatible cards are made for either ISA slots or PCI slots; be sure to choose the latter (provided that your computer supports PCI).

There is always the possibility that some NE2000-compatible cards may not function well with Linux. We recommend reading the how-tos and the FAQs (you'll find them on the Linux Documentation Project (**www.linuxdoc.org**) or choosing three or four commonly available brands and asking Red Hat (provided you purchased and registered the CD-ROM) which if any of these cards have been proven to work. In this way, you'll quickly find one suitable for the Windows PC being used as the client.

Hubs

- Select a hub with sufficient ports for the number of devices to be connected. A hub with eight ports should suffice. A hub is a device used to connect multiple personal computers and devices. Many models are available, from hubs with four ports to hubs with dozens of ports.

A hub with only a few ports will soon prove to be insufficient, and we recommend a relatively inexpensive eight-port hub. If more ports are required with expansion of the LAN, purchase a hub with greater capacity or use several eight-port hubs in series. As a basic rule, a 10Base-T hub can only be used with a 10Base-T connection, and a 100Base-TX

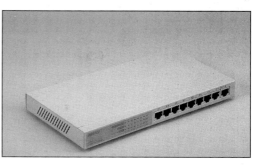

hub can only be used with a 100Base-TX connection. A dual-speed hub is required if a dual 10Base and 100Base LAN is constructed, but this kind of setup is not recommended.

Using A Switching Hub To Expand A LAN

A switching hub is a hub that controls the flow of data in a network. This traffic control feature alleviates network congestion. It's time to purchase a switching hub when the network has definitely slowed down and the cause has proven to be an excessive number of connected PCs. Almost all 100Base-TX switching hubs are equipped with the dual-speed hub function and can be connected to 10Base-T or 100Base-TX LANs.

Cables

• Use twisted-pair cables (although with any 10Base hubs, you may be able to use straight-coaxial-cable that uses a BNC connector). 10Base-2 cable cannot carry a 100Mbs signal, so this option isn't available with 100Base products.
• Match the cable length to the distance between the hub and the personal computers. Short

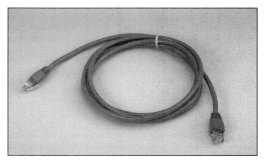

distances do not matter, but long ones may cause timing problems.

Many types of cables are available. Almost all cables on the market support both 10Base-T and 100Base-TX connections, so acquisition is not a problem. Be sure, however, to purchase twisted-pair cables.

Deciding On The Right Network

Setting Up A Network

Configuring a personal computer to a Linux server enables a plural number of both Windows and Macintosh PCs to be connected to the same network for the execution of a variety of applications. Look at your existing network and determine whether a Linux server would better serve your needs.

To avoid problems, consult with your LAN administrator before installing Linux into an existing LAN. This book does not discuss the use of Linux with Windows 3.1, which requires special software for connection to a network.

Example 1: Windows-Only Network

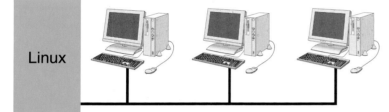

Required Setup
Installation Of Linux (p. 29)
Setup Of Clients (p. 98)
Setup Of Shared Services (p. 111)

Example 2: Macintosh-Only Network

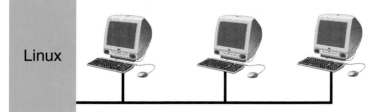

Required Setup
Installation Of Linux (p.29)
Setup Of Clients (p.106)
Setup Of Shared Services (p.127)

Example 3: Windows And Macintosh Network

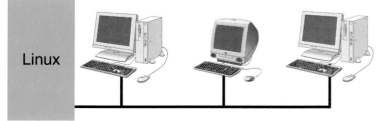

Required Setup
Installation Of Linux (p.29)
Setup Of Clients (p.106)
Setup Of Shared Services (p.111, p.127)

Notes On Using An Ethernet

Increasing Hubs To Match Increasing Clients

More hubs will have to be installed if your number of potential client machines exceeds the number of available hub ports. This does not mean, however, that you must discard your existing hubs and purchase new hubs with more ports. Hubs can be interconnected to increase the number of ports using a procedure known as *cascading*, in which one hub is connected to the special cascading port of another hub. A *stackable hub*, in which the number of ports can be increased without cascading by using a special port called a *stack port*, is also available.

Cascading Hub Restrictions

If you've decided to use cascading hubs, be aware of the restrictions on the number of interconnected hubs. For example, in the following diagram there is one hub between computer A and computer B, but there are two hubs between computer A and computer C, which is connected to a cascaded hub. An Ethernet is restricted to four interconnected hubs. A 100Base-TX, even more constrictive, allows only two interconnecting hubs.

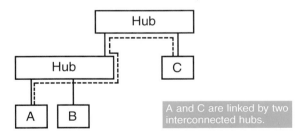

A and C are linked by two interconnected hubs.

Effective Use Of Switching Hubs

In addition to its data traffic control function, a switching hub can be inserted into a cascaded hub configuration to interrupt the counting of contiguous hubs; that is, counting of the number of interconnected hubs starts from one PC up to the switching hub only, then counting restarts at one from the switching hub to the other computer. Insert a switching hub if you want to exceed the specification in configuring cascading hubs. Because access will be concentrated on the Linux server, in using both switching hubs and other hubs, be sure to connect Linux to the port of a switching hub.

Checking PC Specs

Hardware Environment

Red Hat Linux 6 can be installed on any PC/AT-compatible computer. It can even be installed and operated on older PCs that cannot use Windows. The specifications will differ, however, depending on how you will use Linux, so make sure that you confirm that the PC you plan to use will be sufficient for your needs.

However, before dealing with this topic, it's time to install Linux for the first time. By actually installing, you will gradually understand what Linux is and what hardware configuration you will require.

Installable Computers

PC/AT-Compatible Computer

Red Hat Linux 6 can be installed on any PC/AT-compatible desktop or laptop computer.

Recommended PC Specifications

Minimum Of 2GB Of Available Hard Disk Space

Linux itself requires approximately 300MB of hard disk space, but further disk space is required for file sharing and other applications and functions. For practical use in the context of this installation, Linux requires at least 2GB of hard disk space for the server configuration discussed in this book.

NE2000-Compatible Network Card

The authors suggest that you acquire only NE2000-compatible network cards with a PCI slot to use with Linux.

Minimum Of Two PCI Slots

At minimum, one slot will be used for the network card. You will probably add more SCSI cards in the future as you expand your hard disk or otherwise modify your hardware configuration, so make sure that you choose a PC with several open PCI slots.

Familiarization Through Installation And Use

Red Hat Linux can be installed on any PC/AT-compatible computer (although a Pentium-based machine is a reasonable starter). The quickest way to discover what Linux is and what it can do is to install and start using Linux.

Follow The Procedures In This Book To Become Familiar With Linux

Installing Linux does not require much time, and procedures to set up the server as described in this book are quite simple. However, if you are unfamiliar with Linux, mistakes can occur as you perform your first installation-specifically, the use of a command line and the feeling for setting up a Linux server will be unfamiliar. Even so, you can complete the operations explained in this book in approximately a day. You should be able to set up the server and gain an even better understanding of how to use Linux by thoroughly reading this book.

Repeated Use Helps To Master Linux

Procedures that are difficult to understand the first time will become clearer as you repeat the installation process, giving you a greater sense of how to set up a customized server. Repeating the Linux installation process is great training if you really want to set up a server that meets your needs.

Merits Of Repeated Installations

• You can become familiar with the operations of Linux.
• You can learn how Linux works quickly.
• Various problems become evident.

To Use Linux As The Core Server Of A Network

Hard disk capacity of the computer you plan to use as the Linux server can be a problem. You can either acquire a computer with the requisite hard disk capacity or expand the hard disk capacity of an existing computer. For example, because the Linux system requires from 300MB to 400MB, and, assuming that each user will require 100MB, for 10 users you will need at least a 2GB hard disk to allow for some reserve space.

Because Linux does not require that much CPU performance, however, you can install it on older PCs if the hard disk capacity can be adequately expanded.

It is recommended that you install Linux as described in this book to get a sense of how to set up a server, then perform an installation taking into consideration hard disk capacity.

STEP UP

Linux Is A Type Of Unix OS

Although Linux is an OS (like Windows or Mac OS), it is an independently developed Unix-like OS that you can use for diverse applications ranging from operating personal computers to running specialized computers, such as workstations, minicomputers, and even supercomputers. Since its origin in 1971 at AT&T Bell Laboratories, Unix has undergone a variety of complex derivations and combinations; that is, the modern Unix is the result of a global development effort. Linux, as a Unix work-alike, falls under this umbrella.

Various functions included in modern operating systems such as Windows are based on technology developed for Unix. The Internet was originally a network of Unix-operated computers. Unix is currently used for Internet servers and in research laboratories and universities.

Open Source

Some Unix applications are open source software (OSS), but most are proprietary. Most Linux applications, however, are OSS, and the source code is publicly disclosed. There are many licensing regulations for OSS, as explained in the Open Source Definition (OSD).

OSS programs are publicly available, and permission is granted to anyone to modify these programs. The software itself is usually no-cost, and the acquired programs can be improved and distributed in accordance with the licensing regulations, making it possible for people anywhere to participate and build upon programs that move ever higher in terms of quality.

What Is Linux?

Linux is a Unix-like OS for personal computers created through the global cooperative efforts of people working through the Internet, led by Linus B. Torvalds of Finland. The first version of Linux was released on October 5th, 1991, and daily evolution has continued ever since.

Almost all of the many tools required to use Linux and the applications that run on Linux are OSS applications in accordance with the licensing regulations stipulated in the General Public License (GPL) of the Free Software Foundation (FSF).

Chapter 2
Installing Linux

To use Linux, you must determine which PC you will use as an intranet server. Then, you need to install Linux Red Hat. This chapter describes the installation procedures and how to boot up after you have installed Linux.

Contents Of This Chapter

Pre-Installation Procedures For Linux

Checking The Installation Order

Before you begin to install Linux, review the installation procedures. The general flow is similar to the installation of Windows and comprises (in order) the initial setup of the keyboard and other accessories, initialization of the hard disk, copying files, setup of the hardware, and other setups related to the network and Linux startup. Network cards and SCSI cards should be installed before installation of Red Hat to allow the installer to find the cards automatically.

Pre-Installation Preparations

- Gather all hardware specification information.
- Create the boot disk.
- Prepare the PC for installation.
- Create a boot disk for installing Linux on a Windows PC.
- Verify that the PC is ready for installation.

Installing The Network Card Into The PC

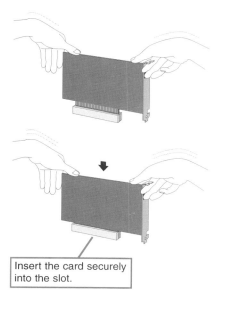

Insert the card securely into the slot.

Connecting Cables

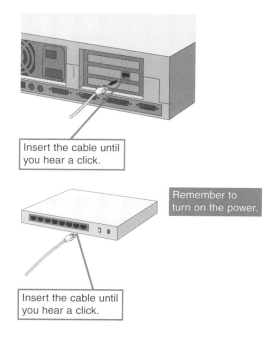

Insert the cable until you hear a click.

Remember to turn on the power.

Insert the cable until you hear a click.

Linux Installation Sequence

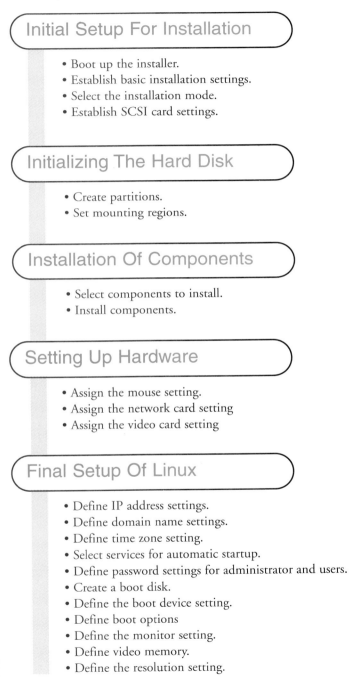

Initial Setup For Installation

- Boot up the installer.
- Establish basic installation settings.
- Select the installation mode.
- Establish SCSI card settings.

Initializing The Hard Disk

- Create partitions.
- Set mounting regions.

Installation Of Components

- Select components to install.
- Install components.

Setting Up Hardware

- Assign the mouse setting.
- Assign the network card setting
- Assign the video card setting

Final Setup Of Linux

- Define IP address settings.
- Define domain name settings.
- Define time zone setting.
- Select services for automatic startup.
- Define password settings for administrator and users.
- Create a boot disk.
- Define the boot device setting.
- Define boot options
- Define the monitor setting.
- Define video memory.
- Define the resolution setting.

Creating An Installation Disk

Creating A Boot Disk

To boot up the Red Hat Linux installer, first create a boot disk on a floppy disk, and then boot up the computer from the boot disk. To create the boot disk, use the special tool called rawrite.exe to write the image file (boot.img) onto a floppy disk.

If you purchased the Red Hat CD-ROM kit, skip down to section 2.3, "installing Linux part 1."

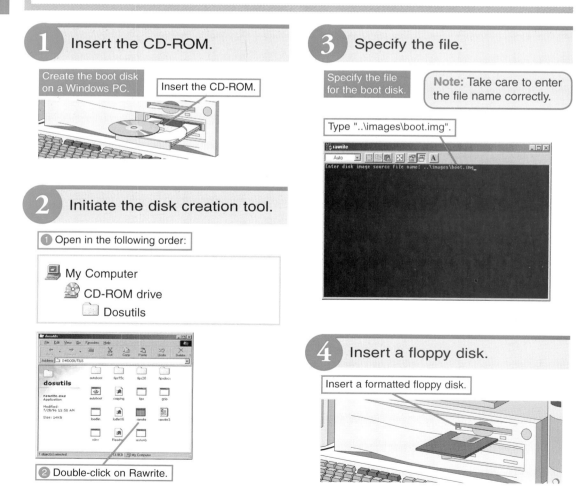

1 Insert the CD-ROM.

Create the boot disk on a Windows PC.

Insert the CD-ROM.

2 Initiate the disk creation tool.

① Open in the following order:

🖳 My Computer
　🖸 CD-ROM drive
　　📁 Dosutils

② Double-click on Rawrite.

3 Specify the file.

Specify the file for the boot disk.

Note: Take care to enter the file name correctly.

Type "..\images\boot.img".

4 Insert a floppy disk.

Insert a formatted floppy disk.

32

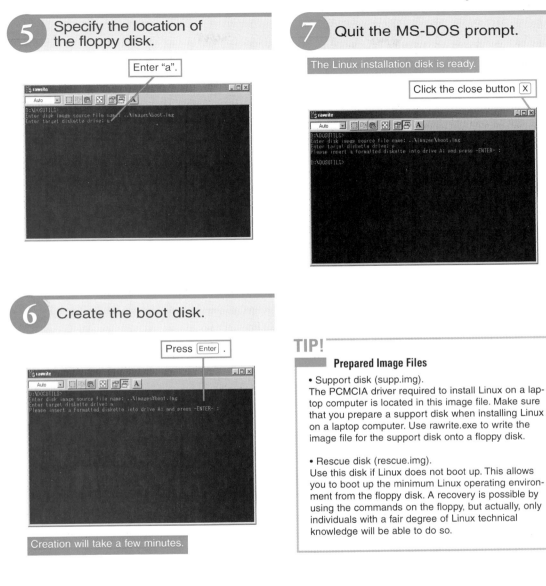

5 Specify the location of the floppy disk.

Enter "a".

7 Quit the MS-DOS prompt.

The Linux installation disk is ready.

Click the close button X

6 Create the boot disk.

Press Enter .

Creation will take a few minutes.

TIP!

Prepared Image Files

• Support disk (supp.img).
The PCMCIA driver required to install Linux on a laptop computer is located in this image file. Make sure that you prepare a support disk when installing Linux on a laptop computer. Use rawrite.exe to write the image file for the support disk onto a floppy disk.

• Rescue disk (rescue.img).
Use this disk if Linux does not boot up. This allows you to boot up the minimum Linux operating environment from the floppy disk. A recovery is possible by using the commands on the floppy, but actually, only individuals with a fair degree of Linux technical knowledge will be able to do so.

Installing Linux Part 1

Booting The Installer

The Red Hat Linux installer is booted up from the boot disk. This installer deletes the Windows OS that is not required to use the PC as a server. If necessary, transfer data used with Windows to a separate location before the installation. Depending on the installation procedure, the Windows partition may or may not be deleted. The authors assume that you want to use this machine only as an intranet server, so in this case, Windows will be deleted.

1 Insert the boot disk.

Insert the boot disk created on the preceding page into the floppy disk drive of the PC into which you will install Linux.

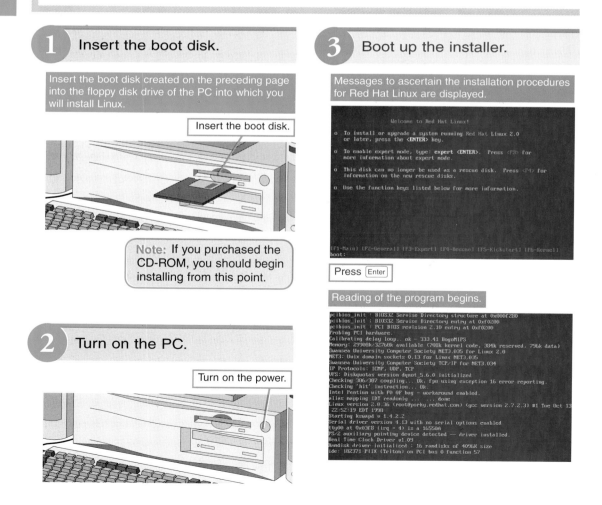

Insert the boot disk.

Note: If you purchased the CD-ROM, you should begin installing from this point.

2 Turn on the PC.

Turn on the power.

3 Boot up the installer.

Messages to ascertain the installation procedures for Red Hat Linux are displayed.

Welcome to Red Hat Linux!

o To install or upgrade a system running Red Hat Linux 2.0 or later, press the <ENTER> key.

o To enable expert mode, type: expert <ENTER>. Press <F3> for more information about expert mode.

o This disk can no longer be used as a rescue disk. Press <F4> for information on the new rescue disks.

o Use the function keys listed below for more information.

[F1-Main] [F2-General] [F3-Expert] [F4-Rescue] [F5-Kickstart] [F6-Kernel]
boot:

Press Enter

Reading of the program begins.

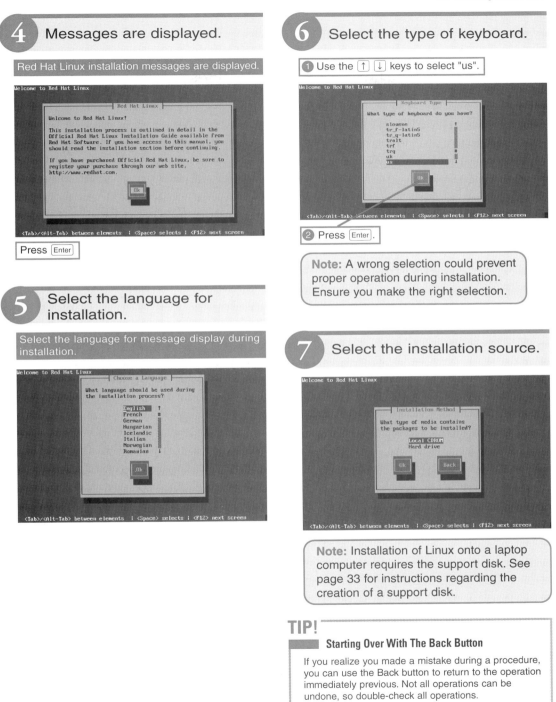

4 Messages are displayed.

Red Hat Linux installation messages are displayed.

Press Enter

5 Select the language for installation.

Select the language for message display during installation.

6 Select the type of keyboard.

① Use the ↑ ↓ keys to select "us".

② Press Enter.

Note: A wrong selection could prevent proper operation during installation. Ensure you make the right selection.

7 Select the installation source.

Note: Installation of Linux onto a laptop computer requires the support disk. See page 33 for instructions regarding the creation of a support disk.

TIP!

Starting Over With The Back Button

If you realize you made a mistake during a procedure, you can use the Back button to return to the operation immediately previous. Not all operations can be undone, so double-check all operations.

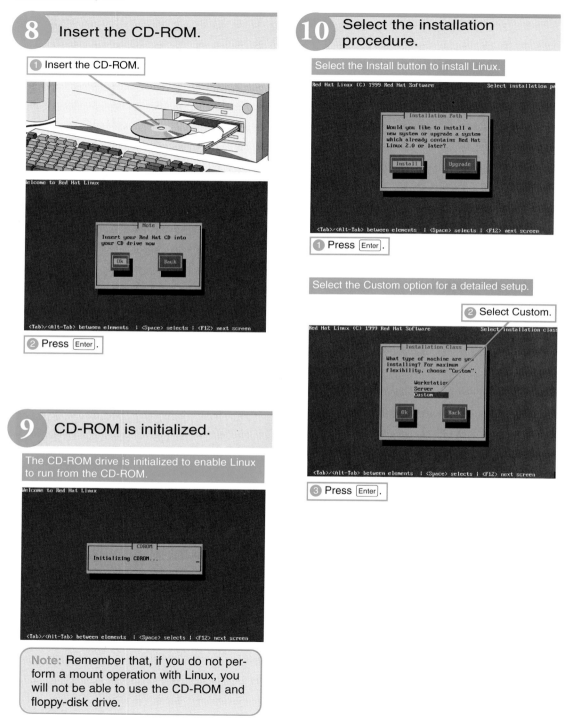

8 Insert the CD-ROM.

① Insert the CD-ROM.

② Press Enter.

9 CD-ROM is initialized.

The CD-ROM drive is initialized to enable Linux to run from the CD-ROM.

Note: Remember that, if you do not perform a mount operation with Linux, you will not be able to use the CD-ROM and floppy-disk drive.

10 Select the installation procedure.

Select the Install button to install Linux.

① Press Enter.

Select the Custom option for a detailed setup.

② Select Custom.

③ Press Enter.

11 Select the presence or absence of a SCSI adapter.

A message to ascertain whether a SCSI adapter is connected is displayed.

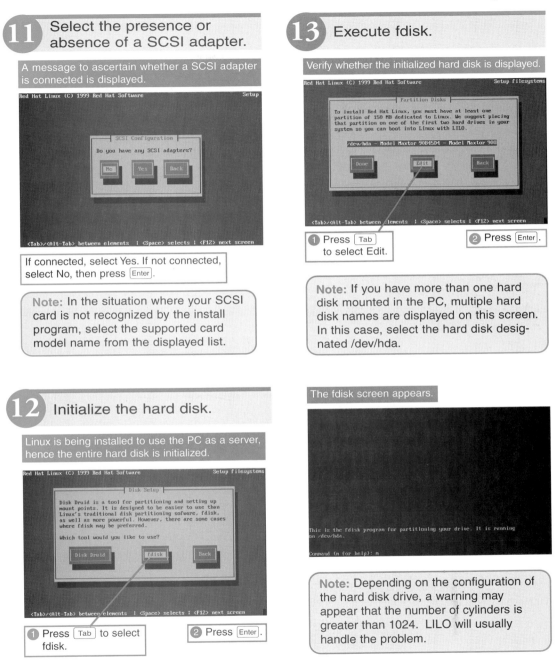

If connected, select Yes. If not connected, select No, then press Enter.

Note: In the situation where your SCSI card is not recognized by the install program, select the supported card model name from the displayed list.

12 Initialize the hard disk.

Linux is being installed to use the PC as a server, hence the entire hard disk is initialized.

1 Press Tab to select fdisk.

2 Press Enter.

13 Execute fdisk.

Verify whether the initialized hard disk is displayed.

1 Press Tab to select Edit.

2 Press Enter.

Note: If you have more than one hard disk mounted in the PC, multiple hard disk names are displayed on this screen. In this case, select the hard disk designated /dev/hda.

The fdisk screen appears.

Note: Depending on the configuration of the hard disk drive, a warning may appear that the number of cylinders is greater than 1024. LILO will usually handle the problem.

37

Installing Linux Part 2

The fdisk tool is used to divide the entire hard disk into separate partitions for different functions. For use as a server, Linux must be the default operation; therefore, in this installation step, all hard disk partitions are released and allocated to Linux. The hard disk is formatted for use with Linux, and all existing data is erased.

The fdisk tool is complicated to use, but no alterations will be written to the hard disk until the w command is issued. Don't be concerned with using the tool up to this point.

Changing The Hard Disk Partitions For Linux Use

The hard disk of a Windows PC is divided into one partition or several partitions, depending on the manufacturer. Because we are installing Linux as a server OS, you can delete all partitions used by Windows. If you want to save data or programs used by Windows, be sure to back them up on separate storage media.

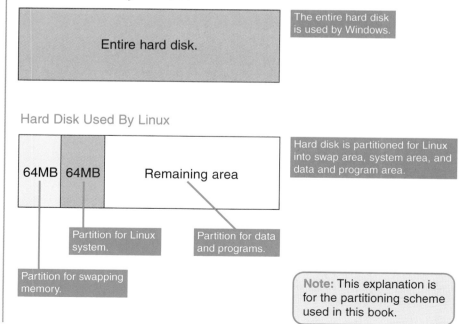

Hard Disk Used By Windows

Entire hard disk.

The entire hard disk is used by Windows.

Hard Disk Used By Linux

| 64MB | 64MB | Remaining area |

Hard disk is partitioned for Linux into swap area, system area, and data and program area.

Partition for Linux system.

Partition for data and programs.

Partition for swapping memory.

Note: This explanation is for the partitioning scheme used in this book.

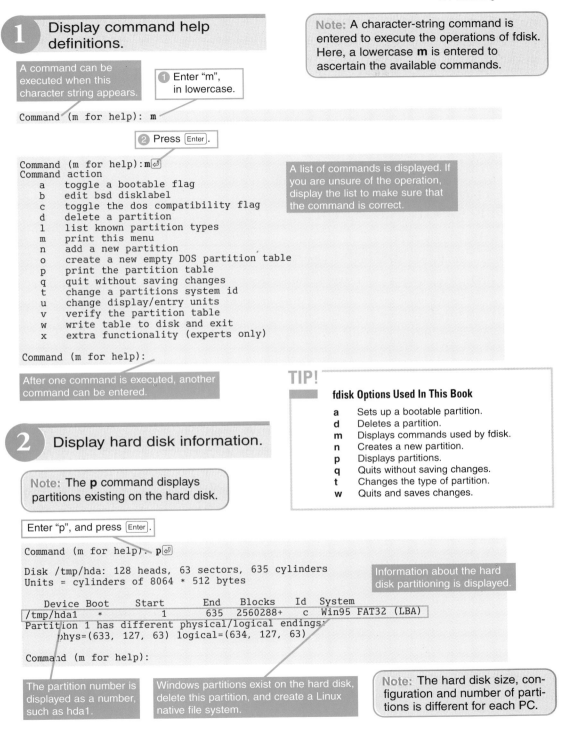

1 Display command help definitions.

Note: A character-string command is entered to execute the operations of fdisk. Here, a lowercase **m** is entered to ascertain the available commands.

A command can be executed when this character string appears.

① Enter "m", in lowercase.

```
Command (m for help): m
```

② Press Enter.

```
Command (m for help): m⏎
Command action
   a   toggle a bootable flag
   b   edit bsd disklabel
   c   toggle the dos compatibility flag
   d   delete a partition
   l   list known partition types
   m   print this menu
   n   add a new partition
   o   create a new empty DOS partition table
   p   print the partition table
   q   quit without saving changes
   t   change a partitions system id
   u   change display/entry units
   v   verify the partition table
   w   write table to disk and exit
   x   extra functionality (experts only)

Command (m for help):
```

A list of commands is displayed. If you are unsure of the operation, display the list to make sure that the command is correct.

After one command is executed, another command can be entered.

TIP!

fdisk Options Used In This Book

a	Sets up a bootable partition.
d	Deletes a partition.
m	Displays commands used by fdisk.
n	Creates a new partition.
p	Displays partitions.
q	Quits without saving changes.
t	Changes the type of partition.
w	Quits and saves changes.

2 Display hard disk information.

Note: The **p** command displays partitions existing on the hard disk.

Enter "p", and press Enter.

```
Command (m for help): p⏎

Disk /tmp/hda: 128 heads, 63 sectors, 635 cylinders
Units = cylinders of 8064 * 512 bytes

    Device Boot    Start      End    Blocks   Id   System
/tmp/hda1    *       1        635   2560288+    c   Win95 FAT32 (LBA)
Partition 1 has different physical/logical endings:
     phys=(633, 127, 63) logical=(634, 127, 63)

Command (m for help):
```

Information about the hard disk partitioning is displayed.

The partition number is displayed as a number, such as hda1.

Windows partitions exist on the hard disk, delete this partition, and create a Linux native file system.

Note: The hard disk size, configuration and number of partitions is different for each PC.

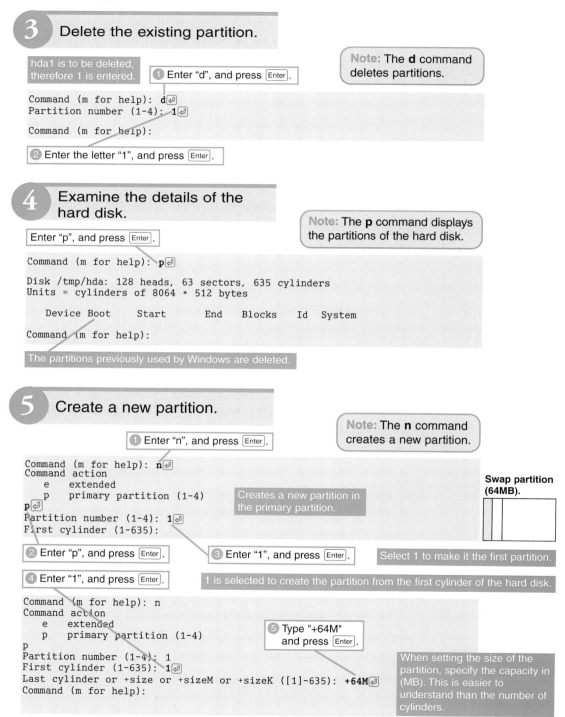

3 Delete the existing partition.

hda1 is to be deleted, therefore 1 is entered.

① Enter "d", and press Enter.

Note: The **d** command deletes partitions.

```
Command (m for help): d↵
Partition number (1-4): 1↵

Command (m for help):
```

② Enter the letter "1", and press Enter.

4 Examine the details of the hard disk.

Enter "p", and press Enter.

Note: The **p** command displays the partitions of the hard disk.

```
Command (m for help): p↵

Disk /tmp/hda: 128 heads, 63 sectors, 635 cylinders
Units = cylinders of 8064 * 512 bytes

    Device Boot    Start      End    Blocks   Id  System

Command (m for help):
```

The partitions previously used by Windows are deleted.

5 Create a new partition.

① Enter "n", and press Enter.

Note: The **n** command creates a new partition.

```
Command (m for help): n↵
Command action
   e   extended
   p   primary partition (1-4)
p↵
Partition number (1-4): 1↵
First cylinder (1-635):
```

Creates a new partition in the primary partition.

Swap partition (64MB).

② Enter "p", and press Enter.

③ Enter "1", and press Enter.

Select 1 to make it the first partition.

④ Enter "1", and press Enter.

1 is selected to create the partition from the first cylinder of the hard disk.

```
Command (m for help): n
Command action
   e   extended
   p   primary partition (1-4)
p
Partition number (1-4): 1
First cylinder (1-635): 1↵
Last cylinder or +size or +sizeM or +sizeK ([1]-635): +64M↵
Command (m for help):
```

⑤ Type "+64M" and press Enter.

When setting the size of the partition, specify the capacity in (MB). This is easier to understand than the number of cylinders.

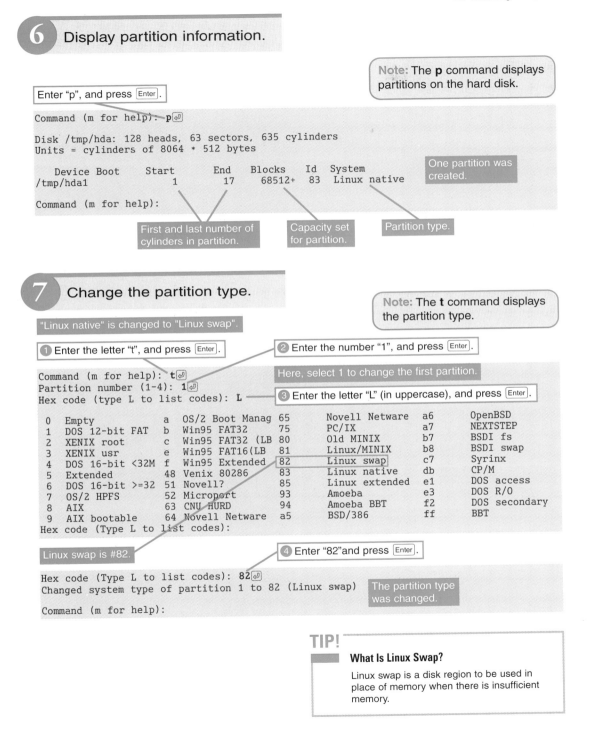

6 Display partition information.

Note: The **p** command displays partitions on the hard disk.

Enter "p", and press Enter.

```
Command (m for help): p⏎

Disk /tmp/hda: 128 heads, 63 sectors, 635 cylinders
Units = cylinders of 8064 * 512 bytes

    Device Boot    Start     End   Blocks   Id  System
/tmp/hda1                1      17   68512+   83  Linux native

Command (m for help):
```

One partition was created.

First and last number of cylinders in partition.

Capacity set for partition.

Partition type.

7 Change the partition type.

Note: The **t** command displays the partition type.

"Linux native" is changed to "Linux swap".

① Enter the letter "t", and press Enter.

② Enter the number "1", and press Enter.

```
Command (m for help): t⏎
Partition number (1-4): 1⏎
Hex code (type L to list codes): L
```

Here, select 1 to change the first partition.

③ Enter the letter "L" (in uppercase), and press Enter.

```
0   Empty           a   OS/2 Boot Manag 65   Novell Netware   a6   OpenBSD
1   DOS 12-bit FAT  b   Win95 FAT32     75   PC/IX            a7   NEXTSTEP
2   XENIX root      c   Win95 FAT32 (LB 80   Old MINIX        b7   BSDI fs
3   XENIX usr       e   Win95 FAT16(LB  81   Linux/MINIX      b8   BSDI swap
4   DOS 16-bit <32M f   Win95 Extended  82   Linux swap       c7   Syrinx
5   Extended        48  Venix 80286     83   Linux native     db   CP/M
6   DOS 16-bit >=32 51  Novell?         85   Linux extended   e1   DOS access
7   OS/2 HPFS       52  Microport       93   Amoeba           e3   DOS R/O
8   AIX             63  CNU HURD        94   Amoeba BBT       f2   DOS secondary
9   AIX bootable    64  Novell Netware  a5   BSD/386          ff   BBT
Hex code (Type L to list codes):
```

Linux swap is #82.

④ Enter "82" and press Enter.

```
Hex code (Type L to list codes): 82⏎
Changed system type of partition 1 to 82 (Linux swap)

Command (m for help):
```

The partition type was changed.

TIP!

What Is Linux Swap?

Linux swap is a disk region to be used in place of memory when there is insufficient memory.

8 Continue to create partitions.

Note: The **n** command creates a new partition.

1 Enter "n", and press Enter.

```
Command (m for help): n⏎
Command action
   e   extended
   p   primary partition (1-4)
p⏎
Partition number (1-4): 2⏎
First cylinder (18-635): 18⏎
Last cylinder or +size or +sizeM or +sizeK ([18]-635): +64M⏎

Command (m for help):
```

2 Enter "p", and press Enter.

3 Enter "2", and press Enter.

Here, 2 is selected to create the second partition.

System partition (64MB).

The number of unused cylinders is displayed.

4 Enter the number "18" of the first cylinder, and press Enter.

5 Enter "+64M", and press Enter.

Note: A minimum of 400MB program application space is required for Linux, as well as 100MB per user on the network.

Note: The values of the cylinders differ depending on the hard disk used. Use the values that match your PC.

6 Enter "n", and press Enter.

7 Enter "p", and press Enter.

```
Command (m for help): n⏎
Command action
   e   extended
   p   primary partition (1-4)
p⏎
Partition number (1-4): 3⏎
First cylinder (35-635): 35⏎
Last cylinder or +size or +sizeM or +sizeK ([35]-635): 635⏎

Command (m for help):
```

8 Enter "3", and press Enter.

Select 3 to make a third partition.

10 Enter the number "635" of the last cylinder, and press Enter.

Data and program partition (remaining disk space).

This number represents the end of the range.

9 Enter the number "35" of the first cylinder, and press Enter.

The last cylinder number is entered because all of the remaining partition is to be used.

9 Verify the details of the partitions.

Note: The **p** command displays partitions existing on the hard disk.

1 Enter "p", and press Enter.

```
Command (m for help): p⏎
Disk /tmp/hda: 128 heads, 63 sectors, 635 cylinders
Units = cylinders of 8064 * 512 bytes

   Device Boot    Start     End    Blocks   Id  System
/tmp/hda1            1       17    68512+   82  Linux swap
/tmp/hda2           18       34    68544    83  Linux native
/tmp/hda3           35      635  2423232    83  Linux native

Command (m for help):
```

Three partitions were created on the hard disk.

Because there is no boot partition, one must be set.

10 Create a boot partition.

The second partition will be used for the Linux system, hence it is set as the boot partition.

❶ Enter "a", and press [Enter].

Note: The **a** command sets the bootable partition.

```
Command (m for help): a↵
Partition number (1-4): 2↵
```

❷ Enter "2", and press [Enter].

```
Command (m for help): p↵
```

❸ Enter "p", and press [Enter].

```
Disk /tmp/hda: 128 heads, 63 sectors, 635 cylinders
Units = cylinders of 8064 * 512 bytes

   Device Boot    Start      End    Blocks   Id  System
/tmp/hda1              1       17    68512+   82  Linux swap
/tmp/hda2     *       18       34    68544    83  Linux native
/tmp/hda3             35      635  2423232    83  Linux native

Command (m for help):
```

An asterisk (*) is appended for the boot partition.

11 Save the changes and quit fdisk.

Enter "w", and press [Enter].

```
Command (m for help): w↵
The partition table has been altered!
```

Settings of the specified partitions are saved.

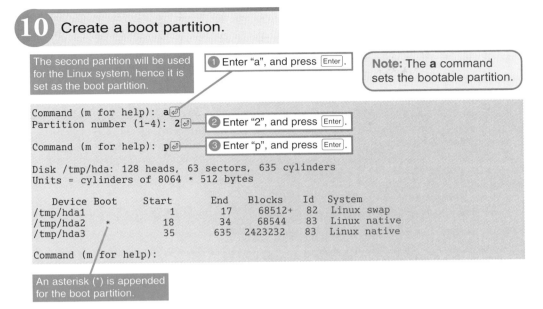

TIP!

Return To Original State Before Pressing w

When you save the changes to partitions, you will not be able to re-access programs and data that were stored on the deleted partitions. Use the **p** command to display partition information, and carefully examine the details. Save the changes only after confirming that there are no mistakes.

Note: The **w** command quits fdisk and saves changes.

Installing Linux Part 3

Installing Red Hat Linux

When partitioning is complete, the next step is to allocate the partitions to be used with Linux and the installation components.

Most of the peripheral devices will be probed and found automatically, but if not, the device can be selected from the displayed list.

The network card is the only important peripheral device for the use of Linux as a server. Mouse and video card settings are not critical, and you don't need to be concerned about detailed setups.

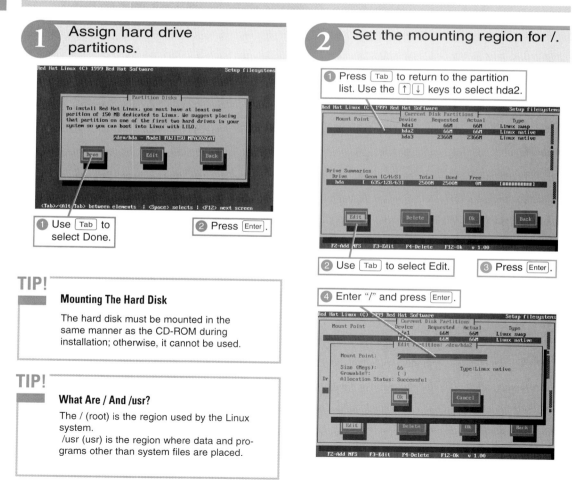

1 Assign hard drive partitions.

① Use [Tab] to select Done.

② Press [Enter].

2 Set the mounting region for /.

① Press [Tab] to return to the partition list. Use the [↑][↓] keys to select hda2.

② Use [Tab] to select Edit.

③ Press [Enter].

④ Enter "/" and press [Enter].

TIP!

Mounting The Hard Disk

The hard disk must be mounted in the same manner as the CD-ROM during installation; otherwise, it cannot be used.

TIP!

What Are / And /usr?

The / (root) is the region used by the Linux system.
/usr (usr) is the region where data and programs other than system files are placed.

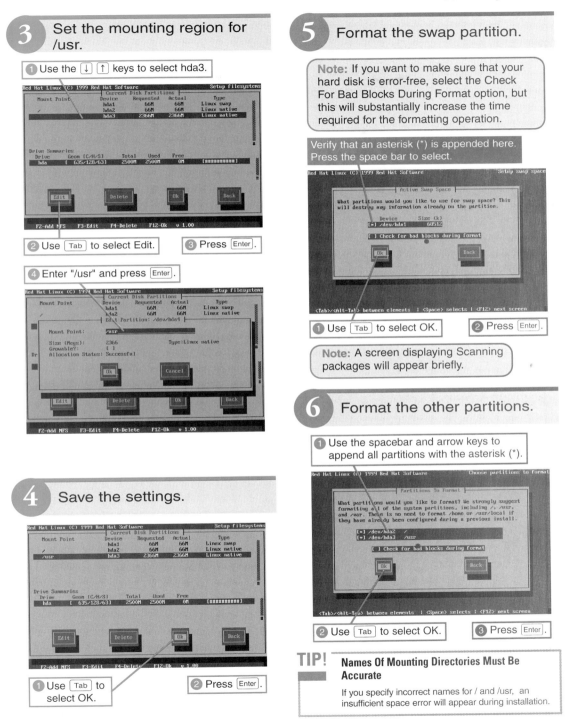

3 Set the mounting region for /usr.

① Use the [↓] [↑] keys to select hda3.

② Use [Tab] to select Edit. ③ Press [Enter].

④ Enter "/usr" and press [Enter].

4 Save the settings.

① Use [Tab] to select OK. ② Press [Enter].

5 Format the swap partition.

Note: If you want to make sure that your hard disk is error-free, select the Check For Bad Blocks During Format option, but this will substantially increase the time required for the formatting operation.

Verify that an asterisk (*) is appended here. Press the space bar to select.

① Use [Tab] to select OK. ② Press [Enter].

Note: A screen displaying Scanning packages will appear briefly.

6 Format the other partitions.

① Use the spacebar and arrow keys to append all partitions with the asterisk (*).

② Use [Tab] to select OK. ③ Press [Enter].

TIP! **Names Of Mounting Directories Must Be Accurate**

If you specify incorrect names for / and /usr, an insufficient space error will appear during installation.

45

7 Select the components to install.

Note: Components are program sets divided according to objective.

❶ Use the spacebar to select the components you want to install with an asterisk (*).

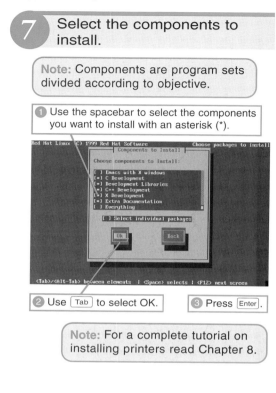

❷ Use Tab to select OK.

❸ Press Enter.

Note: For a complete tutorial on installing printers read Chapter 8.

The components used in this book are shown below. Use the spacebar to remove the appended asterisk from all other components not listed (and add an asterisk to items you want marked).

- X Window System
- DOS/Windows Connectivity
- Networked Workstation
- SMB (Samba) Connectivity
- Anonymous FTP Server
- Web Server
- Network Management Workstation
- C Development
- Development Libraries
- C++ Development
- X Development
- Extra Documentation

8 Verify the location to save the log file.

A message indicating the location where the log file will be saved is displayed.

Note: There may be a short delay before the message appears. If the delay lasts more than five or six minutes, something went wrong and you should restart the install from the beginning.

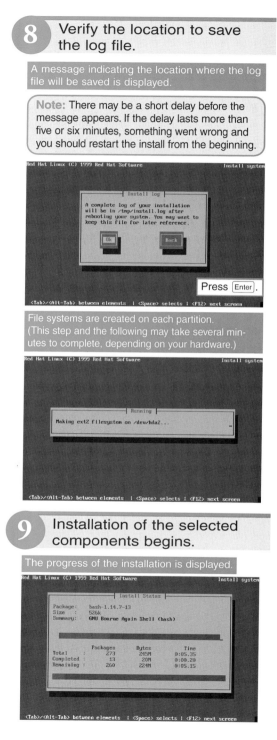

Press Enter.

File systems are created on each partition. (This step and the following may take several minutes to complete, depending on your hardware.)

9 Installation of the selected components begins.

The progress of the installation is displayed.

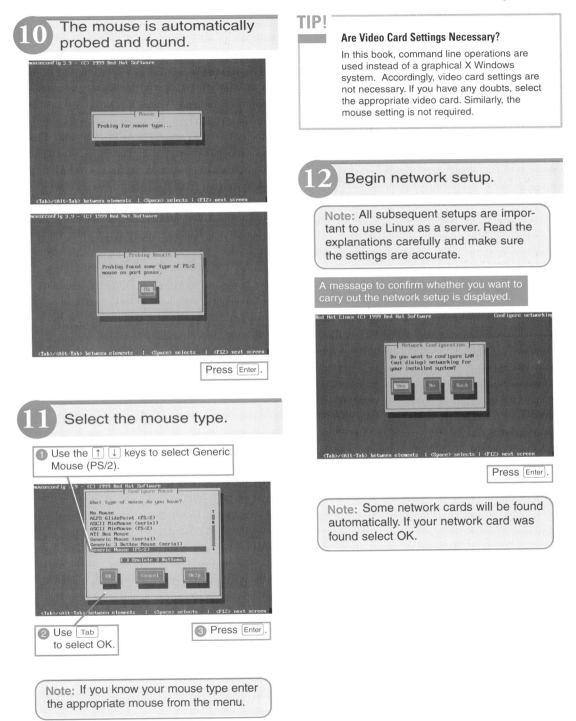

10 The mouse is automatically probed and found.

Press [Enter].

11 Select the mouse type.

1 Use the [↑] [↓] keys to select Generic Mouse (PS/2).

2 Use [Tab] to select OK.

3 Press [Enter].

Note: If you know your mouse type enter the appropriate mouse from the menu.

TIP!

Are Video Card Settings Necessary?

In this book, command line operations are used instead of a graphical X Windows system. Accordingly, video card settings are not necessary. If you have any doubts, select the appropriate video card. Similarly, the mouse setting is not required.

12 Begin network setup.

Note: All subsequent setups are important to use Linux as a server. Read the explanations carefully and make sure the settings are accurate.

A message to confirm whether you want to carry out the network setup is displayed.

Press [Enter].

Note: Some network cards will be found automatically. If your network card was found select OK.

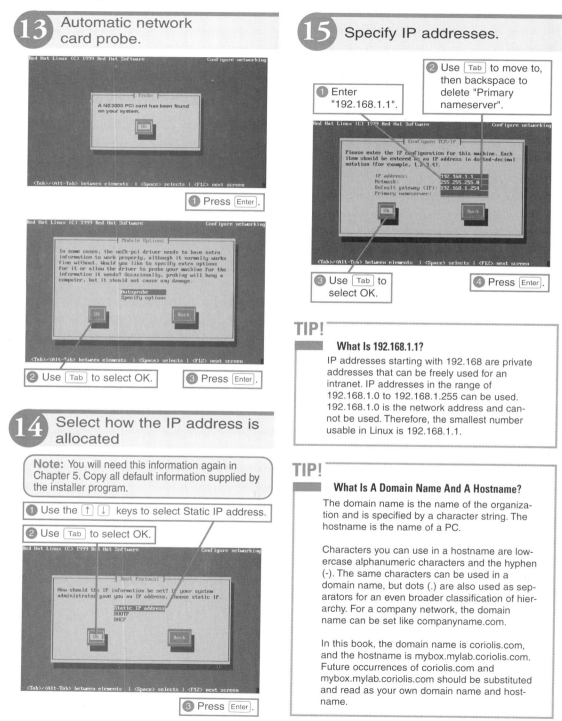

13 Automatic network card probe.

❶ Press [Enter].

❷ Use [Tab] to select OK.

❸ Press [Enter].

14 Select how the IP address is allocated

Note: You will need this information again in Chapter 5. Copy all default information supplied by the installer program.

❶ Use the [↑] [↓] keys to select Static IP address.

❷ Use [Tab] to select OK.

❸ Press [Enter].

15 Specify IP addresses.

❶ Enter "192.168.1.1".

❷ Use [Tab] to move to, then backspace to delete "Primary nameserver".

❸ Use [Tab] to select OK.

❹ Press [Enter].

TIP!

What Is 192.168.1.1?

IP addresses starting with 192.168 are private addresses that can be freely used for an intranet. IP addresses in the range of 192.168.1.0 to 192.168.1.255 can be used. 192.168.1.0 is the network address and cannot be used. Therefore, the smallest number usable in Linux is 192.168.1.1.

TIP!

What Is A Domain Name And A Hostname?

The domain name is the name of the organization and is specified by a character string. The hostname is the name of a PC.

Characters you can use in a hostname are lowercase alphanumeric characters and the hyphen (-). The same characters can be used in a domain name, but dots (.) are also used as separators for an even broader classification of hierarchy. For a company network, the domain name can be set like companyname.com.

In this book, the domain name is coriolis.com, and the hostname is mybox.mylab.coriolis.com. Future occurrences of coriolis.com and mybox.mylab.coriolis.com should be substituted and read as your own domain name and hostname.

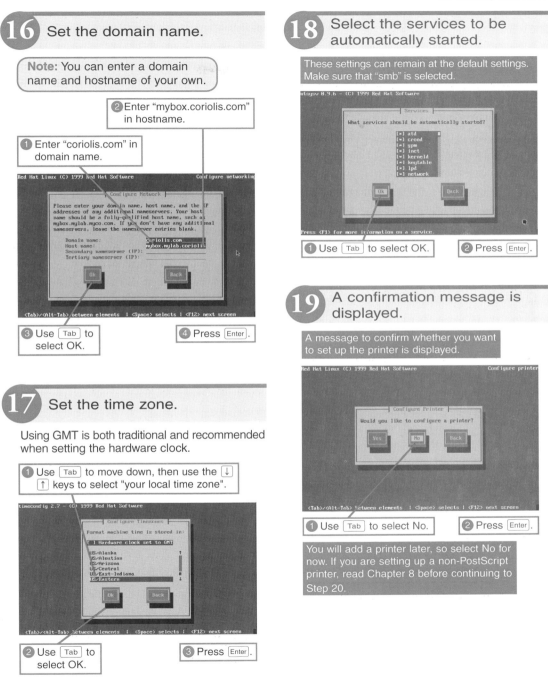

16 Set the domain name.

Note: You can enter a domain name and hostname of your own.

2 Enter "mybox.coriolis.com" in hostname.

1 Enter "coriolis.com" in domain name.

3 Use [Tab] to select OK.

4 Press [Enter].

17 Set the time zone.

Using GMT is both traditional and recommended when setting the hardware clock.

1 Use [Tab] to move down, then use the [↓] [↑] keys to select "your local time zone".

2 Use [Tab] to select OK.

3 Press [Enter].

18 Select the services to be automatically started.

These settings can remain at the default settings. Make sure that "smb" is selected.

1 Use [Tab] to select OK.

2 Press [Enter].

19 A confirmation message is displayed.

A message to confirm whether you want to set up the printer is displayed.

1 Use [Tab] to select No.

2 Press [Enter].

You will add a printer later, so select No for now. If you are setting up a non-PostScript printer, read Chapter 8 before continuing to Step 20.

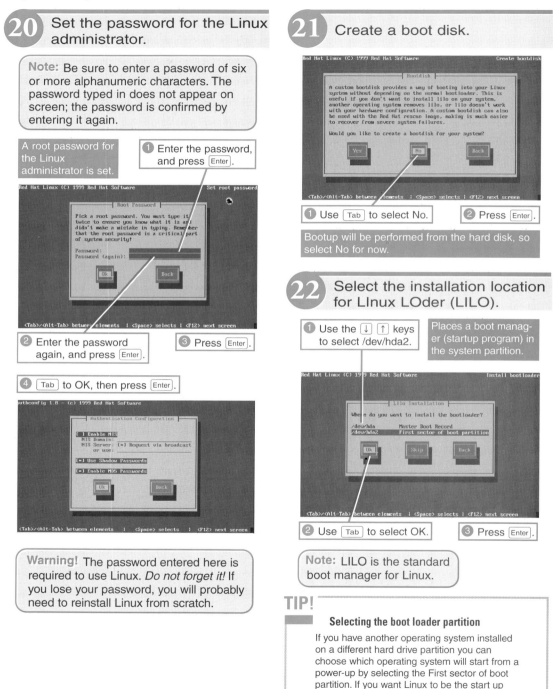

20 Set the password for the Linux administrator.

Note: Be sure to enter a password of six or more alphanumeric characters. The password typed in does not appear on screen; the password is confirmed by entering it again.

A root password for the Linux administrator is set.

❶ Enter the password, and press [Enter].

❷ Enter the password again, and press [Enter].

❸ Press [Enter].

❹ [Tab] to OK, then press [Enter].

Warning! The password entered here is required to use Linux. *Do not forget it!* If you lose your password, you will probably need to reinstall Linux from scratch.

21 Create a boot disk.

❶ Use [Tab] to select No.

❷ Press [Enter].

Bootup will be performed from the hard disk, so select No for now.

22 Select the installation location for LInux LOder (LILO).

❶ Use the [↓] [↑] keys to select /dev/hda2.

Places a boot manager (startup program) in the system partition.

❷ Use [Tab] to select OK.

❸ Press [Enter].

Note: LILO is the standard boot manager for Linux.

TIP!

Selecting the boot loader partition

If you have another operating system installed on a different hard drive partition you can choose which operating system will start from a power-up by selecting the First sector of boot partition. If you want Linux to be the start up operating system choose Master boot record.

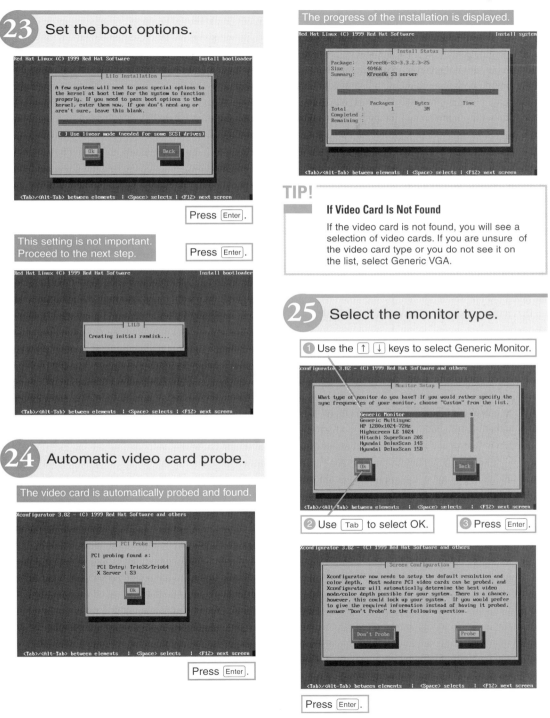

23 Set the boot options.

Red Hat Linux (C) 1999 Red Hat Software   Install bootloader

Lilo Installation

A few systems will need to pass special options to
the kernel at boot time for the system to function
properly. If you need to pass boot options to the
kernel, enter them now. If you don't need any or
aren't sure, leave this blank.

[ ] Use linear mode (needed for some SCSI drives)

Ok   Back

<Tab>/<Alt-Tab> between elements | <Space> selects | <F12> next screen

Press Enter.

This setting is not important.
Proceed to the next step.

Press Enter.

Red Hat Linux (C) 1999 Red Hat Software   Install bootloader

LILO

Creating initial ramdisk...

<Tab>/<Alt-Tab> between elements | <Space> selects | <F12> next screen

24 Automatic video card probe.

The video card is automatically probed and found.

Xconfigurator 3.82 - (C) 1999 Red Hat Software and others

PCI Probe

PCI probing found a:

PCI Entry: Trio32/Trio64
X Server : S3

Ok

<Tab>/<Alt-Tab> between elements | <Space> selects | <F12> next screen

Press Enter.

The progress of the installation is displayed.

Red Hat Linux (C) 1999 Red Hat Software   Install system

Install Status

Package: XFree86-S3-3.3.2.3-25
Size   : 4046k
Summary: XFree86 S3 server

           Packages   Bytes   Time
Total   :   1   3M
Completed :
Remaining :

<Tab>/<Alt-Tab> between elements | <Space> selects | <F12> next screen

TIP!

If Video Card Is Not Found

If the video card is not found, you will see a
selection of video cards. If you are unsure of
the video card type or you do not see it on
the list, select Generic VGA.

25 Select the monitor type.

❶ Use the ↑ ↓ keys to select Generic Monitor.

Xconfigurator 3.82 - (C) 1999 Red Hat Software and others

Monitor Setup

What type of monitor do you have? If you would rather specify the
sync frequencies of your monitor, choose "Custom" from the list.

Generic Monitor
Generic Multisync
HP 1280x1024-72Hz
Highscreen LE 1024
Hitachi SuperScan 20S
Hyundai DeluxScan 14S
Hyundai DeluxScan 15D

Ok   Back

<Tab>/<Alt-Tab> between elements | <Space> selects | <F12> next screen

❷ Use Tab to select OK.   ❸ Press Enter.

Xconfigurator 3.82 - (C) 1999 Red Hat Software and others

Screen Configuration

Xconfigurator now needs to setup the default resolution and
color depth. Most modern PCI video cards can be probed, and
Xconfigurator will automatically determine the best video
mode/color depth possible for your system. There is a chance,
however, this could lock up your system. If you would prefer
to give the required information instead of having it probed,
answer "Don't Probe" to the following question.

Don't Probe   Probe

<Tab>/<Alt-Tab> between elements | <Space> selects | <F12> next screen

Press Enter.

51

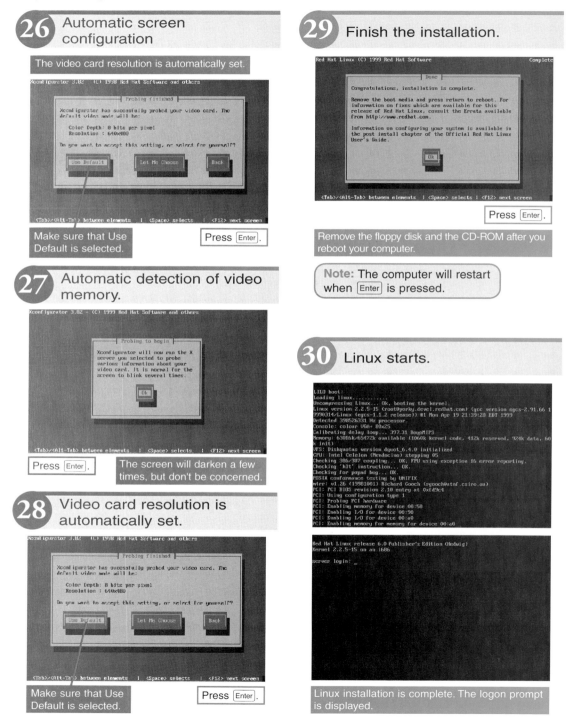

26 Automatic screen configuration

The video card resolution is automatically set.

Make sure that Use Default is selected.

Press Enter.

27 Automatic detection of video memory.

Press Enter.

The screen will darken a few times, but don't be concerned.

28 Video card resolution is automatically set.

Make sure that Use Default is selected.

Press Enter.

29 Finish the installation.

Press Enter.

Remove the floppy disk and the CD-ROM after you reboot your computer.

Note: The computer will restart when Enter is pressed.

30 Linux starts.

Linux installation is complete. The logon prompt is displayed.

Trouble With Booting Up After Installation

Linux uses LILO to boot up. If LILO is operating correctly, the character string "LILO:" is displayed before Linux boots. Enter "linux", then press [Enter] and Linux will start. Alternatively, Linux will start after five seconds if nothing is entered. Failure of Linux to start after installation is almost always tied to LILO.

The Installer Starts (LILO Does Not Display)

This happens because Linux is being booted up from the floppy disk or CD-ROM. Remove the medium, then press [Ctrl]+[Alt]+[Delete] to restart Linux.

LILO Does Not Display And "No Boot Device" Displays
(Message Differs From Computer To Computer)

This may occur because a boot flag was not attached when partitioning the hard disk. Start the installer again, and attach a boot flag to the region assigned to / (in the example in this book, /dev/hda2), using the a command of fdisk in the steps outlined on page 45. Then press [Ctrl]+[Alt]+[Delete] to restart.

LILO Is Only Displayed Briefly During Boot Up
And Then Numbers Are Shown Or Frozen

In almost all cases, this occurs because LILO cannot correctly recognize the information on the boot disk. There is no definitive way to solve this problem, but there has been some success in checking the Use Linear Mode option during the installation of LILO as explained on page 51.

Linux Does Not Boot Up At All

Linux might not boot up successfully if you create and use the boot disk that was not created in Step (21) on page 50. In this case, insert the created boot disk into the floppy disk drive and turn the power on. LILO: should display. Enter "Linux" and press [Enter], or wait ten seconds and Linux will start to boot. Remove the floppy disk after the logon screen appears. If this method does not work, try installing Linux again from the beginning. If that does not work, determine whether your PC can use Linux.

STEP UP

Laptops As Servers

Linux is not limited to desktop PCs. It can also be installed on laptop computers for use as a server, because Linux requires neither much CPU performance nor much memory. In some cases, a laptop computer makes a convenient server because it does not need much space, is portable, and is immune to power interruptions (batteries provide a backup power source).

Transportable To Individual Work Places

A Linux server does not have to be used as a fixed server. For example, you can install Linux on a laptop and use it as a server for your own network. You can then carry that laptop with you and utilize your own operating environment when using the remote location computer. In other words, you can take your own operating environment with you.

Installing Linux On A Laptop Computer

The key to installing Linux on a laptop computer is for the computer to have either an internal CD-ROM drive or a CD-ROM drive that can be connected to it easily. If a CD-ROM can be used, Linux can be installed in the same manner as for a desktop computer. If a CD-ROM drive cannot be connected, however, you must use a CD-ROM connected by a PCMCIA card or some other method of installation. In other words, be sure to first check whether a CD-ROM drive can be used before starting the installation.

Chapter 3
Mastering The Basic
Operations Of Linux

Operations in Linux are performed primarily by entering
commands from a keyboard. This chapter explains the file
system, which is essential to Linux operations, and provides
examples of how to use the command line.

Contents Of This Chapter

Running Linux

Login And Logout

In Linux, you must log in and log out to start and quit operations. Only previously registered users can use Linux, so user verification takes place during login. The login procedure not only enables users to begin operations, but also identifies which users are accessing the system. If you do not log in, you will not be able to use Linux. When you are finished using Linux, you must log out.

Starting Linux Operations

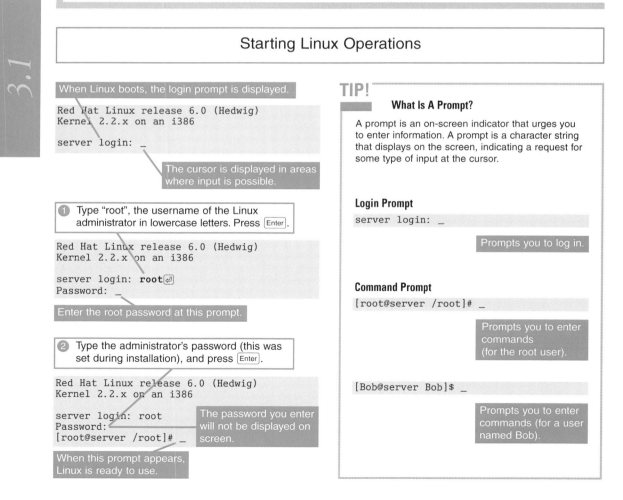

When Linux boots, the login prompt is displayed.

```
Red Hat Linux release 6.0 (Hedwig)
Kernel 2.2.x on an i386

server login: _
```

The cursor is displayed in areas where input is possible.

① Type "root", the username of the Linux administrator in lowercase letters. Press [Enter].

```
Red Hat Linux release 6.0 (Hedwig)
Kernel 2.2.x on an i386

server login: root↵
Password: _
```

Enter the root password at this prompt.

② Type the administrator's password (this was set during installation), and press [Enter].

```
Red Hat Linux release 6.0 (Hedwig)
Kernel 2.2.x on an i386

server login: root
Password: _
[root@server /root]# _
```

The password you enter will not be displayed on screen.

When this prompt appears, Linux is ready to use.

TIP!

What Is A Prompt?

A prompt is an on-screen indicator that urges you to enter information. A prompt is a character string that displays on the screen, indicating a request for some type of input at the cursor.

Login Prompt
```
server login: _
```
Prompts you to log in.

Command Prompt
```
[root@server /root]# _
```
Prompts you to enter commands (for the root user).

```
[Bob@server Bob]$ _
```
Prompts you to enter commands (for a user named Bob).

Starting Linux Operations From Login

A user must log in before they can begin to use Linux. The login procedure verifies whether the user is registered and identifies which users are using Linux. All users have a username and password, which are entered for verification during login. When this process is complete, the user can begin using Linux. When you finish your work in Linux, make sure that you log out by typing "exit" or "logout" at the command prompt. If you fail to do this, someone else can use your account without permission.

```
[root@server /root]# exit⏎
```

Type "exit" or "logout" and press Enter.

```
Red Hat Linux release 6.0 (Hedwig)
Kernel 2.2.x on an i386

server login:
```

The screen changes, and the login prompt is displayed.

Linux Users

Although Linux allows many people to use it simultaneously through a network, it cannot be accessed by just anyone. Access is limited to previously registered individuals called *users*. When Linux is installed, the only user initially set up is the *root* user. The root user is the administrator of Linux and is referred to as a *super user* to distinguish them from normal users. Chapter 4 explains how to register users.

Understanding Directories

All Linux files are kept in directories, which are equivalent to folders in Windows and Macintosh. Directories can be placed within directories in a structure called *nesting*. At the base of this *nesting* structure is the *root directory*. The positional relationship of directories and files is known as a *path*. This path is essential to command line operations, so make sure that you understand what this term means.

Linux Directories: The Same As Windows Folders

Linux directories are equivalent to folders in Windows and Macintosh, and, just like folders, directories can be placed within directories. If directory B is within directory A, then A is called a *parent directory*, while B is called a *subdirectory* of A. In Linux, all directories and files are located within the root directory, so moving up through parent directories will eventually lead to the root directory.

Directory Hierarchy Of Linux

From the root directory, all other directories form a hierarchy. Frequently used directory names are predetermined. Identical directory names can appear at various directory levels, but the directories' contents differ depending on their location.

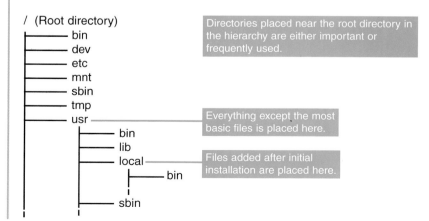

/ (Root directory)

Directories placed near the root directory in the hierarchy are either important or frequently used.

Everything except the most basic files is placed here.

Files added after initial installation are placed here.

3.2

General Directory Names

bin	Commands
sbin	Commands for the system administrator
dev	Files for accessing devices
etc	Configuration files
lib	Libraries (program segments and data)
mnt	Temporary mount location
tmp	Temporary storage location

The root directory is represented by a slash symbol (/) in Linux. If there is a directory A within the root directory, it is represented as /A. Further, if there is a subdirectory B within directory A, a slash symbol is used to separate the two directory names, and it is represented as /A/B. This method of using a slash symbol and the directory names to represent a location is known as a *path*. In Linux, all directories and files can be designated using a path starting at the slash symbol. The path starting at / (root directory), as in /A/B, is called an *absolute path*.

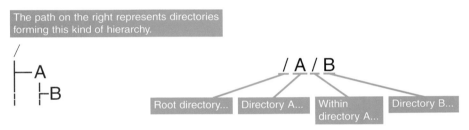

Current Directory: Base Of Operations

Rather than designating an absolute path every time, you can use the double-dot symbol to indicate the parent directory of the directory you are currently in.

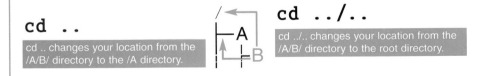

The directory where you are currently working is called the *current directory*. When a slash symbol is not appended to the beginning of the path, the location is represented relative to the current directory and is therefore called a *relative* path.

Uppercase And Lowercase

File and directory names in Linux are case sensitive. For example, /usr and /USR are treated as different items, so pay close attention to case when entering commands.

Mastering Commands

The command line interface–in which commands are entered and a response results–is central to all operations in Linux. Commands are character strings entered at the command prompt to execute an operation.

To specify what type of action the command should perform, arguments are entered after the command with character strings separated by spaces. You can modify the action of a standard command by specifying an option as an argument.

Understanding Command And Argument Relationships

All operations in Linux are executed by entering a command at the command prompt and pressing [Enter]. A command is a character string that designates an operation. After the command is executed, the results are displayed on screen. The command prompt is then ready to accept the next command.

Many commands accept arguments, which are used to specify what type of action the command should perform. Arguments are entered after the command, with the character strings separated by spaces. To specify that a space is included within an argument, surround it by single quotation marks (').

Insert a space between a command and an argument (more than one space can be inserted).

```
[root@server/root]# command   argument   argument...
```

When placing a space within an argument, surround it by single quotation marks (').

How To Use Options

An option is one type of argument. When you want to modify the function of a standard command, specify an option. The method used to specify an option differs depending on the command, although most options are entered with a hyphen (-) followed by a character string.

Example: **ls** command.

This command verifies which files and directories are in the current directory.

① Type "ls" in lowercase.

```
[root@server /root]# ls_
```

② Insert a space after the **ls** command.

```
[root@server /root]# ls _
```

③ Type "-a".

```
[root@server /root]# ls -a _
```

The results of the executed command (the contents of the current directory) are displayed on screen.

④ Press Enter.

```
[root@server /root]# ls -a↵
.                 .Xdefaults      .bash_logout    .bashrc         .tcshrc
..                .bash_history   .bash_profile   .cshrc
[root@server /root]# _
```

The command prompt will appear after the command is executed.

Commands That Do Not Display Their Result

Command operations include the result of an input; a response resulting from a command depends on the input command. Some commands do not display a response, even when the command is issued and the operation is executed. In Linux, if you make a mistake while entering a command or if the operation is not executed properly, you will always receive an error message. If nothing is displayed, the operation was executed correctly.

Changing Current Directories

change directory command (cd)

Using the absolute path in Linux to execute an operation can be cumbersome; using the relative path from the current directory, however, is quite easy. The current directory can be changed readily using the **cd** (change directory) command. When changing to a new directory, either an absolute path or a relative path from the current directory can be specified. With efficient changes in the current directory, specifying an absolute path when entering commands is easier.

Using The **cd** Command To Change The Current Directory

The current directory can be changed readily by using the **cd** command. To specify a new directory, you can use either an absolute path, which indicates the location from the root directory, or a relative path, which indicates the location from the current directory.

Example: Changing the current directory to the root directory.

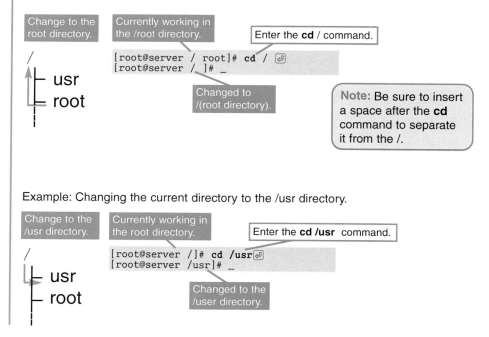

Change to the root directory.

Currently working in the /root directory.

Enter the **cd** / command.

```
[root@server / root]# cd / ⏎
[root@server / ]# _
```

Changed to /(root directory).

Note: Be sure to insert a space after the **cd** command to separate it from the /.

usr
root

Example: Changing the current directory to the /usr directory.

Change to the /usr directory.

Currently working in the root directory.

Enter the **cd /usr** command.

```
[root@server /]# cd /usr⏎
[root@server /usr]# _
```

Changed to the /user directory.

usr
root

Proper Use Of Absolute Paths And Relative Paths

Using an absolute path from /(root directory) to specify a file or directory every time you execute an operation is a tedious prospect. You can, however, specify a file or directory using a relative path from the current directory. For example, if you specify only local when the current directory is /usr, it has the same meaning as /usr/local. Consequently, moving the current directory to a location that makes it easier to enter a specified path simplifies operations.

Example: Changing the current directory to the root directory.

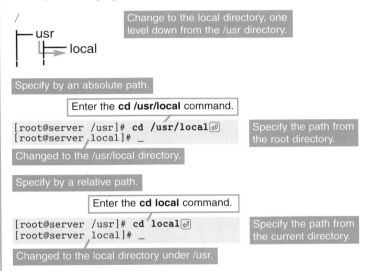

Example: Changing the current directory to the root directory.

How To Change To Your Home Directory

A home directory is the user's main working directory. When a user issues a **cd** command without specifying a directory, the directory is changed to the user's home directory. For example, the home directory of root is /root. The home directories of other users are located within the /home directory, and the directory names are identical to the username.

Example: Changing the current directory to the home directory.

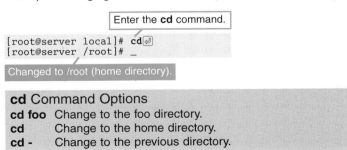

cd Command Options

cd foo	Change to the foo directory.
cd	Change to the home directory.
cd -	Change to the previous directory.

Displaying Directory Contents

list command (ls)

The **ls** (list) command is used to display information about the files and directories located within a directory. Execute this command without an argument to display information about the current directory. You can also specify a directory to display.

The **ls** command can display various types of information by passing options to the command as arguments. More than one option can be specified. The **ls** command is probably the most frequently used command in Linux.

Using The **ls** Command To Display Directory Contents

Files in Linux are the same as files in Windows and Macintosh: consisting of many applications, and text and data files. A directory can contain numerous files and sub-directories. Appending the -l option to the **ls** command results in the display of detailed information about the files and directories. Further, appending the -F option results in the display of a slash symbol (/) at the end of directories, allowing you to distinguish between files and directories.

Example: Displaying the contents of the /usr directory.

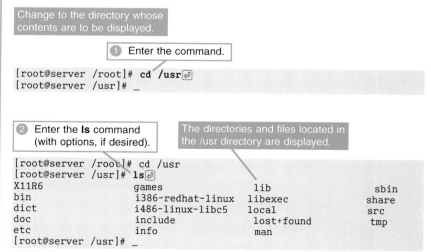

Change to the directory whose contents are to be displayed.

① Enter the command.

```
[root@server /root]# cd /usr↵
[root@server /usr]# _
```

② Enter the **ls** command (with options, if desired).

The directories and files located in the /usr directory are displayed.

```
[root@server /root]# cd /usr
[root@server /usr]# ls↵
X11R6          games          lib            sbin
bin            i386-redhat-linux  libexec    share
dict           i486-linux-libc5   local      src
doc            include        lost+found     tmp
etc            info           man
[root@server /usr]# _
```

Example: Display detailed information about the contents of the /usr directory.

Enter the command.

Detailed information about the directories and files located in the /usr directory is displayed.

```
[root@server /usr]# ls -l↵
total 58
drwxr-xr-x    8 root    root       1024 Oct 10 16:54 X11R6
drwxr-xr-x    2 root    root      13312 Feb 12  1999 bin
drwxr-xr-x    2 root    root       1024 Feb 12  1999 dict
drwxr-xr-x  116 root    root       3072 Feb 12  1999 doc
drwxr-xr-x    2 root    root       1024 Feb 12  1999 etc
drwxr-xr-x    2 root    root       1024 Feb 12  1999 games
drwxr-xr-x    4 root    root       1024 Feb 12  1999 i386-redhat-linux
drwxr-xr-x    3 root    root       1024 Feb 12  1999 i486-linux-libc5
drwxr-xr-x   22 root    root       4096 Feb 12  1999 include
drwxr-xr-x    2 root    root       6144 Feb 12  1999 info
drwxr-xr-x   32 root    root       6144 Feb 12  1999 lib
drwxr-xr-x    3 root    root       1024 Feb 12  1999 libexec
drwxr-xr-x   12 root    root       1024 Feb 12  1999 local
drwxr-xr-x    2 root    root      12288 Feb 12  1999 lost+found
drwxr-xr-x   12 root    root       1024 Feb 12  1999 man
drwxr-xr-x    2 root    root       2048 Feb 12  1999 sbin
drwxr-xr-x   20 root    root       1024 Feb 12  1999 share
drwxr-xr-x    4 root    root       1024 Feb 12  1999 src
lrwxrwxrwx    1 root    root         10 Feb 12  1999 tmp -> ../var/tmp
[root@server /usr]# _
```

Indicates a directory.

Example: Display the contents of the /usr directory by file type.

Enter the command.

/ appended to the end of a name indicates a directory.

```
[root@server /usr]# ls -F↵
X11R6/              games/                  lib/            sbin/
bin/                i386-redhat-linux/      libexec/        share/
dict/               i486-linux-libc5/       local/          src/
doc/                include/                lost+found/     tmp@
etc/                info/                   man/
[root@server /usr]# _
```

Example: Display the contents of a specific directory.

Enter the **ls /usr/local** (absolute pathnames) or **ls local** (relative pathnames) command.

The contents of the local directory within /usr are displayed.

```
[root@server /usr]# ls local↵
bin     doc     etc     games   info    lib     man     sbin    src
[root@server /usr]# _
```

ls Command Options

ls -a   Displays all files, including hidden files (those starting with a dot), and directories.

ls -l   Displays detailed information.

ls -t   Displays by modification date.

ls -F   Displays by file type.

ls -R   Displays everything including the contents of subdirectories.

Understanding Permissions

Permissions

All files and directories in Linux have user owners and group owners to whom permissions are granted. Permissions specify whether a particular user can access a file or directory.

Permissions are used in Linux to maintain control over files and directories. The -l option of the **ls** command is used to display permissions.

Permissions Show Access Privileges To Files And Directories

Information about the user owner, group owner, and permissions is included in all files and directories. When a user attempts to access a file or directory, the permission indicates whether they are authorized to do so. When directory contents are displayed using the **ls** command with the -1 option appended, a row of nine characters consisting of r, w, x, and - is displayed. These characters indicate permissions. From the left, three groups of the rwx character string are displayed in which each letter represents a different permission type; while a hyphen (-) indicates that there is no permission. From the left, the three groups indicate owner access privileges, group access privileges, and other user access privileges, respectively.

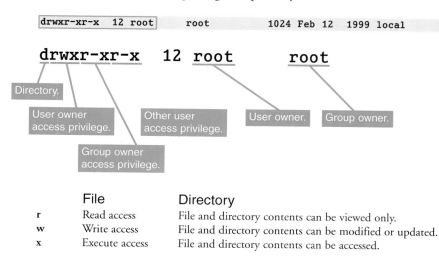

	File	Directory
r	Read access	File and directory contents can be viewed only.
w	Write access	File and directory contents can be modified or updated.
x	Execute access	File and directory contents can be accessed.

rwxr-xr-x for a directory (user owner is root, group owner is root).

```
drwxr-xr-x 12 root   root
```

- When the user is root, the user can view, modify, and access internal files or directories.
- When the user belongs to the root group, the user can view and access internal files or directories.
- When the user is neither of the above, the user can view and access internal files or directories.

rwxr-xr-x for a file (user owner is root, group owner is root).

```
-rwxr-xr-x  1  root    root
```

- When the user is root, the user can read, write, and execute the file.
- When the user belongs to the root group, the user can read and execute the file.
- When the user is neither of the above, the user can read and execute the file.

How To Set Permissions

With permissions, a single number can represent the rwx character string, with the total permission consisting of three numbers. Here, r is equal to 4, w is equal to 2, and x is equal to 1; the sum of the numbers represents the permission. For example, the number 7 represents rwx.

```
4       2       1
r       w       x       4+2+1=7
r       -       x       4+0+1=5
r       w       -       4+2+0=6
r       -       -       4+0+0=4
```

Because rwx is 7 and r-x is 5, the permission of rwxr-xr-x is represented by the number 755.

```
r w x       r - x       r - x
4+2+1       4+0+1       4+0+1
  7           5           5
```

The permission number is used when changing file and directory permissions and when specifying permissions.

Basic File Operations

Copy (cp), Move (mv), Delete/Remove (rm), And Make Directory (mkdir) Commands

Copy, move, and delete are basic tools used to work with files and directories. Copy (**cp**) creates a duplicate of a selected file or directory. Move (**mv**) transfers a selected file to a different location. When using the copy or move tools, the affected files can be saved using the same or a different file name. Delete (**rm**) eliminates a file or directory from the Linux system altogether.

Use this tool carefully because, once deleted, you cannot recover these files.
The make directory (**mkdir**) command is used to create a new directory.

- **cp**   Copy files or directories
- **rm**   Delete files or directories
- **mv**   Move files
- **mkdir**   Make directory

Using The cp Command To Copy Files

The **cp** command copies a file specified in the first argument to a path specified in the second argument (as in **cp** *optional_pathname/from_this_filename optional_pathname/to_this_filename*). If you specify a file name in the pathname of the second argument, you can change the file name when you copy.

Example: Copy a file named motd located in the /etc directory to the /tmp directory.

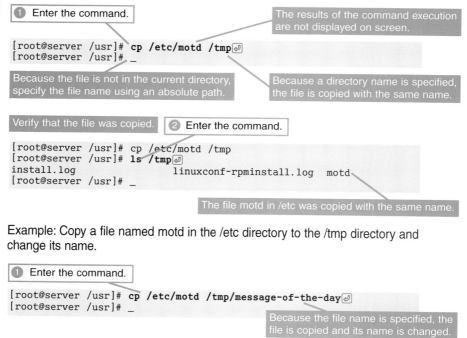

① Enter the command.

The results of the command execution are not displayed on screen.

```
[root@server /usr]# cp /etc/motd /tmp⏎
[root@server /usr]# _
```

Because the file is not in the current directory, specify the file name using an absolute path.

Because a directory name is specified, the file is copied with the same name.

Verify that the file was copied.

② Enter the command.

```
[root@server /usr]# cp /etc/motd /tmp
[root@server /usr]# ls /tmp⏎
install.log              linuxconf-rpminstall.log   motd
[root@server /usr]# _
```

The file motd in /etc was copied with the same name.

Example: Copy a file named motd in the /etc directory to the /tmp directory and change its name.

① Enter the command.

```
[root@server /usr]# cp /etc/motd /tmp/message-of-the-day⏎
[root@server /usr]# _
```

Because the file name is specified, the file is copied and its name is changed.

② Enter the command.

```
[root@server /usr]# cp /etc/motd /tmp/message-of-the-day
[root@server /usr]# ls /tmp⏎
install.log              message-of-the-day
linuxconf-rpminstall.log  motd
[root@server /usr]# _
```

The file motd in /etc was copied with the specified name.

Using The **mkdir** Command To Create Directories

The **mkdir** (make directory) command creates the directory specified in the first argument.

Example: Create a new directory in the /tmp directory.

① Enter the command.

② Enter the command.

Move to the /tmp directory and create a directory called test.

```
[root@server /usr]# cd /tmp⏎
[root@server /tmp]# mkdir test⏎
[root@server /tmp]# _
```

The result of the command execution is not displayed on screen.

③ Enter the command.

The directory test was created in /tmp.

```
[root@server /usr]# cd /tmp
[root@server /tmp]# mkdir test
[root@server /tmp]# ls -F⏎
install.log              message_of_the_day      test/
linuxconf-rpminstall.log  motd
[root@server /tmp]#
```

Using The **mv** Command To Move Files

The **mv** (move) command moves a file specified in the first argument to a path specified in the second argument. If you specify a file name in the pathname of the second argument, you can change the file name when you move the file.

Example: Move a file to the test directory.

① Enter the command.

Move file motd to the test directory.

```
[root@server /tmp]# mv motd test⏎
[root@server /tmp]# _
```

The result of the command execution is not displayed on screen.

② Enter the command.

```
[root@server /tmp]# mv motd test
[root@server /tmp]# ls -FR⏎
install.log              message_of_the_day
linuxconf-rpminstall.log  test/

test:
motd
[root@server /tmp]# _
```

Display the test directory contents, including subdirectories.

File motd was moved to the test directory.

Using The **rm** Command To Delete Files

The **rm** (remove) command deletes the path specified in the first argument. Deleted files cannot be recovered in Linux, so exercise care when using this command.

Example: Delete a file in the test/ directory.

① Change the directory.

Delete motd in the test directory.

```
[root@server /tmp]# cd test↵
[root@server test]# ls↵
motd
[root@server test]# _
```

② Enter the **cd test** or (using absolute path names) **cd /tmp/test** command.

③ Enter the command.

```
[root@server /tmp]# cd test
[root@server test]# ls
motd
[root@server test]# rm motd↵
rm: remove 'motd'? y↵
[root@server test]# _
```

④ Confirmation message is displayed. Type "y" and press Enter.

The result of the command execution is not displayed on screen.

```
[[root@server /tmp]# cd test
[root@server test]# ls
motd
[root@server test]# rm motd
rm: remove 'motd'? y
[root@server test]# ls↵
[root@server test]# _
```

⑤ Enter the **ls** or (to be absolutely certain, the **ls –a**) command.

The file motd is deleted. Nothing is displayed on screen.

Using The **mv** Command To Change File Names

In Linux, the **mv** command can be used both to move files and to change file names. You can change a file name by moving the file to the same directory and assigning it a different name. When using the **mv** command to change a file name, avoid the common mistake of specifying a directory that does not exist.

cp, mv, rm Command Options

cp (mv, rm)	**-i**	Receive confirmation, then copy (move, delete).
cp (mv, rm)	**-f**	Force copy without confirmation (move, delete).
cp (mv, rm)	**-r**	Copy all contents of directory (move, delete).

Input Support Function: Making File And Directory Names Easier To Enter

The program that displays the command prompt and accepts command input is called a *shell* in Linux. The shell has a function called the *input support function for file names* that automatically supplies the remaining characters of a file name after you enter the first character.

If you enter the first character of a file name and press [Tab], the input support function automatically enters the remaining characters and displays the file name if there is only one that begins with that character within the directory path. If there are other file names beginning with the same character, press [Tab] twice to view a list of possible file names. Learning to use this command will enable you to avoid repeatedly entering long file names and also using the **ls** command over and over.

Example: Enter a directory name called /usr/i386-redhat-linux.

① Type "cd /u" and then press [Tab].

```
[root@server test]# cd /u[Tab]
```

```
[root@server test]# cd /usr/
```

/usr/ is entered automatically.

② Type "i" and then press [Tab].

```
[root@server test]# cd /usr/i[Tab]
```

When there is more than one
file, a beep sounds.

③ Press [Tab] again.

```
[root@server test]# cd /usr/i[Tab]
i386-redhat-linux   i486-linux-libc5     include           info
[root@server test]# cd /usr/i
```

Files are displayed, and the file being requested
is displayed at the command prompt.

④ Type "3" and then press [Tab].

```
[root@server test]# cd /usr/i
i386-redhat-linux   i486-linux-libc5     include           info
[root@server test]# cd /usr/i3[Tab]
```

```
[root@server test]# cd /usr/i
i386-redhat-linux   i486-linux-libc5     include           info
[root@server test]# cd /usr/i386-redhat-linux/ _
```

The remainder of the file
name is entered automatically.

Setting Up The CD-ROM Drive

mount

The concept of drives as they are known in Windows and Macintosh does not exist in Linux. When using a CD-ROM in Linux, the CD-ROM must be grafted on to the directory structure before it can be accessed.

This grafting process is called *mounting*. Mounting is executed with the **mount** command; unmounting is executed with the **umount** command, usually available only to the Super-user. Floppy disks must also be mounted.

Mounting And Using The CD-ROM And Other Disk Drives

In Linux, all disks form one part of the directory hierarchy within /. The Linux directory structure is like a large tree with disks branched off as directories. When a disk and a directory are linked together in the mount operation, the disk can then be accessed as part of that directory.

Types Of Mounted Disks

There are many types of disks. Specify the type of disk to mount using the -t option appended to the **mount** command. For example, specify iso9660 to mount CD-ROMs. For Windows formatted floppy disks use the **mount -t ext2 /dev/fd0 /mnt** command.

Using CD-ROMs With Linux

1 Insert the CD-ROM.

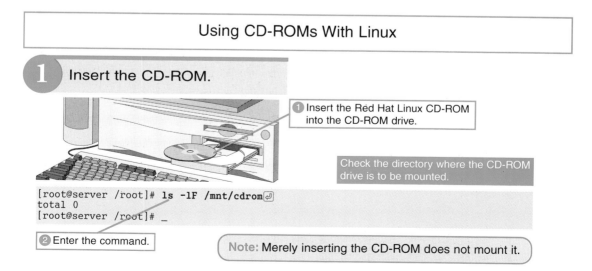

❶ Insert the Red Hat Linux CD-ROM into the CD-ROM drive.

Check the directory where the CD-ROM drive is to be mounted.

```
[root@server /root]# ls -1F /mnt/cdrom⏎
total 0
[root@server /root]# _
```

❷ Enter the command.

Note: Merely inserting the CD-ROM does not mount it.

2 Mount the CD-ROM.

Note: The device name of the CD-ROM is /dev/cdrom.

❶ Enter the command.

```
[root@server /root]# ls -lF /mnt/cdrom
total 0
[root@server /root]# mount -t iso9660 /dev/cdrom /mnt/cdrom⏎
mount: block device /dev/cdrom is write-protected, mounting read-only
ISO9660 Extensions: Microsoft Joliet Level 3
[root@server /root]# _
```

A message is displayed, indicating the format state and other information.

❷ Enter the command.

```
[root@server /root]# mount -t iso9660 /dev/cdrom /mnt/cdrom
mount: block device /dev/cdrom is write-protected, mounting read-only
ISO9660 Extensions: Microsoft Joliet Level 3
[root@server /root]# ls -lF /mnt/cdrom⏎
total 113
-rw-r--r--   1 root     root        19686 May 29  1997 COPYING
-rw-r--r--   1 root     root         3017 Oct 13 05:14 README
-rw-r--r--   1 510      510          2751 Sep 20  1997 RPM-PGP-KEY
drwxr-xr-x   5 root     root         2048 Jan 29 09:06 RedHat/
drwxr-xr-x   2 root     root        63488 Jan 29 09:06 SRPMS/
-r--r--r--   1 root     root          580 Feb 13  1999 TRANS.TBL
-rwxr--r--   1 root     root         2048 Jan 29 09:06 boot.cat*
drwxrwxrwx   4 root     root         2048 Feb 11 05:04 dekiru/
drwxr-xr-x   6 root     root         2048 Jan 29 09:06 doc/
drwxr-xr-x   6 root     root         4096 Jan 29 09:06 dosutils/
drwxr-xr-x   2 root     root         2048 Jan 29 09:06 images/
drwxrwxrwx   2 root     root         2048 Feb 11 05:05 macintosh/
drwxr-xr-x   5 root     root         2048 Jan  2  1970 misc/
dr-xr-xr-x   2 root     root         2048 Oct 15 17:43 rr_moved/
drwxrwxrwx   2 root     root         2048 Feb 11 15:24 windows/
[root@server /root]# _
```

The contents of the CD-ROM are displayed.

Unmounting To Remove The Disk

To remove the CD-ROM or floppy disks in a mounted state, you must use the **umount** command (**umount - no** *n*), which for a CD-ROM would be **umount /mnt/cdrom**.

```
[root@server /root]# umount /mnt/cdrom⏎
[root@server /root]# _
```

Shutting Down Linux

Shutdown

Even if you log out, Linux continues its functions as a server. The **shutdown** command is used to quit all server operations and to stop and restart Linux.

In most cases, Linux does not require the OS itself to be restarted after settings are changed; only user logout is required. Because of this, the **shutdown** command is used only when the power of the PC where Linux is installed must be turned off.

1 Log in as root.

Type "root", and then enter the root password.

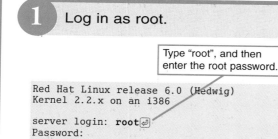

```
Red Hat Linux release 6.0 (Hedwig)
Kernel 2.2.x on an i386

server login: root⏎
Password:
Last login: Fri Feb 12 15:32:51 on tty1
[root@server /root]# _
```

2 Execute the **shutdown** command.

```
Red Hat Linux release 6.0 (Hedwig)
Kernel 2.2.x on an i386

server login: root
Password:
Last login: Fri Feb 12 15:32:51 on tty1
[root@server /root]# shutdown -h now⏎
```

Enter the command.

```
The system is halted
System halted
```

When this message is displayed, the power can be turned off.

The Little-Used **Shutdown** Command

In Linux, when a setting is changed, only the portion related to that change needs to be restarted (unlike Windows and Macintosh, where the entire operating system must be restarted); therefore, the need to restart Linux itself is rare. If a problem develops in the system, finding the source of the problem and taking steps to resolve it, rather than restarting the system, allows Linux to continue operations without hindrance.

Even when you stop working and log out, you should not shut Linux down because the server functions will continue to operate. This is why the **shutdown** command is infrequently used.

How To Use The **Shutdown** Command

The options for the **shutdown** command are shown below:

> shutdown -option time [message].

Be sure to specify a time to stop the system when using the **shutdown** command. If you specify "now", operations begin to stop just after the **shutdown** command is executed. If you specify "+30", operations begin to stop 30 minutes later. If you specify "6:00 a.m.", operations begin to stop at that clock time.

A message used to notify all users logged in to Linux of the system shutdown can be attached to the **shutdown** command.

MESSAGE

The following message will display on all computers connected to Linux via a telnet connection:

```
shutdown +5 because of a power cut
```

The following message will display on all computers connected to Linux via a telnet connection:

```
Broadcast message from root (ttyp0) Tue Jan 26 15:07:08 1999...
because of a power cut
The system is going DOWN to maintenance mode in 5 minutes !!
```

MESSAGE

Shutdown Command Options

shutdown -h	Quit Linux.
shutdown -r	Restart Linux after quitting.
shutdown -c	Specify a time and cancel an already executing shutdown.

STEP UP

Applying The **man** Command

In Linux, you can use the **man** command to search all types of manuals, starting with the manual for commands.

Basics In Using The **man** Command

man *[option] [section] keyword*

Usage Example

```
[root@server /root]# man ls⏎
```
Search the manual for the ls command.

man Command Options

If you're not certain of the exact command you're looking for, specify a keyword when using the **-k** option with the **man** command to view a list of related items. You also can use the - **man apropos** command for more information.

man Command Sections

The **man** command includes *sections*, which are parts of the manual divided into applications. To specify a section, put the section number before the keyword. Sections are numbered from 1 through 9. For example, commands are 1, file formats are 5, and management commands are 8.

Example Of Specifying A Section

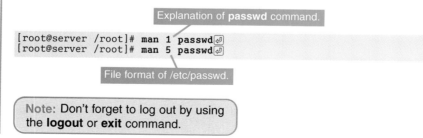

Explanation of **passwd** command.

```
[root@server /root]# man 1 passwd⏎
[root@server /root]# man 5 passwd⏎
```

File format of /etc/passwd.

> **Note:** Don't forget to log out by using the **logout** or **exit** command.

Chapter 4
Registering As A Linux User

When using Linux, it is absolutely necessary to register users. These registered users form the basic unit when using Linux. This chapter explains how to register users.

Contents Of This Chapter

Understanding The Role Of The User

A Look At Users

In Linux, only previously registered individuals, called *users*, have access to the system. Linux allows multiple users access to one computer through a network and identifies users by their username. The login procedure not only enables users to begin operations, but also identifies which users are accessing the system.

When managing users in Linux (although a single user is the basic unit), groups with multiple users can also be set up.

The Role Of Linux Users

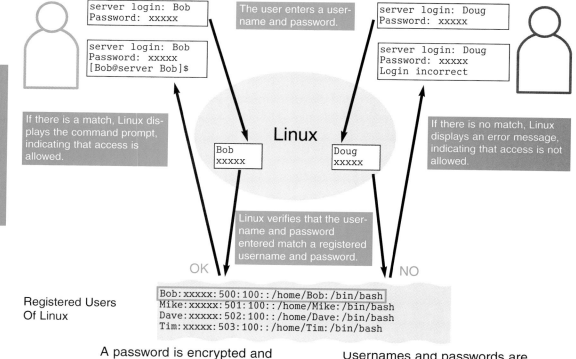

Registered User

Unregistered User

```
server login: Bob
Password: xxxxx
```

```
server login: Bob
Password: xxxxx
[Bob@server Bob]$
```

The user enters a user-name and password.

```
server login: Doug
Password: xxxxx
```

```
server login: Doug
Password: xxxxx
Login incorrect
```

If there is a match, Linux displays the command prompt, indicating that access is allowed.

Linux

```
Bob
xxxxx
```

```
Doug
xxxxx
```

If there is no match, Linux displays an error message, indicating that access is not allowed.

Linux verifies that the user-name and password entered match a registered username and password.

OK

NO

Registered Users Of Linux

```
Bob:xxxxx:500:100::/home/Bob:/bin/bash
Mike:xxxxx:501:100::/home/Mike:/bin/bash
Dave:xxxxx:502:100::/home/Dave:/bin/bash
Tim:xxxxx:503:100::/home/Tim:/bin/bash
```

A password is encrypted and saved, known only to the person entering it.

Usernames and passwords are necessary to identify users and to ensure the security of Linux.

User Environment

- The range in which a single user operates can be limited.

- Operations are carried out primarily in home directories.
  A user with the username "Bob" will work primarily in /home/Bob.

- Users can be specified to carry out operations.
  (To carry out operations as root, change to root by using
  the **su** command after first logging in as a user.)

A user with the username Bob,
will work primarily in /home/Bob.

`[Bob@server Bob]$`

Understanding User And Group Relationships

- The range in which a group operates can be limited.

- Groups can be freely created, and one user can belong to
  many groups.

Because Linux exists in a client/server environment, to even
log on to Linux you need to be a registered user.

Bob
Mike
Dave
Tim
Ian

Bob
Mike
Dave
Tim
Ian

users

Bob
Mike
Ian

young

Dave
Tim

senior

One user can belong to
numerous groups.

Setup

- Register users to use Linux.

- Set passwords.

- Create groups.

Registering Linux Users

useradd

Users are registered in Linux to allow them to log in and to identify which users are using Linux. All operations in Linux are managed in terms of the individual user, which forms the basic unit when dealing with work areas, file access privileges, and other aspects of Linux. Even when operating as root, as a basic principle (because of security) you do not log in as root initially. You log in first as a user, and then change to root using the **su** command.

The **useradd** command is used in Linux to register new users.

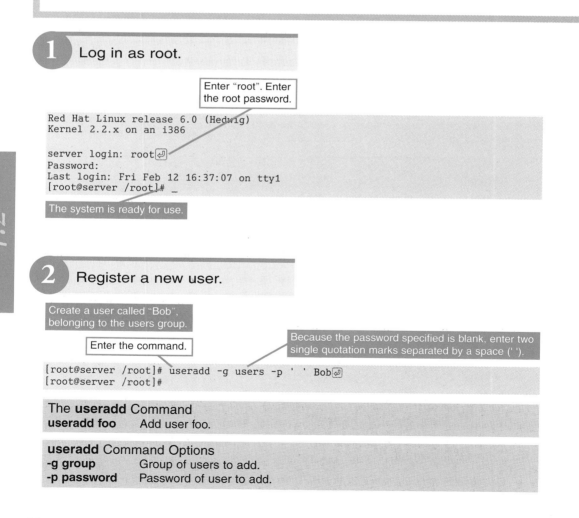

1 Log in as root.

> Enter "root". Enter the root password.

```
Red Hat Linux release 6.0 (Hedwig)
Kernel 2.2.x on an i386

server login: root⏎
Password:
Last login: Fri Feb 12 16:37:07 on tty1
[root@server /root]# _
```

The system is ready for use.

2 Register a new user.

Create a user called "Bob", belonging to the users group.

> Enter the command.

Because the password specified is blank, enter two single quotation marks separated by a space (' ').

```
[root@server /root]# useradd -g users -p ' ' Bob⏎
[root@server /root]#
```

The **useradd** Command
useradd foo   Add user foo.

useradd Command Options
-g group   Group of users to add.
-p password   Password of user to add.

User Roles

Because Linux allows multiple individuals to access the system through a network, users are identified by their usernames. The following list shows the process employed to identify users:

• Divide work areas into home directories. (A home directory is created in /home automatically when the user is registered.)
• Identify file access privileges.
• Identify user services. (Email addresses is one of these services.)

Verifying New Users

Use the **id** command to verify whether a user was registered correctly. Specify the username you want to verify, and execute the **id** command. If the user is registered, their username and the groups to which they belong are displayed.

```
[root@server /root]# id Bob⏎
uid=500(Bob) gid=100(users)
[root@server /root]# _
```

Username.   Group name.

Deleting Users

Use the **userdel** command to delete registered users. Even if you delete a user, his or her home directory and any contents remain on the hard disk.

```
[root@server /root]# userdel Bob⏎
[root@server /root]# _
```

Principle Of Not Directly Logging In As Root

After registering users, do not directly log in as root. If you do log in as root, someone else will be able to carry out operations as root without your knowledge. For this reason, log in first as a user, and then change to root using the **su** command. The **su** command is not an abbreviation for super user, but means substitute user or switch user.

The **su** command changes users. If executed without arguments, this command changes the user to root.

Changing Passwords

passwd

Passwords are set so that only registered users can access the system. Linux requests the password to be entered, along with the username, at login. The password can be a combination of alphanumeric characters and symbols. Passwords are set and changed using the **passwd** command.

The password is the sole key protecting each user's information. Do not choose an obvious password, and keep your password to yourself.

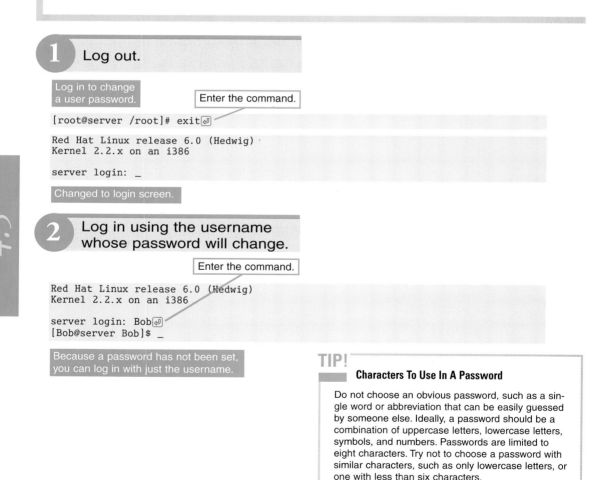

1 Log out.

Log in to change a user password.

Enter the command.

```
[root@server /root]# exit⏎

Red Hat Linux release 6.0 (Hedwig)
Kernel 2.2.x on an i386

server login: _
```

Changed to login screen.

2 Log in using the username whose password will change.

Enter the command.

```
Red Hat Linux release 6.0 (Hedwig)
Kernel 2.2.x on an i386

server login: Bob⏎
[Bob@server Bob]$ _
```

Because a password has not been set, you can log in with just the username.

TIP!

Characters To Use In A Password

Do not choose an obvious password, such as a single word or abbreviation that can be easily guessed by someone else. Ideally, a password should be a combination of uppercase letters, lowercase letters, symbols, and numbers. Passwords are limited to eight characters. Try not to choose a password with similar characters, such as only lowercase letters, or one with less than six characters.

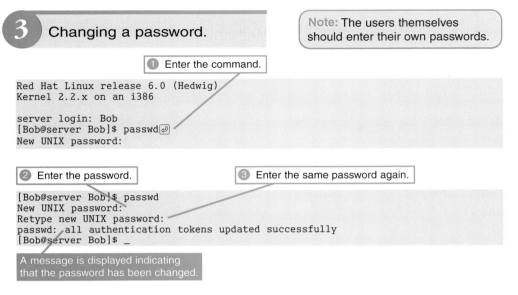

3 Changing a password.

Note: The users themselves should enter their own passwords.

① Enter the command.

```
Red Hat Linux release 6.0 (Hedwig)
Kernel 2.2.x on an i386

server login: Bob
[Bob@server Bob]$ passwd⏎
New UNIX password:
```

② Enter the password.

③ Enter the same password again.

```
[Bob@server Bob]$ passwd
New UNIX password:
Retype new UNIX password:
passwd: all authentication tokens updated successfully
[Bob@server Bob]$ _
```

A message is displayed indicating that the password has been changed.

Passwords: Important Keys

Passwords are the only keys safeguarding each user's information. If someone else discovers your password, they can log in to Linux using your username. Even though you are working on the same network, it's impossible to know what they are doing. For this reason, even on an intranet, passwords should be managed carefully. Also, it is a mistake to think that you will be the only one affected. If someone harms the system while using an assumed username, you will not be able to find any evidence of this, so not only you, but also others, will be inconvenienced.

Forgetting Passwords

If a user forgets his or her password, log in as root and set a new, simple password. Specify the username and execute the **passwd** command to set a password. Allow the user to log in and set a new password.

```
[root@server /root]# passwd Bob⏎
New UNIX password:
Retype new UNIX password:
passwd: all authentication tokens updated successfully
[root@server /root]# _
```

Creating New Groups

Editing Groups Using vi

Because identifying individual Linux users can be a cumbersome task, it's sometimes useful to identify users as a group. This can be done by setting up groups with multiple users. Groups can be created freely and can have any number of members.

Groups are set up by adding them to the group registration file called /etc/group. Use one of the two special versions of vi to edit this file (vipw) and set up groups (vigr). Of these two editors, vigr is the best choice for editing the group file and vipw for editing the password file.

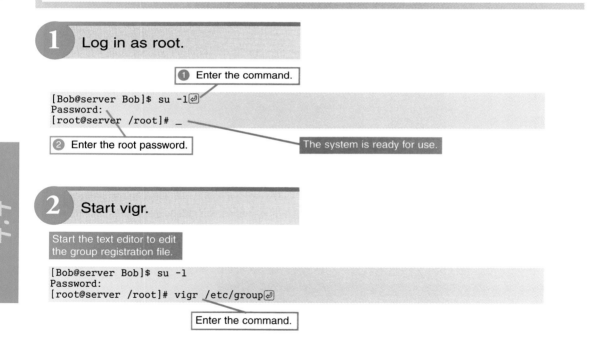

1 Log in as root.

❶ Enter the command.

```
[Bob@server Bob]$ su -l↵
Password:
[root@server /root]# _
```

② Enter the root password.

The system is ready for use.

2 Start vigr.

Start the text editor to edit the group registration file.

```
[Bob@server Bob]$ su -l
Password:
[root@server /root]# vigr /etc/group↵
```

Enter the command.

3 The vi edit screen is displayed.

The vi text editor (vigr) starts, and the group registration file is opened.

Tip!

The Two Modes Of The vi Editor

The vi editors have two modes: command and insert. Characters cannot be entered while in the command mode; rather, commands are entered that allow you to begin entering text by changing to the insert mode. Press ⎄Esc⎄ to return to the command mode from the insert mode.

```
root::0:root
bin::1:root,bin,daemon
daemon::2:root,bin,daemon
sys::3:root,bin,adm
adm::4:root,adm,daemon
tty::5:
disk::6:root
lp::7:daemon,lp
mem::8:
kmem::9:
wheel::10:root
mail::12:mail
news::13:news
uucp::14:uucp
man::15:
games::20:
gopher::30:
dip::40:
ftp::50:
nobody::99:
users::100:
floppy:x:19:
pppusers:x:230:
popusers:x:231
"/etc/group" 25 lines, 352 characters
```

TIP!

How To Move The Cursor

Use the ↑,↓, ←, →, and other keys in vi to move the cursor.

j	Down.
k	Up.
h	Back.
l	Right.
w	Moves right to next word.
b	Moves left to next word.
$	Moves to the end of the line.
0	Moves to the beginning of the line.
:$⏎	Moves to the end of the file.
:n⏎	Moves to the nth line number.
	(Press 1 to move to beginning of line.)
⎄Ctrl⎄ + **f**	Scrolls forward one screen.
⎄Ctrl⎄ + **b**	Scrolls back one screen.

TIP!

Commands Used In vi

Command Mode→Insert Mode

a	Inserts characters to the right of the cursor.
i	Inserts characters at the cursor.
o	Inserts characters on the next line.

Command Mode

x	Deletes characters at the cursor.
dd	Deletes the line where the cursor is located.
yy	Copies the line where the cursor is located.
p	Pastes at the cursor.
P	Pastes after the cursor.
	(Pastes text just deleted or text copied.)

/word⏎ **Searches for a specified word.**

	(Press n to display the next word.)
:w ⏎	Saves the file.
:q ⏎	Quits the vi editor.

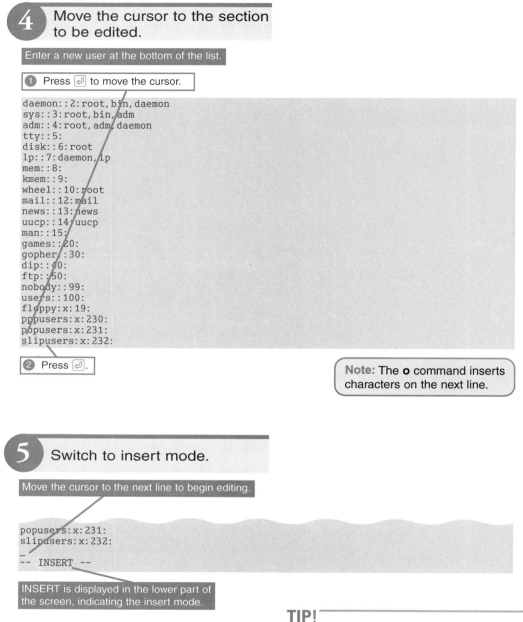

4 Move the cursor to the section to be edited.

Enter a new user at the bottom of the list.

1 Press ↵ to move the cursor.

```
daemon::2:root,bin,daemon
sys::3:root,bin,adm
adm::4:root,adm,daemon
tty::5:
disk::6:root
lp::7:daemon,lp
mem::8:
kmem::9:
wheel::10:root
mail::12:mail
news::13:news
uucp::14:uucp
man::15:
games::20:
gopher::30:
dip::40:
ftp::50:
nobody::99:
users::100:
floppy:x:19:
popusers:x:230:
popusers:x:231:
slipusers:x:232:
```

2 Press ↵.

Note: The **o** command inserts characters on the next line.

5 Switch to insert mode.

Move the cursor to the next line to begin editing.

```
popusers:x:231:
slipusers:x:232:

-- INSERT --
```

INSERT is displayed in the lower part of the screen, indicating the insert mode.

TIP!
Primary Group

Users belong to groups specified by **useradd** and added in /etc/group. Groups specified by **useradd** are called primary groups and do not need to be written in /etc/group like other groups.

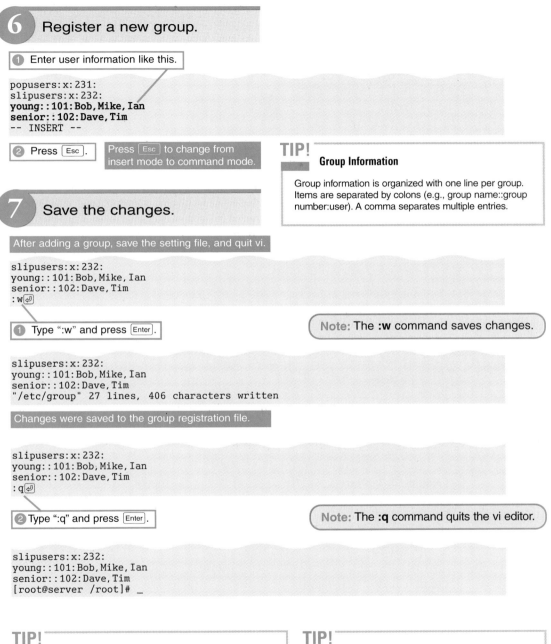

6 Register a new group.

① Enter user information like this.

```
popusers:x:231:
slipusers:x:232:
young::101:Bob,Mike,Ian
senior::102:Dave,Tim
-- INSERT --
```

② Press Esc.

Press Esc to change from insert mode to command mode.

TIP!

Group Information

Group information is organized with one line per group. Items are separated by colons (e.g., group name::group number:user). A comma separates multiple entries.

7 Save the changes.

After adding a group, save the setting file, and quit vi.

```
slipusers:x:232:
young::101:Bob,Mike,Ian
senior::102:Dave,Tim
:w⏎
```

① Type ":w" and press Enter.

Note: The **:w** command saves changes.

```
slipusers:x:232:
young::101:Bob,Mike,Ian
senior::102:Dave,Tim
"/etc/group" 27 lines, 406 characters written
```

Changes were saved to the group registration file.

```
slipusers:x:232:
young::101:Bob,Mike,Ian
senior::102:Dave,Tim
:q⏎
```

② Type ":q" and press Enter.

Note: The **:q** command quits the vi editor.

```
slipusers:x:232:
young::101:Bob,Mike,Ian
senior::102:Dave,Tim
[root@server /root]# _
```

TIP!

Reflecting Changes In Group Information

If group information is changed by editing /etc/group while an applicable user is logged in, the changes will not be reflected until the user logs out and logs back in again.

TIP!

How To Verify Registered Groups

The **groups** command allows you to verify whether groups were registered correctly. Specify the username to verify.

Using vi

The vi editor has two modes: command and insert. Characters cannot be entered while in the command mode; rather, commands are entered that allow you to begin entering text by changing to the insert mode. Press [Esc] to return to the command mode from the insert mode.

Insert Characters

i   Inserts characters at the cursor

a   Inserts characters to the right of the cursor.

o   Inserts character on the next line.

Delete Characters

x   Deletes characters at the cursor.

Search Text

/word Searches for a specified word.

Type n to continue searching.

vi Command List

Basic Operations

Command Mode / Insert Mode

a	Inserts characters to the right of the cursor.
A	Inserts characters at the end of line where the cursor is located.
i	Inserts characters at the cursor.
I	Inserts characters at the beginning of the line.
o	Inserts characters on the next line.
O	Inserts characters on the previous line.

Command Mode

x	Deletes characters at the cursor.
dd	Deletes the line where the cursor is located.
yy	Copies the line where the cursor is located.
p	Pastes text just deleted or copied at the cursor.
P	Pastes text just deleted or copied to the right of the cursor.
/word ⏎	Searches previous text for the specified word. (Press n to display the next word.)
?word ⏎	Searches subsequent text for the specified word. (Press n to display the next word.)
:$s/old/new/g ⏎	Replaces an old character string with a new character string (no verification).
:$s/old/new/cg ⏎	Replaces an old character string with a new character string (with y or n verification).

Saving Files And Quitting vi

:w ⏎	Saves the file.
:q ⏎	Quits vi editor.
:w! ⏎, :q! ⏎	Forcibly executes :w and :q.

Cursor Movement

j	Down.
k	Up.
h	Back.
l	Right.
w	Moves right to next word.
b	Moves left to next word.
$	Moves to end of line.
O	Moves to beginning of the line.
:$ ⏎	Moves to the end of the file.
:n ⏎	Moves to the nth line number. (Press 1 to move to the beginning of the line.)
Ctrl + f	Scrolls forward one screen.
Ctrl + b	Scrolls rearward one screen.

The vi editor in the command mode can combine command and cursor operations.

c	Replaces text from the cursor to a specified position.
d	Deletes text from the cursor to a specified position.

(Usage Examples)

cw	Replaces text from the cursor to the end of the word, then changes to insert mode.
dw	Deletes text from the cursor to the end of the word.
c ⏎	Replaces text from the cursor to the end of the line, then changes to insert mode.
d ⏎	Deletes text from the cursor to the end of the line.

STEP UP

Managing Users And Passwords

Information about Linux users is stored in the file /etc/passwd. The **useradd** command introduced in this chapter automatically edits the /etc/passwd file. Each line contains the information about one user.

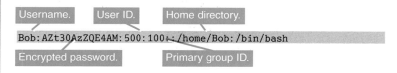

Managing Passwords

Passwords of Linux users are also stored in the /etc/passwd file. Because this file can be viewed, passwords are saved in encrypted format. The encryption itself is not difficult, but decryption is extremely difficult. This is not to say that a password cannot be decrypted, but a great amount of time would be required to carry out the calculations involved.

During password verification at login, the password entered is encrypted and verified against the stored password.

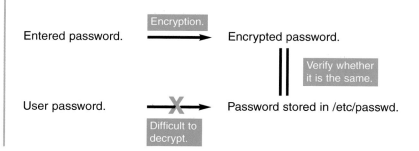

Chapter 5
Using Linux From Windows And Macintosh

Even when you are not working from a Linux personal computer (PC) directly, you can use the same Linux working environment by accessing Linux from a client PC through a network. This chapter explains how to set up Windows and Macintosh to access Linux through a network.

Contents Of This Chapter

Using Linux From A Client PC

Using Telnet

Even when you are not working from a Linux PC directly, you can use the Linux working environment from a client PC through a network. Using telnet software, a client personal PC can execute operations directly on the Linux system. To use Linux in this manner, Windows and Macintosh networks must be set up. First, prepare the Dynamic Host Configuration Protocol (DHCP) server in Linux to assign IP addresses automatically. Second, set up the Windows and Macintosh networks. Finally, install telnet software to connect to Linux directly.

Operating Linux From A Client PC

When Linux is connected to a network, accessing it from Windows or Macintosh is the same as using it directly on the Linux PC. The software used to achieve this is telnet. Telnet software duplicates the Linux screen (terminal) inside a telnet window. This is called a *virtual terminal*. Linux can support multiple virtual terminals, allowing many individuals to use Linux simultaneously via telnet.

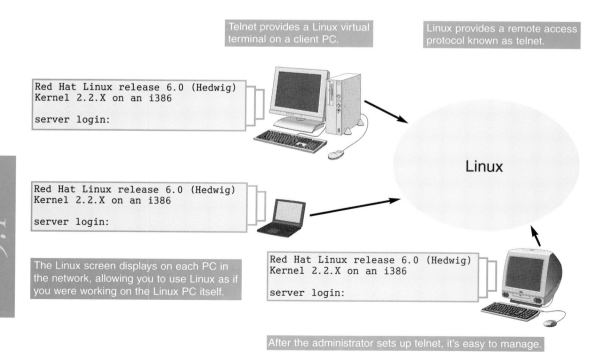

Telnet provides a Linux virtual terminal on a client PC.

Linux provides a remote access protocol known as telnet.

```
Red Hat Linux release 6.0 (Hedwig)
Kernel 2.2.X on an i386

server login:
```

```
Red Hat Linux release 6.0 (Hedwig)
Kernel 2.2.X on an i386

server login:
```

Linux

```
Red Hat Linux release 6.0 (Hedwig)
Kernel 2.2.X on an i386

server login:
```

The Linux screen displays on each PC in the network, allowing you to use Linux as if you were working on the Linux PC itself.

After the administrator sets up telnet, it's easy to manage.

5.1

Preparations

- Create a DHCP server.
- Setup a network on the PCs.
- Install telnet software.

Obtaining IP Addresses Automatically

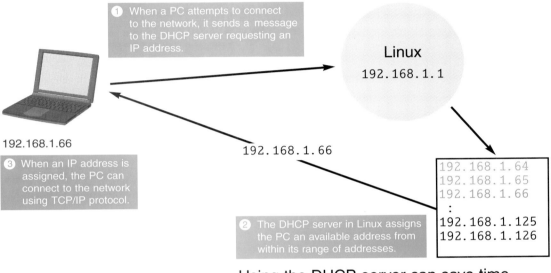

Using the DHCP server can save time setting up ordinary users.

Advantages And Disadvantages Of Assigning IP Addresses With DHCP

Advantages

- No time is required to assign different IP addresses to every PC.
- The possibility of assigning identical IP addresses is eliminated.
- No time is required to manage IP addresses.
- When changing IP addresses, only the DHCP settings need to be changed.

Disadvantages

- Time is required to setup the DHCP server.

Automatic Assignment Of IP Addresses

Setting Up A DHCP Server

DHCP is a service that assigns an IP address automatically to a computer that is connected to the network. After specifying the DHCP settings for Windows and Macintosh once, IP addresses are assigned automatically in accordance with the settings of the DHCP server running in Linux. When changing network settings, it isn't necessary to change the settings of every PC.

Only the DHCP server settings are changed, making it much easier to manage PC IP addresses. You can download this file, named dhcpd.conf, from **ftp.coriolis.com/linux_server_vbb**. Download dhcpd.conf file to an Internet equipped PC, copy the file to a floppy disk, mount the floppy in the Linux machine and copy it to the /etc directory.

1 Mount the CD-ROM.

① Insert the CD-ROM.

② Enter the command.

Note: Work as root for operations related to Linux settings.

```
[root@server /root]# mount -t iso9660 /dev/cdrom /mnt/cdrom⏎
mount: block device /dev/cdrom is write-protected, mounting read-only
ISO9660 Extensions: Microsoft Joliet Level 3
[root@server /root]# _
```

2 Install the DHCP server.

Enter the command.

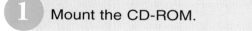

```
[root@server /root]# rpm -i /mnt/cdrom/RedHat/RPMS/dhcp-2.0b1p16-6.i386.rpm⏎
[root@server /root]# _
```

If an error message does not appear, the server was installed correctly.

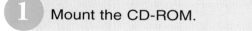

5.2

TIP!

What Is rpm?

An rpm is an archive format that groups programs, source files, and so on. The rpm format can store operations such as installation procedures, which can then be executed by issuing the **rpm** command, thus simplifying operations.

TIP!

Simplifying The Input Of Filenames

Specifying filenames by absolute paths and long filenames when entering commands is cumbersome. Pressing the [Tab] key to activate the input support function helps to shorten the process.

③ Copy and edit the settings file.

① Enter these commands.

```
[root@server /root]# cp /etc/dhcpd.conf⏎
[root@server /root]# vi /etc/dhcpd.conf⏎
```

② Modify the file to match the settings established during installation, and save.

```
# dhcpd.conf

server-identifier mybox.coriolis.com;

option domain-name "coriolis.com";

shared-network DHCP {
    option subnet-mask 255.255.255.0;
    default-lease-time 6000;
    max-lease-time 72000;

    subnet 192.168.1.0 netmask 255.255.255.0 {
        range 192.168.1.64 192.168.1.126;
        option broadcast-address 192.168.1.255;
    }
}
```

Enter the server name specified during Linux installation.

Enter the domain name specified during Linux installation.

Enter the network address and the netmask.

Specify the address range to be assigned by DHCP automatically.

Enter the largest address number (broadcast address) that the network will use from within the range.

TIP!

Commands Used In vi

Command Mode Æ Insert Mode

a	Inserts characters to the right of the cursor.
i	Inserts characters at the cursor.
cw	Replaces text from the cursor to the end of the word.

Command Mode

x	Deletes characters at the cursor.
rX	Replaces the character at the cursor with the entered character X.
O	Moves to the beginning of the line.
w	Moves right to the next word.
/X	Searches for the word specified in X.
:w ⏎	Saves the file.
:q ⏎	Quits the vi editor.

④ Create an empty file.

Create a file for DHCP to use.

Enter the command.

Note: Be careful to avoid mistakes when entering the filename.

```
[root@server /root]# touch /etc/dhcpd.leases⏎
[root@server /root]# _
```

4 Start the DHCP daemon.

① Move to the directory.

② Enter the command.

TIP!

The touch Command

The touch command creates an empty file (file without contents). Use touch when you need to create a file in advance.

```
[root@server /root]# touch /etc/dhcpd.leases
[root@server /root]# cd /etc/rc.d/init.d⏎
[root@server init.d]# ./dhcpd start⏎
Starting dhcpd: [OK]
[root@server init.d]# _
```

The DHCP daemon is started.

DHCP Explained

DHCP is a service that assigns IP addresses automatically within a previously specified range. When DHCP is used with a PC network, it assigns an available IP address automatically to a PC as soon as the PC is turned on. Using DHCP is convenient because the person using the Windows or Macintosh PC does not need to know the IP address.

Contents Of dhcpd.conf

Both network information and the range of IP addresses automatically assigned by DHCP are set in the file dhcpd.conf. The network used in this book has an address range of 256 addresses, starting from 192.168.1.0. The network address is 192.168.1.0. The netmask address is 255.255.255.0.

The largest IP address in this range (192.168.1.255) is the broadcast address. From within this address range, DHCP assigns 63 IP addresses (192.168.1.64 through 192.168.1.126) that do not overlap with other machines, including Linux.

Daemon: A Program That Provides A Service

Special programs called *daemons* provide all server functions in Linux, including DHCP. The daemon programs are executed when Linux boots and maintains continuous operation. Along with DHCP, the programs appearing in this book (in other words, Samba, netatalk, sendmail, and Apache) are all daemons.

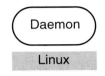

A daemon is a program that provides server functions in Linux.

This daemon is named dhcpd because it provides DHCP functions. The function it provides is called a service.

This sequence of operations is a service.

Nearly all of the programs providing server functions in Linux are provided in this service format. For anything you may want to do in Linux, a daemon can be added to provide that service. All service functions introduced in this book are descriptions of these services (daemons).

Connecting To Linux From Windows

Setting Up The Network

To connect to Linux from Windows through a network, you must take the following steps to set up the Windows network:
- Add a network card to the personal PC.
- Add TCP/IP to Windows.

- Make DHCP the method to obtain IP addresses.

Use DHCP to assign IP addresses. Because the default TCP/IP settings for Windows can be used with DHCP, there is no need to verify them.

Adding Network Cards To Desktop PCs

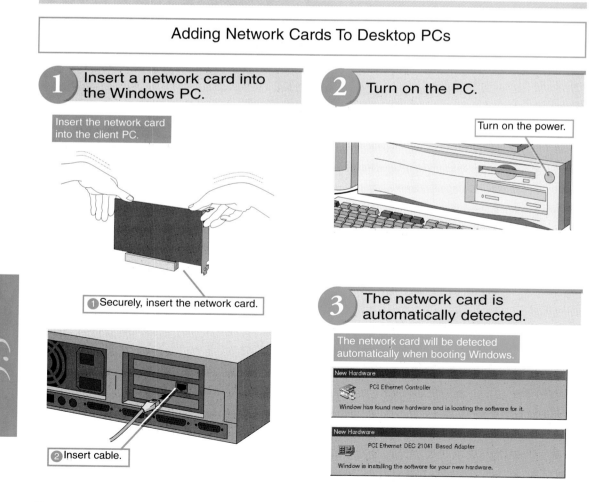

1 Insert a network card into the Windows PC.

Insert the network card into the client PC.

①Securely, insert the network card.

②Insert cable.

2 Turn on the PC.

Turn on the power.

3 The network card is automatically detected.

The network card will be detected automatically when booting Windows.

New Hardware
PCI Ethernet Controller
Window has found new hardware and is locating the software for it.

New Hardware
PCI Ethernet DEC 21041 Based Adapter
Window is installing the software for your new hardware.

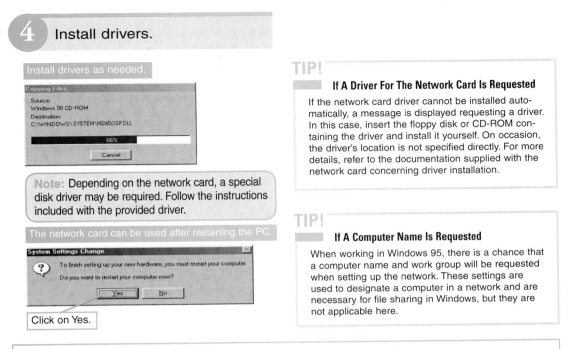

4 Install drivers.

Install drivers as needed.

Copying Files...

Source:
Windows 98 CD-ROM
Destination:
C:\WINDOWS\SYSTEM\MSWSOSP.DLL

66%

Cancel

Note: Depending on the network card, a special disk driver may be required. Follow the instructions included with the provided driver.

The network card can be used after restarting the PC.

System Settings Change

To finish setting up your new hardware, you must restart your computer.

Do you want to restart your computer now?

Yes   No

Click on Yes.

TIP!

If A Driver For The Network Card Is Requested

If the network card driver cannot be installed automatically, a message is displayed requesting a driver. In this case, insert the floppy disk or CD-ROM containing the driver and install it yourself. On occasion, the driver's location is not specified directly. For more details, refer to the documentation supplied with the network card concerning driver installation.

TIP!

If A Computer Name Is Requested

When working in Windows 95, there is a chance that a computer name and work group will be requested when setting up the network. These settings are used to designate a computer in a network and are necessary for file sharing in Windows, but they are not applicable here.

Adding Network Cards To Laptop PCs

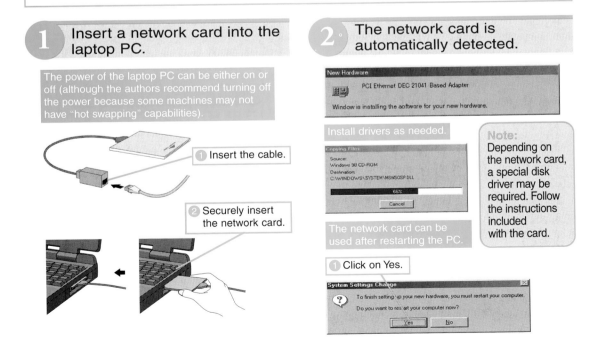

1 Insert a network card into the laptop PC.

The power of the laptop PC can be either on or off (although the authors recommend turning off the power because some machines may not have "hot swapping" capabilities).

① Insert the cable.

② Securely insert the network card.

2 The network card is automatically detected.

New Hardware

PCI Ethernet DEC 21041 Based Adapter

Window is installing the software for your new hardware.

Install drivers as needed.

Copying Files

Source:
Windows 98 CD-ROM
Destination:
C:\WINDOWS\SYSTEM\MSWSOSP.DLL

66%

Cancel

The network card can be used after restarting the PC.

Note: Depending on the network card, a special disk driver may be required. Follow the instructions included with the card.

① Click on Yes.

System Settings Change

To finish setting up your new hardware, you must restart your computer.

Do you want to restart your computer now?

Yes   No

Setting Up TCP/IP

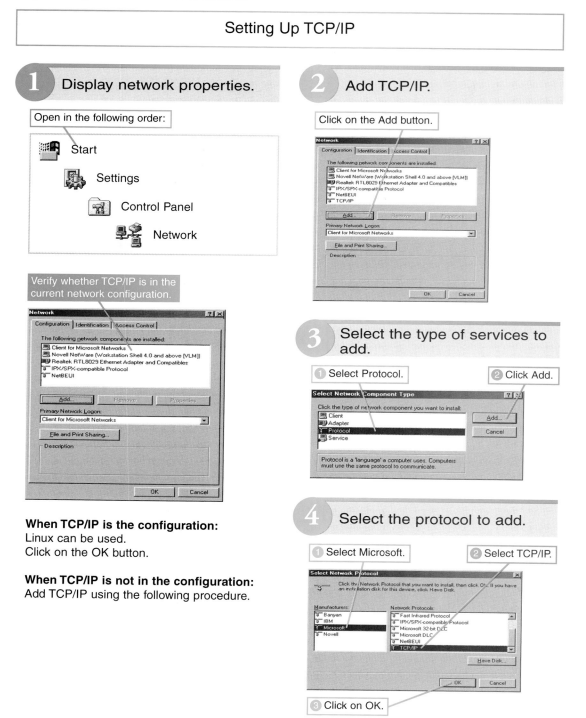

1 Display network properties.

Open in the following order:

Start

Settings

Control Panel

Network

Verify whether TCP/IP is in the current network configuration.

When TCP/IP is the configuration:
Linux can be used.
Click on the OK button.

When TCP/IP is not in the configuration:
Add TCP/IP using the following procedure.

2 Add TCP/IP.

Click on the Add button.

3 Select the type of services to add.

① Select Protocol. ② Click Add.

Protocol is a 'language' a computer uses. Computers must use the same protocol to communicate.

4 Select the protocol to add.

① Select Microsoft. ② Select TCP/IP.

③ Click on OK.

5 Apply the settings.

TCP/IP is added.

① Click on OK.

② Click on Yes.

TIP!

If The PC Is Already Connected To TCP/IP Or DHCP

If the PC is already connected to a local area network (LAN), there is a possibility that TCP/IP or DHCP settings have already been established. If this is the case, setting up a server according to the method in this book may have a negative effect on the existing network environment and server. Proceed with the operation only after consulting with the network administrator.

The Necessity Of Setting Up Each PC On The Network

You cannot use a network simply by installing an Ethernet network card on a PC and then connecting cables.

You must install the network driver card, and then set up Windows to allow Ethernet to be used. Even then the PCs are not ready to exchange information. Because Linux and Windows exchange information through a network in accordance with TCP/IP protocols, the final step is to add and set up TCP/IP.

Using Linux From Windows

Telnet Using Tera Term Pro

Telnet is used to access Linux from Windows through a network. Because the standard telnet program in Windows does not have sufficient functions or operability, install Tera Term Pro, which you can download from tucows at **www.tucows.com** or from **Softseek.com** at

http://192.41.3.165. When you log in using telnet, you cannot initially log in as root. You first need to log in as an ordinary user and then use the **su** command to change to root.

---

1 Installing Tera Term Pro.

① Execute the file in the following order:

Open Microsoft Explorer.

Go to the folder where you originally downloaded Tera Term Pro.

② Use an unzipping utility such as WinZip to extract the compressed Tera Term Pro files.

③ Change to the folder where the expanded set up files are contained.

---

2 Install Tera Term Pro.

Double-click on Setup.

The setup program starts.

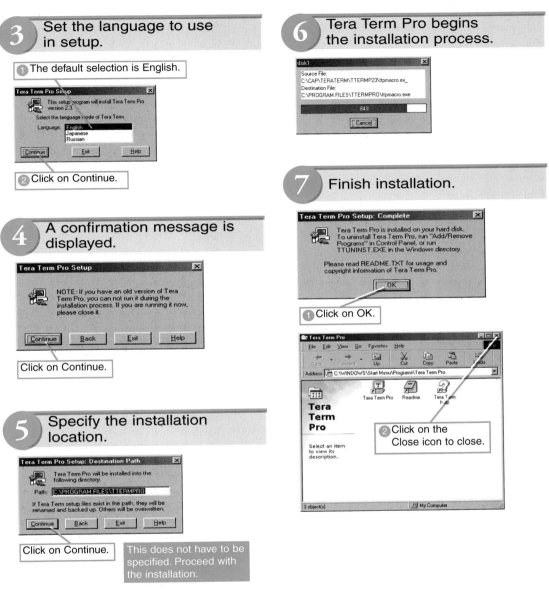

3 Set the language to use in setup.

① The default selection is English.

Tera Term Pro Setup

This setup program will install Tera Term Pro version 2.3.

Select the language mode of Tera Term.

Language: English
Japanese
Russian

Continue   Exit   Help

② Click on Continue.

4 A confirmation message is displayed.

Tera Term Pro Setup

NOTE: If you have an old version of Tera Term Pro, you can not run it during the installation process. If you are running it now, please close it.

Continue   Back   Exit   Help

Click on Continue.

5 Specify the installation location.

Tera Term Pro Setup: Destination Path

Tera Term Pro will be installed into the following directory.

Path: C:\PROGRAM FILES\TTERMPRO

If Tera Term setup files exist in the path, they will be renamed and backed up. Others will be overwritten.

Continue   Back   Exit   Help

Click on Continue.

This does not have to be specified. Proceed with the installation.

6 Tera Term Pro begins the installation process.

disk1

Source File:
C:\CAP\TERATERM\TTERMP23\ttpmacro.ex_
Destination File:
C:\PROGRAM FILES\TTERMPRO\ttpmacro.exe

84%

Cancel

7 Finish installation.

Tera Term Pro Setup: Complete

Tera Term Pro is installed on your hard disk. To uninstall Tera Term Pro, run "Add/Remove Programs" in Control Panel, or run TTUNINST.EXE in the Windows directory.

Please read README.TXT for usage and copyright information of Tera Term Pro.

OK

① Click on OK.

Tera Term Pro

File Edit View Go Favorites Help

Back   Forward   Up   Cut   Copy   Paste   Undo

Address: C:\WINDOWS\Start Menu\Programs\Tera Term Pro

Tera Term Pro   Readme   Tera Term Help

Tera Term Pro

Select an item to view its description.

② Click on the Close icon to close.

3 object(s)   My Computer

9 Start Tera Term Pro.

Open in the following order:

Start

Programs

Tera Term Pro

Tera Term Pro

10 Connect to Linux.

Because this will be a direct connection to the Linux PC, specify the IP address of the Linux PC.

① Type 192.168.1.1.

② Click on OK.

TIP!

If Telnet Does Not Operate Smoothly

If the Windows and Linux machines do not connect properly, the problem could be with either of the two machines. Use the Windows tool winipcfg to verify the following points. Start winipcfg by typing "winipcfg" in the Run field of the Start menu.

Verify Whether The Network Card Is Ready For Use

If the network card to be used does not display in winipcfg, it is not properly set up.

Verify Whether The IP Address Is Assigned Correctly

Although Windows automatically receives an IP address from DHCP, if this process doesn't execute properly, an IP address will not be assigned. Use winipcfg to verify whether an IP address is assigned.

If an address is not assigned, press Renew to request that an IP address be assigned. If an IP address is still not assigned, there is a problem in either the network or the DHCP server.

Verify The Network Connection

Verify whether the Ethernet cable is correctly connected to the network card or hub. Make sure that you verify that the LEDs of each hub port are lit.

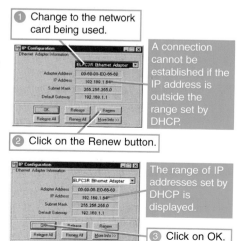

① Change to the network card being used.

A connection cannot be established if the IP address is outside the range set by DHCP.

② Click on the Renew button.

The range of IP addresses set by DHCP is displayed.

③ Click on OK.

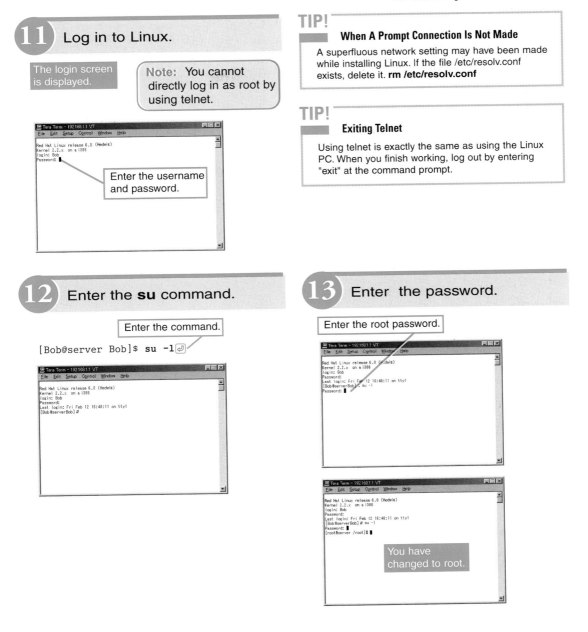

11 Log in to Linux.

The login screen is displayed.

Note: You cannot directly log in as root by using telnet.

Enter the username and password.

TIP!

When A Prompt Connection Is Not Made

A superfluous network setting may have been made while installing Linux. If the file /etc/resolv.conf exists, delete it. **rm /etc/resolv.conf**

TIP!

Exiting Telnet

Using telnet is exactly the same as using the Linux PC. When you finish working, log out by entering "exit" at the command prompt.

12 Enter the **su** command.

Enter the command.

```
[Bob@server Bob]$ su -l
```

13 Enter the password.

Enter the root password.

You have changed to root.

Connecting To Linux From Macintosh

Setting Up The Network

To connect to Linux from Macintosh through a network, you must take the following steps to setup the Macintosh network:

1. Make your Ethernet preparations.
2. Set up TCP/IP.
3. Make DHCP the method to obtain IP addresses.

Because DHCP is used to assign IP addresses, verify whether DHCP is being used in the TCP/IP settings.

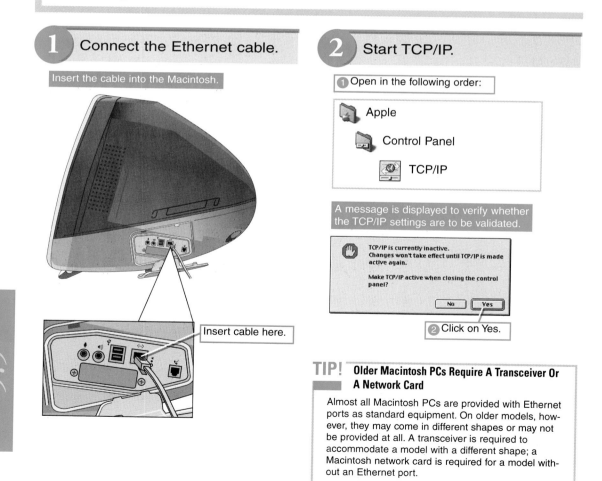

1 Connect the Ethernet cable.

Insert the cable into the Macintosh.

Insert cable here.

2 Start TCP/IP.

① Open in the following order:

Apple

Control Panel

TCP/IP

A message is displayed to verify whether the TCP/IP settings are to be validated.

> TCP/IP is currently inactive.
> Changes won't take effect until TCP/IP is made active again.
>
> Make TCP/IP active when closing the control panel?
>
> No   Yes

② Click on Yes.

TIP! **Older Macintosh PCs Require A Transceiver Or A Network Card**

Almost all Macintosh PCs are provided with Ethernet ports as standard equipment. On older models, however, they may come in different shapes or may not be provided at all. A transceiver is required to accommodate a model with a different shape; a Macintosh network card is required for a model without an Ethernet port.

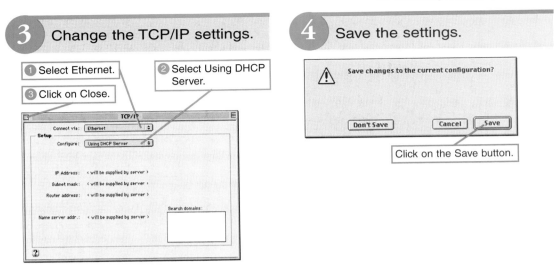

3 Change the TCP/IP settings.

1 Select Ethernet.

2 Select Using DHCP Server.

3 Click on Close.

TCP/IP

Connect via: Ethernet

Setup

Configure: Using DHCP Server

IP Address: < will be supplied by server >
Subnet mask: < will be supplied by server >
Router address: < will be supplied by server >

Name server addr.: < will be supplied by server >

Search domains:

4 Save the settings.

⚠ Save changes to the current configuration?

Don't Save   Cancel   Save

Click on the Save button.

The Necessity Of Setting Up Each Macintosh On The Network

You cannot use the network by simply connecting an Ethernet cable to a Macintosh. Information cannot be exchanged between Linux and Macintosh until a network is setup. Although Appletalk, a Macintosh product, is used for file sharing between Linux and Macintosh, when using Linux from Macintosh through a network or when accessing the Web or email, information is exchanged in accordance with TCP/IP protocol. TCP/IP is set up for this reason.

Using Linux From Macintosh

Using BetterTelnet

Telnet is used to operate Linux from Macintosh through the network. Because a standard Macintosh system does not contain a telnet program, install BetterTelnet, a tool that you can easily download from:
http://www.cstone.net/~rbraun/mac/telnet/
and many other sites.

You will also need Stuffit Expander to upack the compressed Better Telnet file. Download the StuffIt Expander freeware from: **www.aladdin-sys.com/expander/expander_mac_login.html** When you log in using telnet, you cannot directly login as root. Log in first as an ordinary user, and then use the **su** command to change to root.

1 **Download the Better Telnet file to your desktop.**

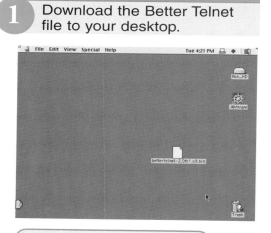

Note: You will also need Stuffit Expander on your hard disk to unpack the archive file.

2 **Extract BetterTelnet.**

StuffIt Expander automatically extracts the files.

The two files, BetterTelnet and Copying, are extracted.

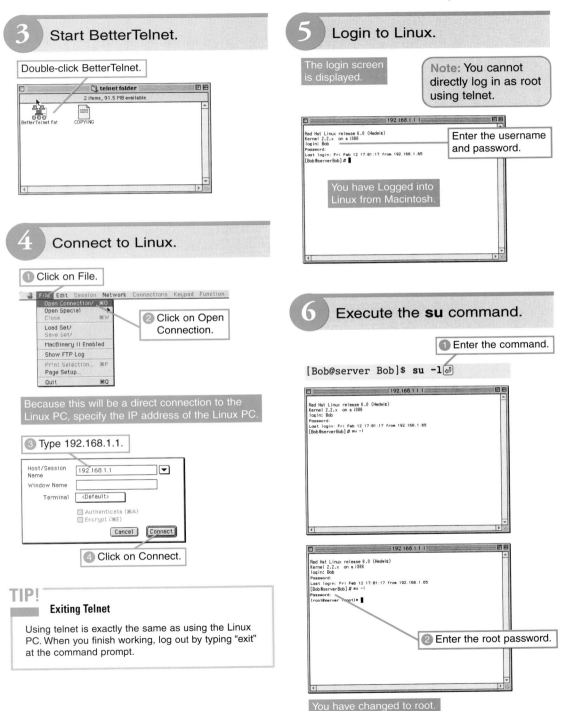

3 Start BetterTelnet.

Double-click BetterTelnet.

4 Connect to Linux.

① Click on File.

② Click on Open Connection.

Because this will be a direct connection to the Linux PC, specify the IP address of the Linux PC.

③ Type 192.168.1.1.

Host/Session Name	192.168.1.1
Window Name	
Terminal	<Default>

④ Click on Connect.

TIP!

Exiting Telnet

Using telnet is exactly the same as using the Linux PC. When you finish working, log out by typing "exit" at the command prompt.

5 Login to Linux.

The login screen is displayed.

Note: You cannot directly log in as root using telnet.

Enter the username and password.

You have Logged into Linux from Macintosh.

6 Execute the **su** command.

① Enter the command.

[Bob@server Bob]$ **su -l**⏎

② Enter the root password.

You have changed to root.

STEP UP

Telnet And Virtual Terminals

Linux is a multiuser operating system (OS) that allows multiple users to work simultaneously. Logging in from the PC where Linux is operating is not the only way to access Linux. You can also log in using a virtual terminal from another computer that has telnet. Using these virtual terminals, multiple users can log in to Linux simultaneously and work independently. A single user can log in and open any number of virtual terminals.

Simultaneously Editing Identical Files At Two Locations

A user can work concurrently on multiple virtual terminals. For ordinary users, one username is used by only one person; therefore, no problems should arise. When working as root, however, problems may occur.

Depending on the working environment, there may be more than one individual who changes to root to work as the administrator. In this case, assume that user A and user B start the vi editor to edit the same file. User A saves the file first. As a result, the file edited by user B is not the original edited file. Depending on the changes made by user A, the original work done by user B could very likely be invalidated.

Exercise caution when multiple users are working as root at the same time.

Chapter 6
Using Linux As A File
Server From Windows

File sharing is one of the merits of using a network.
It is necessary to configure Linux as a file server
in order to allow file sharing.
This chapter explains how to set up
a Windows file server from Linux.

Contents Of This Chapter

How To Configure Linux As A Windows File Server

The Role Of Samba

You can share files and folders between Windows systems connected to a network by configuring Windows for file sharing. However, data cannot be seamlessly exchanged between Linux and Windows systems.

Therefore, a software program that emulates the Windows sharing environment in Linux has been introduced, permitting files to be exchanged between the systems. To the user, it appears as if Windows applications are seamlessly connected to one another.

The Windows And Linux Systems Cannot Seamlessly Exchange Data

The Linux and Windows systems are not equipped to exchange data directly. Consequently, you must add software to Windows systems to allow them to interface with Linux systems, or add software to Linux systems to allow them to interface with Windows systems.

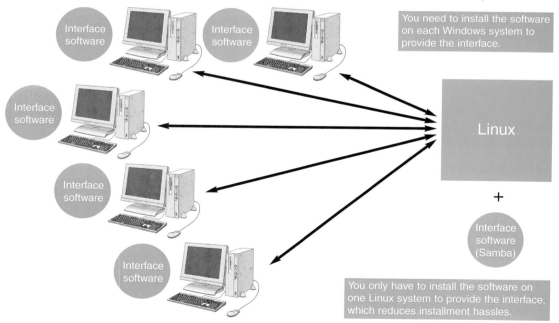

You need to install the software on each Windows system to provide the interface.

Interface software

Interface software

Interface software

Interface software

Interface software

Linux

+

Interface software (Samba)

You only have to install the software on one Linux system to provide the interface, which reduces installment hassles.

This chapter introduces methods for dealing with the interface problem from the Linux perspective, using Samba with priority placed on avoiding trouble for the general user.

The Role Of Samba

• Makes Linux emulate Windows (Windows NT)

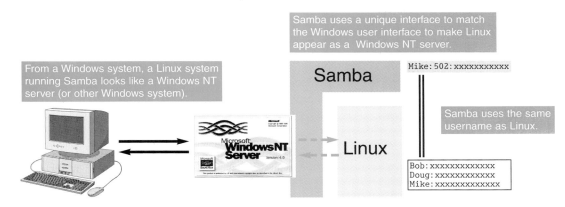

Samba uses a unique interface to match the Windows user interface to make Linux appear as a Windows NT server.

From a Windows system, a Linux system running Samba looks like a Windows NT server (or other Windows system).

Samba uses the same username as Linux.

Samba

`Mike:502:xxxxxxxxxxx`

Linux

```
Bob:xxxxxxxxxxxxxx
Doug:xxxxxxxxxxxxx
Mike:xxxxxxxxxxxxx
```

Samba And Linux Use Different User Management Systems

• Usernames are the same to allow Samba to use Linux directories and files.
• Passwords are different to allow Samba to use settings appropriate for Windows.

Samba

Usernames are the same, but passwords are managed independently.

Linux

```
Bob:501:xxxxxxxxxx
Doug:501:xxxxxxxxxx
Mike:502:xxxxxxxxxx
```

```
Bob:xxxxxxxx
Doug:xxxxxxxx
Mike:xxxxxxx
```

Installation Preparations

• Set the Samba settings.
• Register the Linux users with Samba.
• Set the user passwords.
• Set the shared folder settings.
• Set the sharing settings on the client systems (Windows).

> Note: Please use the DHCP server introduced in Chapter 5 to connect other PCs to the network. They will not connect correctly unless set up in advance.

How To Handle A Linux File In Windows

Samba

The Samba program is used to share Linux files with Windows systems. Samba is equipped with numerous functions to replace those provided by Windows NT servers.

This section explains how to use Samba as a logon server, file server, and print server in an NT domain.
All of the Samba settings are set in a file named smb.conf.

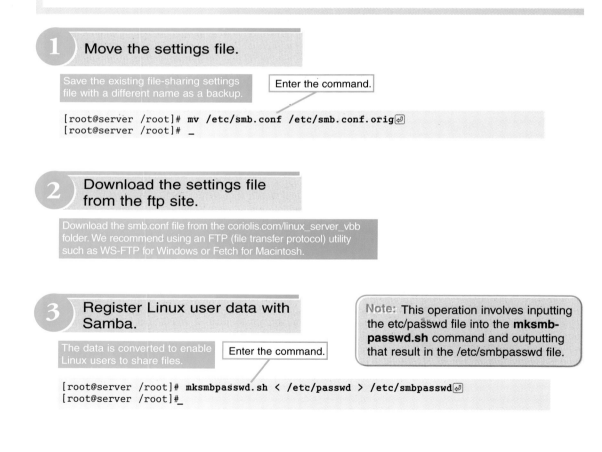

1 Move the settings file.

Save the existing file-sharing settings file with a different name as a backup.

Enter the command.

```
[root@server /root]# mv /etc/smb.conf /etc/smb.conf.orig⏎
[root@server /root]# _
```

2 Download the settings file from the ftp site.

Download the smb.conf file from the coriolis.com/linux_server_vbb folder. We recommend using an FTP (file transfer protocol) utility such as WS-FTP for Windows or Fetch for Macintosh.

3 Register Linux user data with Samba.

The data is converted to enable Linux users to share files.

Enter the command.

Note: This operation involves inputting the etc/passwd file into the **mksmbpasswd.sh** command and outputting that result in the /etc/smbpasswd file.

```
[root@server /root]# mksmbpasswd.sh < /etc/passwd > /etc/smbpasswd⏎
[root@server /root]#_
```

4 Register the Samba user passwords.

① Enter the command.

```
[root@server /root]# mksmbpasswd.sh < /etc/passwd > /etc/smbpasswd
[root@server /root]# smbpasswd Bob⏎
New SMB password:        ⏎
Retype new SMB password:        ⏎
Password changed
[root@server /root]# _
```

The password can be the same as the Linux password.

② Enter a password.

③ Enter the same password again.

5 Edit the settings file.

Enter the command.

```
[root@server /root]# smbpasswd Bob
New SMB password:
Retype new SMB password:
Password changed
[root@server /root]# vi /etc/smb.conf⏎
```

```
;;;
;;;        smb.conf -- Linux

[global]
        hosts allow = 192.168.1.0/255.255.255.0
         workgroup = coriolis.com
        netbios name = mybox.coriolis.com
        server string = Samba%v@%h
        status = yes

        coding system = cap
        preserve case = yes
        short preserve case = yes

        domain logons = yes
        security = user
        domain master = no
        preferred master = yes
        local master  = yes
        os level = 32
        encrypt passwords = yes
        update encrypted = yes
        null passwords = yes
        guest account = nobody
"/etc/smb.conf" 52 lines, 995 characters
```

vi has started to run.

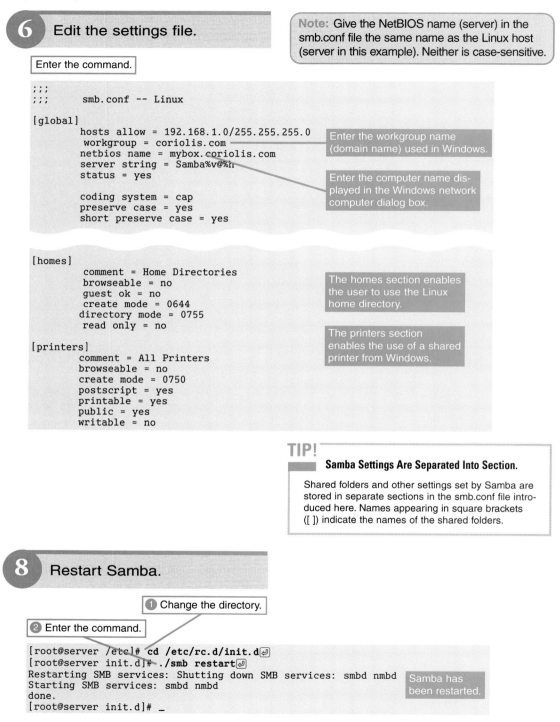

6 Edit the settings file.

Note: Give the NetBIOS name (server) in the smb.conf file the same name as the Linux host (server in this example). Neither is case-sensitive.

Enter the command.

```
;;;
;;;        smb.conf -- Linux

[global]
        hosts allow = 192.168.1.0/255.255.255.0
        workgroup = coriolis.com
        netbios name = mybox.coriolis.com
        server string = Samba%v@%h
        status = yes

        coding system = cap
        preserve case = yes
        short preserve case = yes
```

Enter the workgroup name (domain name) used in Windows.

Enter the computer name displayed in the Windows network computer dialog box.

```
[homes]
        comment = Home Directories
        browseable = no
        guest ok = no
        create mode = 0644
        directory mode = 0755
        read only = no

[printers]
        comment = All Printers
        browseable = no
        create mode = 0750
        postscript = yes
        printable = yes
        public = yes
        writable = no
```

The homes section enables the user to use the Linux home directory.

The printers section enables the use of a shared printer from Windows.

TIP!

Samba Settings Are Separated Into Section.

Shared folders and other settings set by Samba are stored in separate sections in the smb.conf file introduced here. Names appearing in square brackets ([ ]) indicate the names of the shared folders.

8 Restart Samba.

① Change the directory.

② Enter the command.

```
[root@server /etc]# cd /etc/rc.d/init.d⏎
[root@server init.d]# ./smb restart⏎
Restarting SMB services: Shutting down SMB services: smbd nmbd
Starting SMB services: smbd nmbd
done.
[root@server init.d]# _
```

Samba has been restarted.

Setting Up Windows PCs

1 Set the Windows NT domain.

① Open in the following order:

📇 Start
  📥 Settings
    📖 Control Panel
      📇 Network

② Select Client for Microsoft Networks.

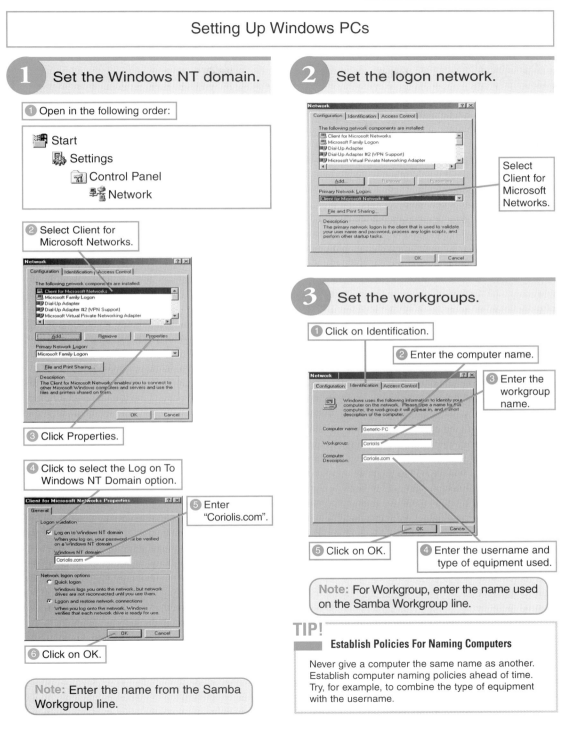

③ Click Properties.

④ Click to select the Log on To Windows NT Domain option.

⑤ Enter "Coriolis.com".

⑥ Click on OK.

Note: Enter the name from the Samba Workgroup line.

2 Set the logon network.

Select Client for Microsoft Networks.

3 Set the workgroups.

① Click on Identification.

② Enter the computer name.

③ Enter the workgroup name.

⑤ Click on OK.

④ Enter the username and type of equipment used.

Note: For Workgroup, enter the name used on the Samba Workgroup line.

TIP!

Establish Policies For Naming Computers

Never give a computer the same name as another. Establish computer naming policies ahead of time. Try, for example, to combine the type of equipment with the username.

117

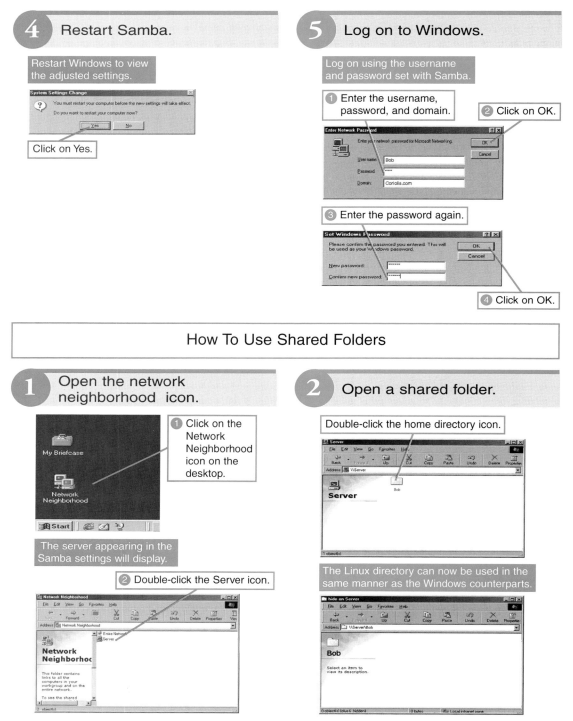

4 Restart Samba.

Restart Windows to view the adjusted settings.

System Settings Change

You must restart your computer before the new settings will take effect.

Do you want to restart your computer now?

Yes   No

Click on Yes.

5 Log on to Windows.

Log on using the username and password set with Samba.

① Enter the username, password, and domain.

② Click on OK.

Enter Network Password

Enter your network password for Microsoft Networking.   OK

Cancel

Username: Bob

Password: ****

Domain: Coriolis.com

③ Enter the password again.

Set Windows Password

Please confirm the password you entered. This will be used as your Windows password.   OK

Cancel

New password: ******

Confirm new password: ******

④ Click on OK.

How To Use Shared Folders

1 Open the network neighborhood icon.

① Click on the Network Neighborhood icon on the desktop.

My Briefcase

Network Neighborhood

Start

The server appearing in the Samba settings will display.

② Double-click the Server icon.

Network Neighborhood

File Edit View Go Favorites Help

Back Forward Up Cut Copy Paste Undo Delete Properties Views

Address Network Neighborhood

Network Neighborhoc

Entire Network
Server

This folder contains links to all the computers in your workgroup and on the entire network.

To see the shared

2 Open a shared folder.

Double-click the home directory icon.

Server

File Edit View Go Favorites Help

Back Forward Up Cut Copy Paste Undo Delete Properties

Address \\Server

Server   Bob

1 object(s)

The Linux directory can now be used in the same manner as the Windows counterparts.

hide on Server

File Edit View Go Favorites Help

Back Forward Up Cut Copy Paste Undo Delete Properties

Address \\Server\Bob

Bob

Select an item to view its description.

0 object(s) (plus 6 hidden)   0 bytes   Local intranet zone

How To Verify smb.conf Settings

Samba features numerous settings categories, and each has a default setup. If the settings do not contain the expected parameters, Samba will not operate as expected. Samba is supplied with a tool that monitors all of the settings within the smb.conf file that are automatically set by the program. This tool is the **testparm** command. Running **testparm** displays all the settings.

```
[root@server /root]# testparm⏎
Load smb config files from /etc/smb.conf
Processing section "[homes]"
Processing section "[printers]"
No path in service printers - using /tmp
Unable to open printcap file /etc/printcap for read!
Loaded services file OK.
Press enter to see a dump of your service definitions
```

Press Enter to display the values for all the settings. To display a manual describing the available settings options and explanations of their use in the smb.conf file, execute the **man smb.conf** command.

```
[root@server /root]# man smb.conf
```

Linux And Samba Usernames Are The Same

Basically, both Linux and Samba usernames are treated as the same for managing and organizing usernames. Files created by a user accessing through the Samba interface can be handled in the same manner as files created by a user with the same name accessing through Linux.

How To Add Users

To add Samba users, first create a username with the **useradd** command in Linux, then use the **smbpasswd –a** command to create a Samba password for the same username.

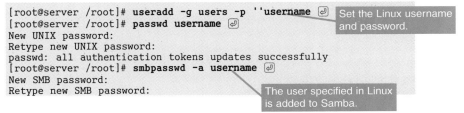

```
[root@server /root]# useradd -g users -p ''username ⏎    Set the Linux username
[root@server /root]# passwd username ⏎                   and password.
New UNIX password:
Retype new UNIX password:
passwd: all authentication tokens updates successfully
[root@server /root]# smbpasswd -a username ⏎             The user specified in Linux
New SMB password:                                        is added to Samba.
Retype new SMB password:
```

119

Changing A Samba Password From Windows

When a Windows system uses the Samba interface as a logon server to an NT domain to access a Linux system as described in this section, the Password icon in the Windows control panel can be used to reset the Samba password.

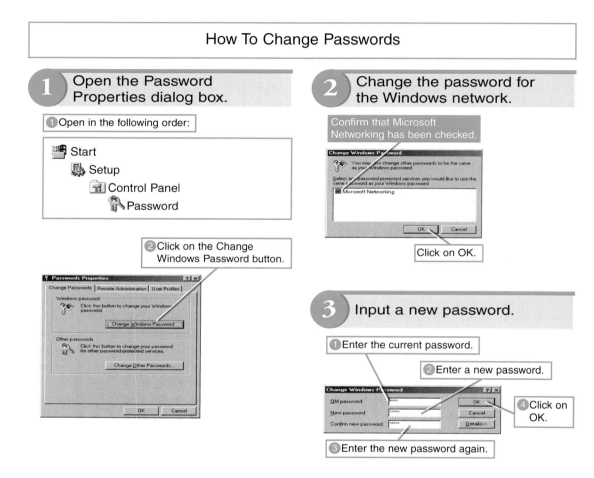

How To Change Passwords

1 Open the Password Properties dialog box.

①Open in the following order:

- Start
  - Setup
    - Control Panel
      - Password

②Click on the Change Windows Password button.

2 Change the password for the Windows network.

Confirm that Microsoft Networking has been checked.

Click on OK.

3 Input a new password.

①Enter the current password.

②Enter a new password.

④Click on OK.

③Enter the new password again.

4   The password will change.

A message indicates that the password
has been changed correctly.

① Click on OK.

② Click on Close.

TIP!

Different Samba And Windows Passwords

If the passwords for Windows and Samba differ, a
dialog box appears allowing you to re-enter either
password. Change the password by entering either
of the Windows or Samba passwords.

Passwords Can Be Managed Together Using Windows NT Server

The merits of operating Samba as a Windows NT Server is that the NT domain, a
unique user-management feature of Windows NT, can also be used as the overall system manager for Linux users. By utilizing this user-management feature, the logon
passwords for Windows and Linux (Samba) can be synchronized. Regular users can
access the file server without having to think about Linux, lessening the burden on
them. Although some may feel uncomfortable with the thought of operating Linux as
a Windows NT Server, the ability to take on the functions of other server systems is
one of Linux's great advantages.

Creating Folders Anyone Can Use

Creating Shared Folders

File sharing is a mechanism that allows an identical folder to be accessed from different computers. When file sharing, not only can you copy files at another location, you can also open and edit files as if they were on your own computer.

Creating a folder that anyone can access makes it easy to collect and install free software, and allows you to use a common work area to transfer files.

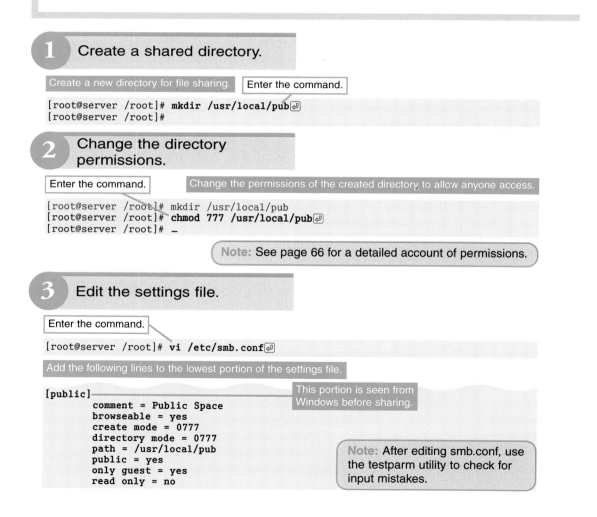

1 **Create a shared directory.**

Create a new directory for file sharing.   Enter the command.

```
[root@server /root]# mkdir /usr/local/pub⏎
[root@server /root]#
```

2 **Change the directory permissions.**

Enter the command.   Change the permissions of the created directory to allow anyone access.

```
[root@server /root]# mkdir /usr/local/pub
[root@server /root]# chmod 777 /usr/local/pub⏎
[root@server /root]# _
```

Note: See page 66 for a detailed account of permissions.

3 **Edit the settings file.**

Enter the command.

```
[root@server /root]# vi /etc/smb.conf⏎
```

Add the following lines to the lowest portion of the settings file.

```
[public]
        comment = Public Space
        browseable = yes
        create mode = 0777
        directory mode = 0777
        path = /usr/local/pub
        public = yes
        only guest = yes
        read only = no
```

This portion is seen from Windows before sharing.

Note: After editing smb.conf, use the testparm utility to check for input mistakes.

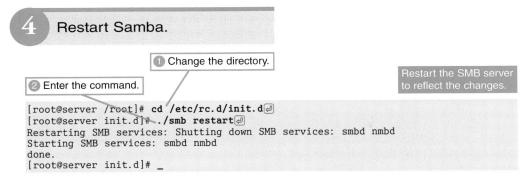

4 Restart Samba.

① Change the directory.

② Enter the command.

Restart the SMB server to reflect the changes.

```
[root@server /root]# cd /etc/rc.d/init.d↵
[root@server init.d]# ./smb restart↵
Restarting SMB services: Shutting down SMB services: smbd nmbd
Starting SMB services: smbd nmbd
done.
[root@server init.d]# _
```

Setting Directory Permissions

Because Linux files and directories are accessed on the authority of the user who is logged in, Samba requires the appropriate permissions to be set for the Linux directories. A user obtains access privileges in Linux by logging into Samba.

File Permissions Created In Shared Folders

If a public folder is set up by using the method shown in this book, a file created in the public folder can be read and written to by anyone accessing it from Linux. When access is granted as a guest, the owner of a Linux file is set to "nobody", which makes it impossible to determine who created the file.

When a user writes a file in their home directory using Samba, they have read and write access to that file from Linux, while other users will have read-only access. You can change these settings in the create and directory modes in the smb.conf file. The create and directory modes use the Linux permission numbers listed on page 67. With the number 0644, you are 6 (rw-), so you have read and write access; group and other users are 4 (r-), so they have read only access. For example, if you do not want other users in Linux to read your home directory, set the create mode of the [homes] section to 600 and the directory mode to 700. See page 66 for a detailed account of permissions.

Creating Folders For Specific Users Only

Settings Access Privileges

Folders for use by specific users only can also be created. To do so, set the shared folder to be inaccessible to users other than those specified in Samba.
This setting is made in smb.conf. Additionally, a shared directory in Linux must be created for use by those users specified in smb.conf.

Although the Samba settings can be as complicated as you like, managing Linux users and groups together will make these settings easier to work with.

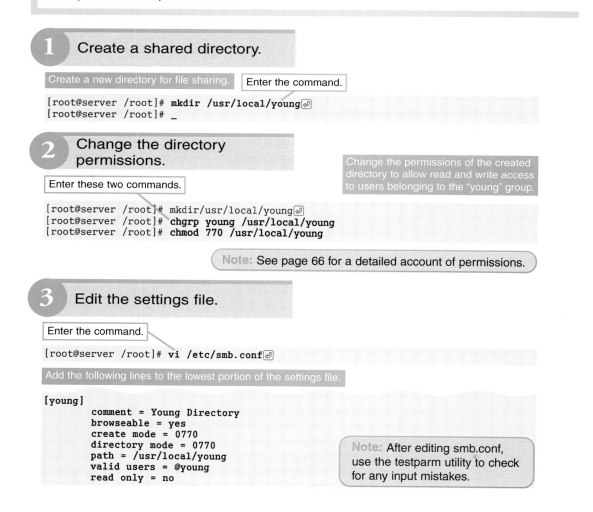

1 Create a shared directory.

Create a new directory for file sharing.   Enter the command.

```
[root@server /root]# mkdir /usr/local/young⏎
[root@server /root]# _
```

2 Change the directory permissions.

Enter these two commands.

Change the permissions of the created directory to allow read and write access to users belonging to the "young" group.

```
[root@server /root]# mkdir/usr/local/young⏎
[root@server /root]# chgrp young /usr/local/young
[root@server /root]# chmod 770 /usr/local/young
```

Note: See page 66 for a detailed account of permissions.

3 Edit the settings file.

Enter the command.

```
[root@server /root]# vi /etc/smb.conf⏎
```

Add the following lines to the lowest portion of the settings file.

```
[young]
        comment = Young Directory
        browseable = yes
        create mode = 0770
        directory mode = 0770
        path = /usr/local/young
        valid users = @young
        read only = no
```

Note: After editing smb.conf, use the testparm utility to check for any input mistakes.

4 Restart Samba.

① Change the directory.

② Enter the command.

Restart the SMB server
to reflect the changes.

```
[root@server /root]# cd /etc/rc.d/init.d⏎
[root@server init.d]# ./smb restart⏎
Restarting SMB services: Shutting down SMB services: smbd nmbd
Starting SMB services: smbd nmbd
done.
[root@server init.d]# _
```

Advantages Of Using Groups

Using groups in Linux to set access privileges in Samba simplifies the settings. The settings for Linux directory permissions are also compatible with smb.conf, making it quite straightforward. When adding a user, add the user to /etc/group in Linux.

More Complicated Access Settings

A variety of access privileges can be set in smb.conf. For example, read and write access for each service can be specified in detail with usernames and group names.

How To Restrict Main Access

Types of users	Access restriction
valid users	Users who can log in.
invalid users	Users who cannot log in.
read only	Read only (yes/no).
read list	Read only users (also valid when read only = no).
write list	Users who can write to files (also valid when read only = yes).

To set up a user, use a comma to separate the username and group name, and put an @ symbol in front of the group name to distinguish it. If nothing is specified, the settings are interpreted as allowing access to all users.

This only allows access from Windows. It is recommended that you also consider access privileges for netatalk (access from Macintosh) and for users logged in to Linux, and use Linux groups to set access privileges while setting directory permissions in the same manner.

125

STEP UP

Why Are Passwords In Samba Set Separately?

The user passwords to access Linux are managed in /etc/passwd; passwords to access Samba are managed separately in /etc/smbpasswd. Why is it necessary to separate the password management files?

Simply, user passwords are saved in an encrypted state. The encryption method is discussed in Chapter 4. The encryption itself is not difficult, but returning to the original file from an encrypted state is difficult. Additionally, Windows and Macintosh use different encryption methods.

Password security has been enhanced with Windows 98. A password entered while sharing is sent through the network in an encrypted state. Samba software running on Linux receives the encrypted password, but, because the encryption method is different, cannot verify it against passwords stored in the Linux file /etc/passwd. Although restoring the encrypted data is not impossible, it is extremely difficult. This makes it impossible to verify the password by restoring the encrypted password and then encrypting it again using Linux's method. Consequently, you must first save passwords encrypted by Windows 98.

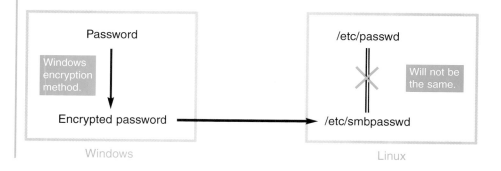

Chapter 7
Using Linux As A
Macintosh File Server

To share files on a Macintosh system,
Linux must be set up as a Macintosh file server.
This chapter explains how to make Linux
a Macintosh file server.

Contents Of This Chapter

How To Configure Linux As A Macintosh File Server

The Role Of netatalk

A Macintosh system can share files and folders when the system is connected through a network and configured for file sharing. Data exchanges between Linux and Macintosh systems, however, are not enabled.

By using software to emulate the Macintosh sharing environment in Linux, Macintosh users can access Linux files, which permits file exchanges between the two systems. To the user, it appears as if Macintosh applications are seamlessly connected.

Macintosh And Linux Systems Cannot Exchange Data Without Assistance

Linux and Macintosh systems are not equipped to exchange data directly. Consequently, software must be added either to Macintosh systems to allow them to interface with Linux systems or to Linux systems to allow them to interface with Macintosh systems.

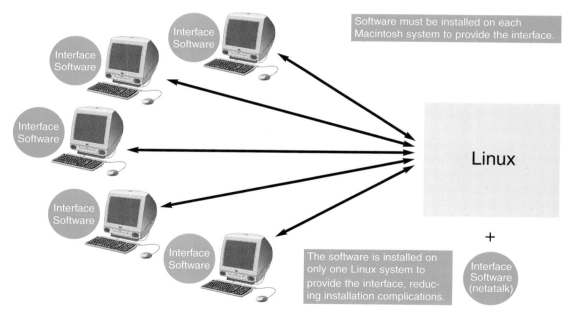

Interface Software

Interface Software

Interface Software

Interface Software

Interface Software

Software must be installed on each Macintosh system to provide the interface.

The software is installed on only one Linux system to provide the interface, reducing installation complications.

Linux

+

Interface Software (netatalk)

This book introduces *netatalk*, a service that enables Linux to use AppleTalk as a way to deal with the interface problem from the perspective of Linux. (Priority is placed on avoiding hassles for the general user.)

The Role Of netatalk

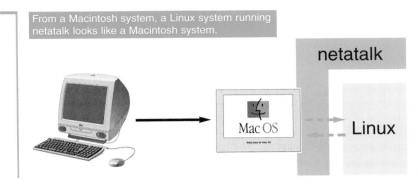

From a Macintosh system, a Linux system running netatalk looks like a Macintosh system.

netatalk

Mac OS

Linux

What You Can Do With netatalk

- Use the network functions provided in a Macintosh system.

- Use the same usernames and passwords as Linux.

- Use the permissions set in Linux directories.
  (Administrators can limit access by using permissions.)

Directory	Write Permission With netatalk	
/pub	drwxrwxrwx	When write permission is granted to owners, groups, and other users, netatalk allows everyone with permission access to this folder.
/young	drwxrwx---	When write permission is granted only to owners and groups, netatalk denies access to this folder to users who do not belong to these groups.

Installation Preparations

- Install netatalk.

- Set the shared folder settings

> Note: Use the DHCP server introduced in Chapter 5 to connect other personal computers to the network. They will not connect properly unless set up in advance.

How To Handle Linux Files From Macintosh Part 1

Open Source (tar)

The netatalk software installed on Linux enables you to work with files located on the Linux server from a Macintosh system. If the same folder is shared using Samba for Windows and netatalk for Macintosh, Windows and Macintosh can share the same file in Linux.

Netatalk is not distributed with Red Hat 6, but you can download it from the Internet. As a preliminary step to installing netatalk, this section explains how to open and compile the netatalk source.

1 Download the compressed program.

Download the netatalk-1.4b2.tar.gz file from the **www.umich.edu/~rsug/netatalk/index.html** site, and place it in the /usr/local/src directory.

2 Change to the directory used to extract the file.

To install the compressed program, change to the directory used to extract the file.

Enter the command.

```
[root@server /root]# cd /usr/local/src⏎
[root@server src]# _
```

Perform these commands as root.

3 Extract the compressed netatalk file.

Enter the command.

```
[root@server /root]# cd /usr/local/src
[root@server src]# tar xzvf netatalk-1.4b2.tar.gz⏎
netatalk-1.4b2/
netatalk-1.4b2/include/
```

The extracted file name is displayed.

```
netatalk-1.4b2/VERSION
[root@server src]# _
```

The Linux Archiving Tool: **tar**

Most programs for Linux are distributed as source code and made publicly available as text files by the authors. The source code may consist of many files, so it is standard practice to collect the files together and release them in a compressed format. Using software to collect files is called archiving.

Generally, Macintosh uses hqx and Windows uses zip or lzh routines for archiving. All these programs have a compression function. In contrast, Linux handles file collection and file compression separately. In nearly all cases, the **tar** command is used to collect files, and a general-purpose file-compression program (gzip) is used to compress files.

To compress a file with gzip, append an option to the **tar** command. Whether you collect the files using the **tar** command and then compress the file or use the **tar** command with an option, the result is exactly the same. Likewise, using the **tar** command with an option to open the files while extracting the compressed file is the same as extracting the compressed file with gzip and then opening the files with the **tar** command.

The **tar** Command Sequence

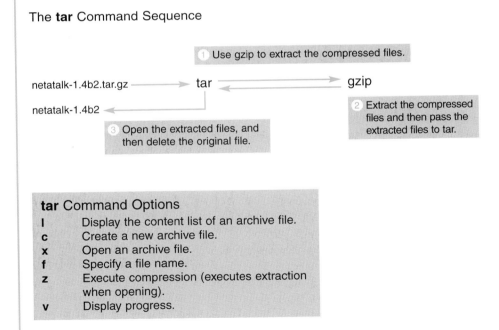

1 Use gzip to extract the compressed files.

netatalk-1.4b2.tar.gz → tar ⇆ gzip

netatalk-1.4b2 ←

2 Extract the compressed files and then pass the extracted files to tar.

3 Open the extracted files, and then delete the original file.

tar Command Options

l	Display the content list of an archive file.
c	Create a new archive file.
x	Open an archive file.
f	Specify a file name.
z	Execute compression (executes extraction when opening).
v	Display progress.

131

How To Handle Linux Files From Macintosh Part 2

Revising The Source (patch)

The netatalk source cannot be compiled in Red Hat Linux without a patch (a diff file for the source code). Normally, a patch is applied to fix software bugs, upgrade versions, or localize a program.

Some software does not need and/or is not provided with patches. You can find the patch shown here (netatalk-1.4b2.linux-patch) on the Internet, at **ftp.coriolis.com,** from the linux_server_vbb directory.

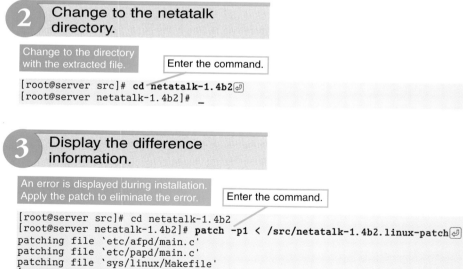

1 Download the patch file.

Download the netatalk-1.4b2.linux-patch file and place it in the /usr/local/src directory .

2 Change to the netatalk directory.

Change to the directory with the extracted file.

Enter the command.

```
[root@server src]# cd netatalk-1.4b2⏎
[root@server netatalk-1.4b2]# _
```

3 Display the difference information.

An error is displayed during installation. Apply the patch to eliminate the error.

Enter the command.

```
[root@server src]# cd netatalk-1.4b2
[root@server netatalk-1.4b2]# patch -p1 < /src/netatalk-1.4b2.linux-patch⏎
patching file `etc/afpd/main.c'
patching file `etc/papd/main.c'
patching file `sys/linux/Makefile'
[root@server netatalk-1.4b2]# _
```

Patches

A *patch* is a text file written to make changes in the source code. The patch contains command information such as which file, what line number, change/add/delete the following line, and so forth. If you change and compile the source code in accordance with the patch file, a revised program is the result.

Using a patch to change a file is called *applying a patch*. The options of the patch command differ depending on how the patch file is created.

Operating Problems

If you did not select development environment components in Chapter 2, you cannot compile programs. A C language compiler is needed to compile programs. A patch must be applied to compile netatalk, so the patch command is also necessary.

Programs Needed To Compile netatalk

gcc   C compiler.
make   Program that executes a compiling procedure.
patch   Program that applies a source file patch.

How To Verify Programs Are Installed

```
[root@server /root]# make -v⏎
[root@server /root]# gcc -v⏎
[root@server /root]# patch -v⏎
```

How To Add A Program

```
[root@server /root]# rpm -i /mnt/cdrom/RedHat/RPMS/make-3.76.1-5.i386.rpm⏎
[root@server /root]# rpm -i /mnt/cdrom/RedHat/RPMS/gcc-2.7.2.3-14.i386.rpm⏎
[root@server /root]# rpm -i /mnt/cdrom/RedHat/RPMS/patch-2.5-5.i386.rpm⏎
```

How To Handle Linux Files From Macintosh Part 3

Compiling The Source (make)

The compiling and installation procedures for netatalk are written in a file called Makefile. The **make** command is used to interpret and execute a Makefile. When the **make** command is executed, the Makefile in the current directory is interpreted and the procedure written in the file is executed.

Because the **make** command is used to compile and install nearly all programs, compiling a program is known as *making* a program.

1 Compile.

Ready the system to install netatalk.

Enter the command.

```
[root@server netatalk-1.4b2]# make⏎
Making all for linux...
```

```
make[1]: Leaving directory '/usr/local/src/netatalk-1.4b2/sys/linux'
[root@server netatalk-1.4b2]# _
```

2 Install.

Install netatalk.

Enter the command.

```
make[1]: Leaving directory '/usr/local/src/netatalk-1.4b2/sys/linux'
[root@server netatalk-1.4b2]# make install⏎
Making install for linux...
```

```
Install is done.  Don t forget to add lines from
services.atalk to /etc/services and to call rc.atalk
in /etc/rc.  See README and README.LINUX for more
information.
make[1]: Leaving directory '/usr/local/src/netatalk-1.4b2/sys/linux'
[root@server netatalk-1.4b2]# _
```

When the installation is complete, the message "Install is done" is displayed.

Compiling: Changing Source Code Into Executable Files

All programs are created by writing source code. The operation to convert source code into an executable file is called *compiling*. The programs we have installed so far (such as DHCP and Samba) do not need to be compiled because they are supplied in rpm file format, which compiles the program from the source code and installs it directly.

The Role Of **make**

The procedure to compile and create a program is written in the Makefile supplied with the source code. The **make** command executes the procedure written in the Makefile.

The compiled program is placed in the same directory as the source code. After compiling, execute the **make install** command to execute the procedure that installs the created program.

How To Distinguish Between The Compiling Method And The Installation Method

The source usually contains text files named INSTALL and README in which the compiling method and the installation method are written. Reading these files is the most reliable way to distinguish between the two methods.

If there is an executable file named configure, perform the following steps.

```
[root@server /root]# ./configure    Set the environment and create Makefile.
[root@server /root]# make            Compile.
[root@server /root]# make install    Install.
```

If there is a file named Imakefile, perform the following steps.

```
[root@server /root]# xmkmf -a        Set the environment and create Makefile.
[root@server /root]# make            Compile.
[root@server /root]# make install    Install.
```

How To Handle Linux Files From Macintosh Part 4

Booting Up netatalk

The netatalk settings files allow registered Linux users to view their home directory from their Macintosh system. Download the Applevolumes.default, Applevolumes.system, and rc.atalk files from the **ftp.coriolis.com/linux_server_vbb** site.

Booting netatalk usually requires about 20 to 30 seconds, depending on the environment. During this time, netatalk examines the network and obtains AppleTalk information. In this section, you will set netatalk to boot automatically when Linux boots.

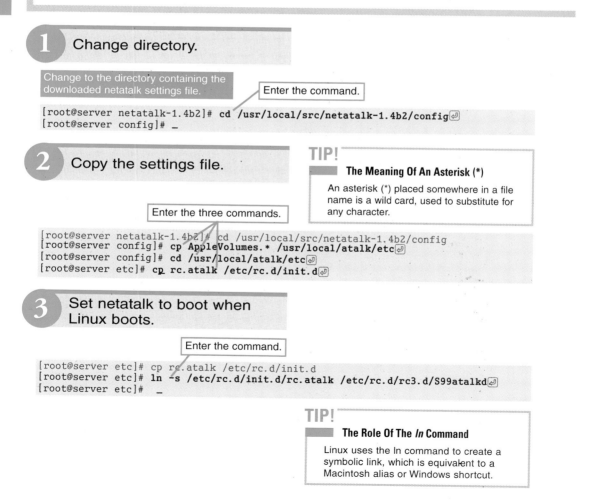

1 Change directory.

Change to the directory containing the downloaded netatalk settings file.

Enter the command.

```
[root@server netatalk-1.4b2]# cd /usr/local/src/netatalk-1.4b2/config⏎
[root@server config]# _
```

2 Copy the settings file.

Enter the three commands.

```
[root@server netatalk-1.4b2]# cd /usr/local/src/netatalk-1.4b2/config
[root@server config]# cp AppleVolumes.* /usr/local/atalk/etc⏎
[root@server config]# cd /usr/local/atalk/etc⏎
[root@server etc]# cp rc.atalk /etc/rc.d/init.d⏎
```

TIP!

The Meaning Of An Asterisk (*)

An asterisk (*) placed somewhere in a file name is a wild card, used to substitute for any character.

3 Set netatalk to boot when Linux boots.

Enter the command.

```
[root@server etc]# cp rc.atalk /etc/rc.d/init.d
[root@server etc]# ln -s /etc/rc.d/init.d/rc.atalk /etc/rc.d/rc3.d/S99atalkd⏎
[root@server etc]# _
```

TIP!

The Role Of The *ln* Command

Linux uses the ln command to create a symbolic link, which is equivalent to a Macintosh alias or Windows shortcut.

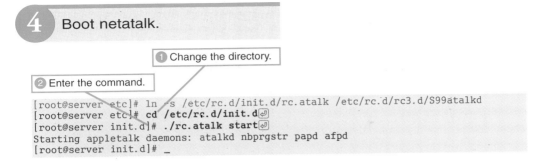

4 Boot netatalk.

① Change the directory.

② Enter the command.

```
[root@server etc]# ln -s /etc/rc.d/init.d/rc.atalk /etc/rc.d/rc3.d/S99atalkd
[root@server etc]# cd /etc/rc.d/init.d⏎
[root@server init.d]# ./rc.atalk start⏎
Starting appletalk daemons: atalkd nbprgstr papd afpd
[root@server init.d]# _
```

Using Linux As A File Server From Macintosh

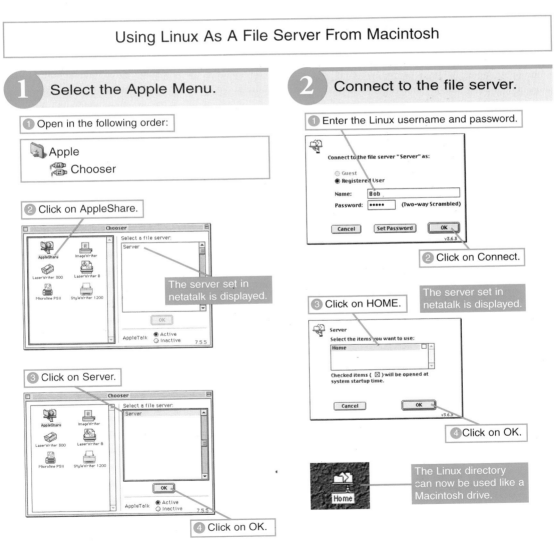

1 Select the Apple Menu.

① Open in the following order:

Apple
　Chooser

② Click on AppleShare.

The server set in netatalk is displayed.

③ Click on Server.

④ Click on OK.

2 Connect to the file server.

① Enter the Linux username and password.

Connect to the file server "Server" as:

○ Guest
● Registered User

Name:　Bob
Password:　●●●●●　(Two-way Scrambled)

Cancel　　Set Password　　OK
v3.6.3

② Click on Connect.

③ Click on HOME.

The server set in netatalk is displayed.

Server
Select the items you want to use:

Home

Checked items (⊠) will be opened at system startup time.

Cancel　　OK
v3.6.3

④ Click on OK.

The Linux directory can now be used like a Macintosh drive.

Home

Creating Shared Folders

Setting Access Rights

The netatalk settings are very simple. To create a new shared folder, enter the shared directory location and shared name in AppleVolumes.default. When entering the shared name, be sure to insert a space after the directory name. If a shared name is not entered, it is set automatically.

Unlike Samba, the settings file for netatalk is not at all complicated. Access privileges are set by setting the permissions for each directory and file.

1 Edit the settings file.

Enter the command.

```
[root@server /root]# vi /usr/local/atalk/etc/AppleVolumes.default⏎
```

2 Enter the name of the folder to be shared.

```
# This file looks empty when viewed with vi .  In fact, there is one
#  ~  , so users with no AppleVolumes file in their home directory get
# their home directory by default.
~ HOME
/usr/local/pub PUBLIC
```

After making changes, save and quit.

Note: After the revision, the rc.atalk daemon does not need to be restarted.

Access Privileges To netatalk Shared Folders

Access privileges to folders and files in netatalk correspond to the file permissions in Linux. To restrict user access, set the permissions in the shared Linux directories. For example, to create a shared folder with read and write access for all users, set the permissions of the shared directory so that anyone is allowed to read or write.

chmod 777 shared directory.

In this case, guests are granted read and write access. Owners of files created by guests become "nobody" in Linux.

To grant specific individuals read and write access, create a Linux group, and then allow access only to users belonging to that group.

chgrp users shared directory.
chmod 770 shared directory.

Permissions of files and folders created in a shared folder are essentially the same as the shared directory. The owner is the user currently logged in.

STEP UP

Why Compile?

The Windows operating system (OS) can only be used on PC/AT-compatible computers, so programs to be used under Windows are distributed in executable format. Macintosh is similar with its operating system. In Unix, however, each version of the Unix OS has a different format for executable files, so distributing programs in executable format is not possible. Programs for a Unix OS are often distributed as source code or pre-compiled for different platforms. You compile the source code in your environment and create an executable file yourself.

Nearly all programs used in Linux are distributed as source code, in case you have a platform for which a binary is unavailable, if you are security conscious, or if you just want to play with the source code. In Red Hat Linux, however, rpm packages are distributed in a compiled and executable format. Why then are we compiling software in this book?

Providing A More Recent Version Than The rpm

The packages are source code complied and created by someone else. The packages may not always be distributed with updated original source code. Because this book discusses setting up an intranet, you need not be too concerned with security, although you should take adequate precautions when using Linux as an Internet server. Occasionally updating to newer and more stable source code and compiling it can be good practice for you.

rpm May Not Always Be Supplied

The packages you need may not always be included with the Red Hat Linux distribution. If this is the case, you can try to find a package at another location, but obtaining the source code and compiling it yourself is easier. One warning, however; compiling from source can be tricky and is usually recommended only for the experienced.

Chapter 8
Using Printers In
Windows And Macintosh

Using Linux to build a network allows
multiple computers to share and
use one (late model) printer efficiently.
Although the focus of this chapter is
on a printer environment that combines Windows and
Macintosh systems, methods to share printers
in a variety of contexts are also described.

Contents Of This Chapter

Using Network Printers

Shared Printer Types

Using Linux to build a network allows multiple personal computers (PCs) to share one printer. In a Windows and Macintosh combined network system, shared settings and usage limitations differ depending on the type of printer and access method. Because of this, be sure to verify what type of printer can be used in your environment.

When adding a new printer, choose the one best suited to the current client needs and that is suitable for use with Linux.

> **Note:** Not all printers are easy to use with Linux. Because this chapter covers shared printers, try to use a PostScript printer for your network. Often, non-PostScript printers can be difficult to setup (or won't work) in the Linux environment.

Non-PostScript Printer

If you use a non-PostScript printer, configure the printer during the Red Hat installation process, where you can choose the type of printer and cause the installation process to set up your system accordingly. However, even by using the preconfigured printer list, you aren't guaranteed that your printer will work correctly or that all functions (color, draft-mode, photo-quality printing, and so on) will be available.

Configuring Your Printer During The Red Hat Installation

During installation, after main installation, setting up a mouse, setting up a network, specifying a time zone, specifying what services will run automatically, you configure the printer.

Here, say "Yes", you want to install a printer now. A list appears that shows all the printers Red Hat may be able to install automatically. Select the printer that matches yours exactly. Specifying a printer from the same manufacturer but with an earlier model often works, but sometimes it will not. If your printer isn't listed, you can try this, but don't be surprised if your printer doesn't work.

After you specify the printer, you are asked to enter the name of the queue and the type of printer to use. The default name and printer is "lp", but you should change it (just these two letters) and enter the name that you want your printer to be known by. The name should make it obvious to users what printer is being referred to; often, the type of printer is a good choice (use HPDeskJet, for example, if your printer is a HP DeskJet).

Next, choose the printer paper size. Use the default of the other two selections, resolution and fix stair stepping. Finally, select color depth (if applicable to your printer) and confirm the information. The most appropriate color depth is usually chosen by default.

Read the rest of the installation information in this chapter; it tells you what files are used and where they are located. You will need this information to troubleshoot your configuration. If you follow the instructions in this chapter carefully and your printer doesn't work correctly, you need to troubleshoot or, perhaps, buy a PostScript printer. Troubleshooting printers is beyond the scope of this book, so you may need to go to the Internet for help. Assuming that you purchased an Official Red Hat CD-ROM set, you can get help from Red Hat (**www.redhat.com**), so you should start there. Also, check the newsgroup dedicated to Red Hat (**news://linux.redhat.misc**).

After you configure your printer, the installation of Red Hat Linux continues as described in Chapter 2.

Advantages Of Shared Printers

- One printer appears to be directly connected to each PC on the network; there is no need to use a print switch each time it uses the printer.

- The printer is used more efficiently, even with heavy use, because the server simultaneously receives multiple print jobs and sends them to the printer in order.

- One high-speed printer can be connected to the server, instead of connecting one printer to every PC.

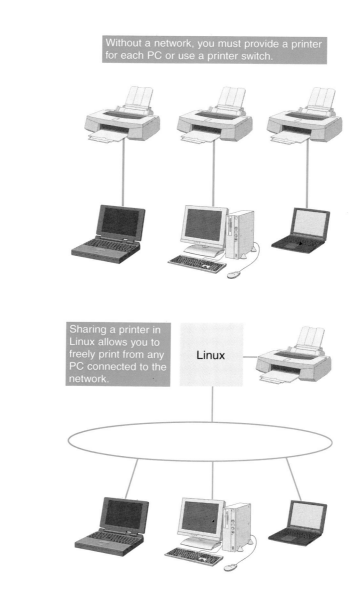

Without a network, you must provide a printer for each PC or use a printer switch.

Sharing a printer in Linux allows you to freely print from any PC connected to the network.

Linux

Network Printers And Their Uses

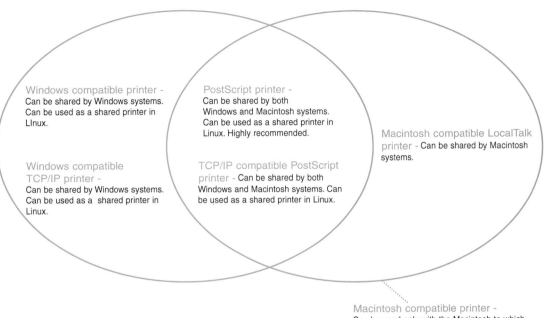

Windows compatible printer -
Can be shared by Windows systems.
Can be used as a shared printer in
LInux.

PostScript printer -
Can be shared by both
Windows and Macintosh systems.
Can be used as a shared printer in
Linux. Highly recommended.

Macintosh compatible LocalTalk
printer - Can be shared by Macintosh
systems.

Windows compatible
TCP/IP printer -
Can be shared by Windows systems.
Can be used as a shared printer in
Linux.

TCP/IP compatible PostScript
printer - Can be shared by both
Windows and Macintosh systems. Can
be used as a shared printer in Linux.

Macintosh compatible printer -
Can be used only with the Macintosh to which
it is connected.

Using Shared Printers In Linux

Printers Shared Only By Windows Systems

Windows compatible printer.
Connect the main printer to Linux and use it as a shared printer.
Windows compatible TCP/IP printer.
Specify an IP address and set this address in Linux as the shared printer.

Printers Compatible With Both Windows And Macintosh Systems

PostScript printer.
Connect the main printer to Linux and use it as a shared printer.
TCP/IP compatible PostScript printer.
Specify an IP address and set this address in Linux as the shared printer.

> **Note:** Use the DHCP Server introduced in Chapter 5 to connect
> other PCs to the network. They will not be connected properly unless
> this is set up in advance.

Sharing Printers

printcap And papd.conf

Printers are registered in Linux by recording the information about printers connected to Linux and TCP/IP printers in the printcap file. When printcap is configured, Samba uses this information to allow printer sharing from Windows. The type of printer being used makes little difference when sharing from Windows. If a PostScript printer is being used, however, by configuring the papd.conf file and allowing the registered information in printcap to be reflected, a Macintosh system can share the printer as well. You can find and download printcap and papd.conf online at **ftp.coriolis.com** in the linux_server_vbb folder. Place these files in the /etc directory.

How To Set Up Different Kinds Of Printers

Windows Compatible Printers (Includes PostScript Printers)

Read the following required configuration steps in the order in which they appear:
(1) Copy printcap.
(2) Edit printcap configuring a printer connected to Linux.

Windows Compatible TCP/IP Printer (Includes PostScript Printers)

Read the following required configuration steps in the order in which they appear:
(1) Copy printcap.
(3) Edit printcap. TCP/IP printer configuration.

PostScript Printers Shared By Both Windows And Macintosh Systems

(1) Copy printcap.
(2) Edit printcap. configure a printer connected to Linux.
(4) Configure a shared Linux PostScript printer from a Macintosh.

TCP/IP Compatible PostScript Printers Shared By Both Windows Macintosh Systems

Read the following required configuration steps in the order in which they appear:
(1) Copy printcap.
(3) Edit printcap. (TCP/IP printer configuration).
(4) Configure a shared Linux PostScript printer from a Macintosh.

(1) Copy printcap.

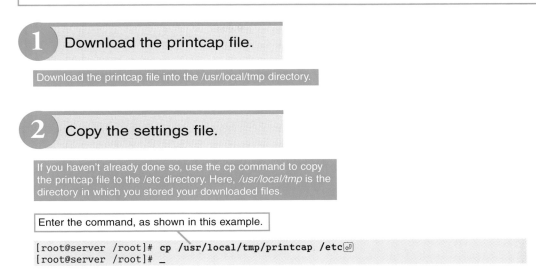

1 Download the printcap file.

Download the printcap file into the /usr/local/tmp directory.

2 Copy the settings file.

If you haven't already done so, use the cp command to copy the printcap file to the /etc directory. Here, *usr/local/tmp* is the directory in which you stored your downloaded files.

Enter the command, as shown in this example.

```
[root@server /root]# cp /usr/local/tmp/printcap /etc⏎
[root@server /root]# _
```

(2) Editing printcap (Configuring a printer connected to Linux)

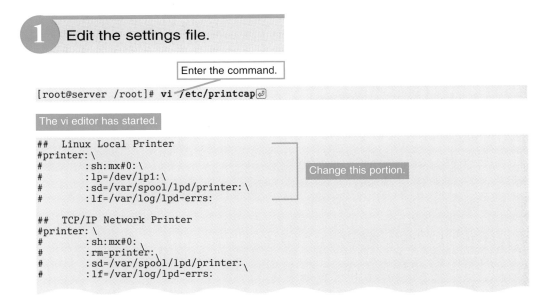

1 Edit the settings file.

Enter the command.

```
[root@server /root]# vi /etc/printcap⏎
```

The vi editor has started.

```
##   Linux Local Printer
#printer:\
#        :sh:mx#0:\
#        :lp=/dev/lp1:\
#        :sd=/var/spool/lpd/printer:\
#        :lf=/var/log/lpd-errs:

##   TCP/IP Network Printer
#printer:\
#        :sh:mx#0:
#        :rm=printer:
#        :sd=/var/spool/lpd/printer:
#        :lf=/var/log/lpd-errs:
```

Change this portion.

147

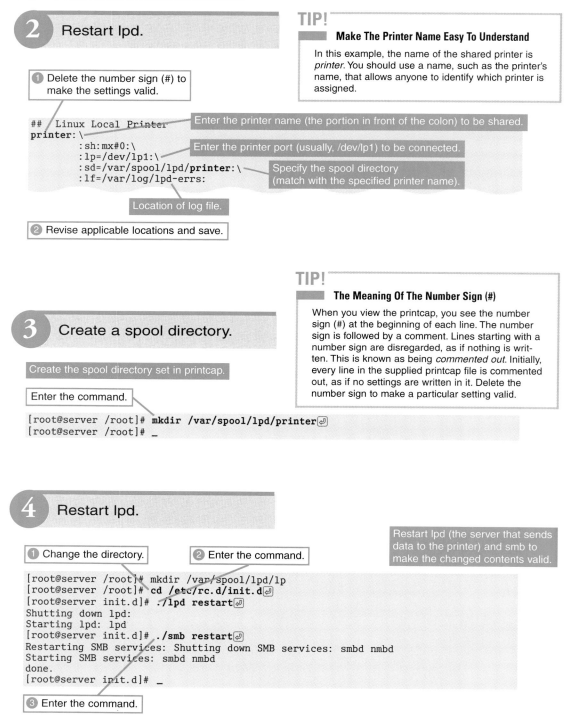

2 Restart lpd.

① Delete the number sign (#) to make the settings valid.

```
##  Linux Local Printer
printer:\
        :sh:mx#0:\
        :lp=/dev/lp1:\
        :sd=/var/spool/lpd/printer:\
        :lf=/var/log/lpd-errs:
```

Enter the printer name (the portion in front of the colon) to be shared.

Enter the printer port (usually, /dev/lp1) to be connected.

Specify the spool directory (match with the specified printer name).

Location of log file.

② Revise applicable locations and save.

TIP!

Make The Printer Name Easy To Understand

In this example, the name of the shared printer is *printer*. You should use a name, such as the printer's name, that allows anyone to identify which printer is assigned.

3 Create a spool directory.

Create the spool directory set in printcap.

Enter the command.

```
[root@server /root]# mkdir /var/spool/lpd/printer⏎
[root@server /root]# _
```

TIP!

The Meaning Of The Number Sign (#)

When you view the printcap, you see the number sign (#) at the beginning of each line. The number sign is followed by a comment. Lines starting with a number sign are disregarded, as if nothing is written. This is known as being *commented out*. Initially, every line in the supplied printcap file is commented out, as if no settings are written in it. Delete the number sign to make a particular setting valid.

4 Restart lpd.

① Change the directory.

② Enter the command.

Restart lpd (the server that sends data to the printer) and smb to make the changed contents valid.

```
[root@server /root]# mkdir /var/spool/lpd/lp
[root@server /root]# cd /etc/rc.d/init.d⏎
[root@server init.d]# ./lpd restart⏎
Shutting down lpd:
Starting lpd: lpd
[root@server init.d]# ./smb restart⏎
Restarting SMB services: Shutting down SMB services: smbd nmbd
Starting SMB services: smbd nmbd
done.
[root@server init.d]# _
```

③ Enter the command.

(3) Edit printcap (TCP/IP printer settings)

1 Edit the settings file.

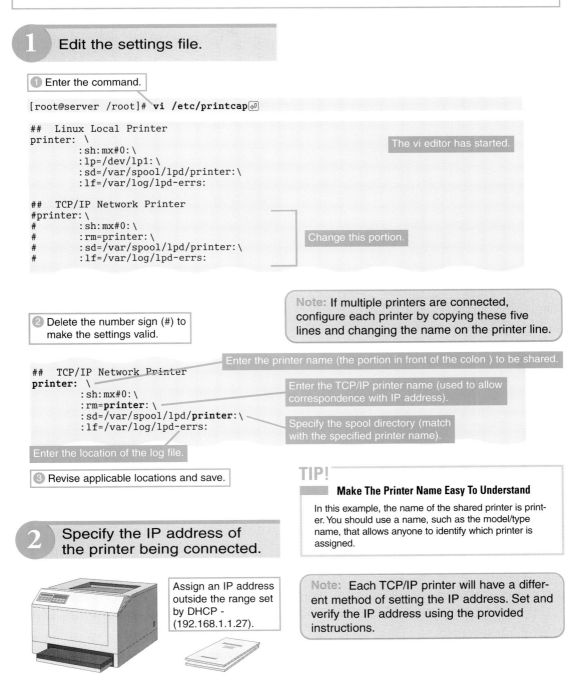

❶ Enter the command.

```
[root@server /root]# vi /etc/printcap↵

##   Linux Local Printer
printer: \
        :sh:mx#0:\
        :lp=/dev/lp1:\
        :sd=/var/spool/lpd/printer:\
        :lf=/var/log/lpd-errs:

##   TCP/IP Network Printer
#printer:\
#        :sh:mx#0:\
#        :rm=printer:\
#        :sd=/var/spool/lpd/printer:\
#        :lf=/var/log/lpd-errs:
```

The vi editor has started.

Change this portion.

❷ Delete the number sign (#) to make the settings valid.

Note: If multiple printers are connected, configure each printer by copying these five lines and changing the name on the printer line.

Enter the printer name (the portion in front of the colon) to be shared.

```
##   TCP/IP Network Printer
printer: \
        :sh:mx#0:\
        :rm=printer:\
        :sd=/var/spool/lpd/printer:\
        :lf=/var/log/lpd-errs:
```

Enter the TCP/IP printer name (used to allow correspondence with IP address).

Specify the spool directory (match with the specified printer name).

Enter the location of the log file.

❸ Revise applicable locations and save.

TIP!

Make The Printer Name Easy To Understand

In this example, the name of the shared printer is printer. You should use a name, such as the model/type name, that allows anyone to identify which printer is assigned.

2 Specify the IP address of the printer being connected.

Assign an IP address outside the range set by DHCP - (192.168.1.1.27).

Note: Each TCP/IP printer will have a different method of setting the IP address. Set and verify the IP address using the provided instructions.

3 Register the IP address of the printer being connected.

Set to allow the use of a TCP/IP printer in Linux.

① Enter the command.

```
[root@server /root]# vi /etc/hosts⏎
```

```
127.0.0.1              localhost localhost.localdomain
209.17.129.210         mybox.mylab.coriolis.com server
192.168.1.1.27         printer.coriolis.com printer
```

The vi editor has started.

② Add this line to the last line and save.

TIP!

What Is /etc/hosts?

/etc/hosts is a file that allows names and IP addresses to correspond. It allows you to specify multiple names to an IP address.

4 Restart lpd.

① Change the directory.

Restart both lpd (the server that sends data to the printer) and smb to make the changed contents valid.

```
[root@server /root]# cd /etc/rc.d/init.d⏎
[root@server init.d]# ./lpd restart⏎
Shutting down lpd: lpd
Starting lpd: lpd
[root@server init.d]# ./smb restart⏎
Restarting SMB services: Shutting down SMB services: smbd nmbd
Starting SMB services: smbd nmbd
done.
[root@server init.d]# _
```

② Enter the command.

③ Enter the command.

---

(4)Establish the settings to share a Linux PostScript printer from a Macintosh system.

---

1 Copy the settings file.

Enter the command.

Copy the PostScript settings file from your download directory, as in this example.

```
[root@server /root]# cp /usr/local/src/netatalk-1.4b2/config/papd.conf
/usr/local/atalk/etc⏎
[root@server /root]# _
```

2 Copy the Macintosh printer description file.

① Open in the following order:

- Macintosh HD
  - System Folder
    - Extensions
      - Printer Description File

② Copy LaserWriter II to the shared folder in Linux.

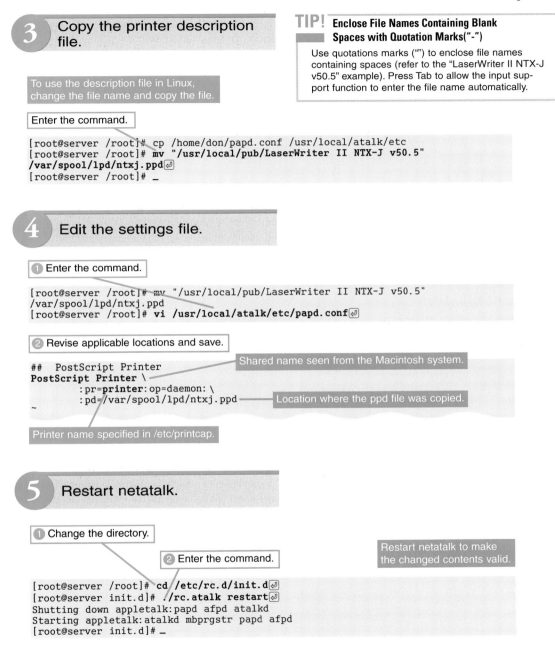

3 Copy the printer description file.

TIP! **Enclose File Names Containing Blank Spaces with Quotation Marks("-")**

Use quotations marks ("") to enclose file names containing spaces (refer to the "LaserWriter II NTX-J v50.5" example). Press Tab to allow the input support function to enter the file name automatically.

To use the description file in Linux, change the file name and copy the file.

Enter the command.

```
[root@server /root]# cp /home/don/papd.conf /usr/local/atalk/etc
[root@server /root]# mv "/usr/local/pub/LaserWriter II NTX-J v50.5"
/var/spool/lpd/ntxj.ppd⏎
[root@server /root]# _
```

4 Edit the settings file.

① Enter the command.

```
[root@server /root]# mv "/usr/local/pub/LaserWriter II NTX-J v50.5"
/var/spool/lpd/ntxj.ppd
[root@server /root]# vi /usr/local/atalk/etc/papd.conf⏎
```

② Revise applicable locations and save.

```
##  PostScript Printer
PostScript Printer \
        :pr=printer:op=daemon: \
        :pd=/var/spool/lpd/ntxj.ppd
~
```

Shared name seen from the Macintosh system.

Location where the ppd file was copied.

Printer name specified in /etc/printcap.

5 Restart netatalk.

① Change the directory.

② Enter the command.

Restart netatalk to make the changed contents valid.

```
[root@server /root]# cd /etc/rc.d/init.d⏎
[root@server init.d]# ./rc.atalk restart⏎
Shutting down appletalk:papd afpd atalkd
Starting appletalk:atalkd mbprgstr papd afpd
[root@server init.d]# _
```

Using Shared Printers

Client PC Settings

Samba and netatalk allow printers set for sharing in Linux to be shared by Windows and Macintosh systems. Special settings are not required to use Linux for sharing. Install the drivers, and establish the settings as if you are connecting a shared printer directly to a PC.

In a Macintosh system, the shared printer is viewed as a LaserWriter 8, regardless of the printer being shared. A PostScript printer, which is essentially the same as a LaserWriter 8, should present no significant problems.

Setting Shared Printers For Windows PCs

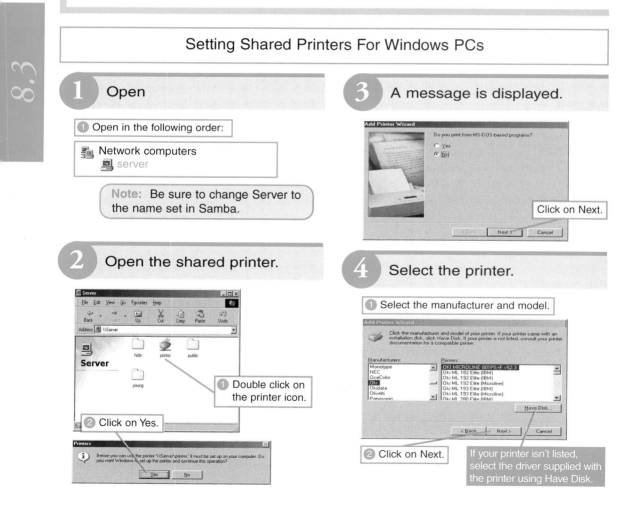

1 Open

① Open in the following order:

Network computers
server

Note: Be sure to change Server to the name set in Samba.

2 Open the shared printer.

① Double click on the printer icon.

② Click on Yes.

3 A message is displayed.

Click on Next.

4 Select the printer.

① Select the manufacturer and model.

② Click on Next.

If your printer isn't listed, select the driver supplied with the printer using Have Disk.

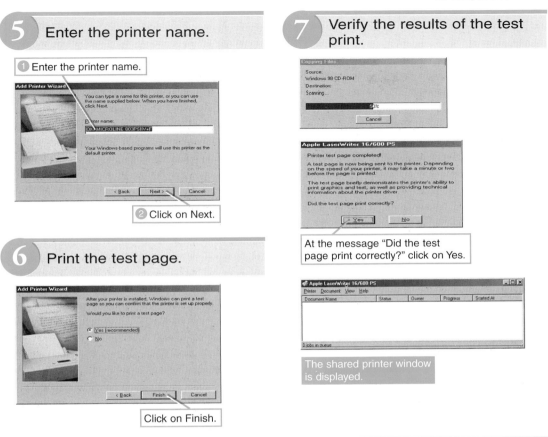

5 Enter the printer name.

❶ Enter the printer name.

❷ Click on Next.

6 Print the test page.

Click on Finish.

7 Verify the results of the test print.

At the message "Did the test page print correctly?" click on Yes.

The shared printer window is displayed.

How To Use A Shared Printer With Macintosh

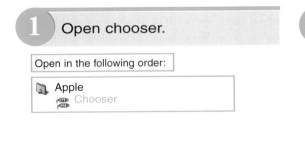

1 Open chooser.

Open in the following order:

🗂 Apple
   📠 Chooser

2 Select LaserWriter 8.

❶ Click on LaserWriter 8.

❷ Click on the printer to use.

The shared printer settings are complete.

Sharing Printers Connected To Windows PCs

Shared Network Service

The Linux PC cannot support multiple network shared printers. However, you can share several printers over the network by using them through Windows.

Check the network settings on the Windows PCs connected to the shared printers to verify whether network sharing is enabled. Using shared printers from Windows is the same as sharing with Linux.

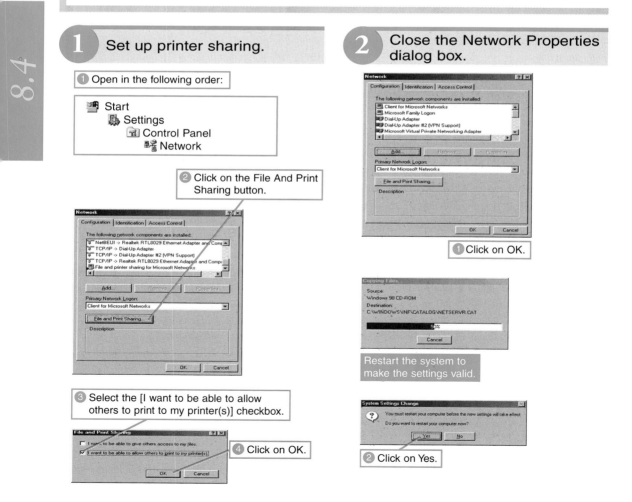

1 Set up printer sharing.

❶ Open in the following order:

Start
　Settings
　　Control Panel
　　　Network

❷ Click on the File And Print Sharing button.

❸ Select the [I want to be able to allow others to print to my printer(s)] checkbox.

❹ Click on OK.

2 Close the Network Properties dialog box.

❶ Click on OK.

Restart the system to make the settings valid.

❷ Click on Yes.

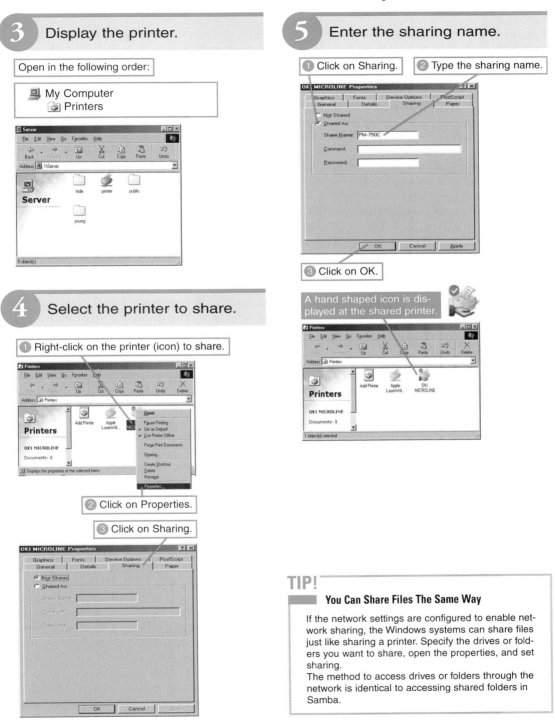

3 Display the printer.

Open in the following order:

🖥️ My Computer
   📁 Printers

4 Select the printer to share.

① Right-click on the printer (icon) to share.

② Click on Properties.

③ Click on Sharing.

5 Enter the sharing name.

① Click on Sharing.

② Type the sharing name.

③ Click on OK.

A hand shaped icon is displayed at the shared printer.

TIP!

You Can Share Files The Same Way

If the network settings are configured to enable network sharing, the Windows systems can share files just like sharing a printer. Specify the drives or folders you want to share, open the properties, and set sharing.

The method to access drives or folders through the network is identical to accessing shared folders in Samba.

155

STEP UP

Sharing Printers On A Macintosh That Doesn't Have A Printer Port

Macintosh systems such as the iMac, G3, and G4, which are equipped with an Ethernet port but not a printer port (serial port), cannot use printers equipped solely with a Macintosh printer port. If you want to use this type of printer, connect it to a Macintosh that has a printer port and share it using the network. You'll need to contact your printer's manufacturer to determine whether your printer will support adding a serial-to-USB converter.

Without the converter, if another Macintosh is not available, you may not be able to use Linux to share the printer using a network. Even if the printer is connected to Linux and if it is not a PostScript printer, it cannot be shared. In this case, you must either provide a PostScript printer and connect it to Linux or purchase a printer (or if possible, a converter) that can be connected to an iMac.
Although an iMac is not equipped with a printer port, it does have a USB port which allows you to use a low-cost inkjet printer to do high quality color printing

When using a network to connect Windows PCs and iMacs, sharing a high-performance PostScript printer throught Linux is more convenient than connecting a printer to the iMacs.

Chapter 9
Making Web Pages
For Intranet Use

When you install Red Hat Linux on a PC as instructed in this book, a Web server is also automatically installed as well, allowing Linux to be used a Web server.

This chapter explains how a Web server operates and the basic settings of a functioning Web server.

Contents Of This Chapter

How Web Pages Are Displayed

The Web is the most familiar service on the Internet. Web pages are provided by a Web server. When Red Hat Linux is installed, a Web server called *Apache* is also automatically installed. Apache appears as a special directory in Linux, as a document root (Web page root). Placing files in this directory allows them to be viewed as Web pages. If you share the directory, you can create Web pages from a PC.

How A Web Page Works

Web pages of the CoriolisOpen Press series of books by Coriolis.

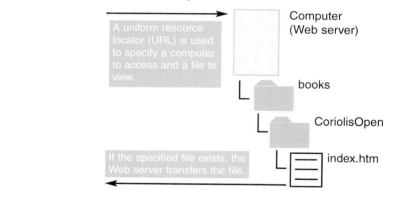

A uniform resource locator (URL) is used to specify a computer to access and a file to view.

Computer (Web server)

books

CoriolisOpen

If the specified file exists, the Web server transfers the file.

index.htm

The transferred file displays in the browser.

The Meaning Of URL

Protocol tag used to open a Web page.

Host computer name (IP address is also valid).

Directory and file name (file of page to display).

http://coriolis.com/books/CoriolisOpen/index.htm

The path accessed by specifying a URL is called the document root.

Red Hat Linux comes equipped with Web server functions (Apache) that are used to supply Web pages.

The Role Of Apache

A Special Directory In Linux Is Assigned For Web Use

Enter the following URL in the browser of the computer connected to the network to display the Apache Web page.

http://192.168.1.1/

Linux PC (specified by IP address).

Apache is set as the root of this Web page.

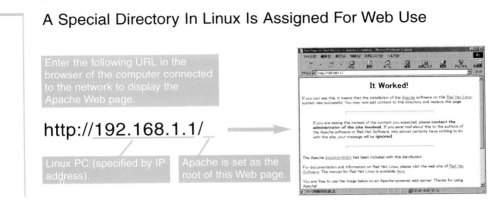

Directory Assigned By Apache As The Document Root

http://192.168.1.1/

This directory is equivalent to the document root.

||

/home/httpd/html

For example, the URL to open a file called /home/httpd/html/manual/index.html is as follows:

http://192.168.1.1/manual/index.html

Linux PC (specified by IP address).

The relative path after /home/httpd/html.

If the directory /home/httpd/html assigned to this document root is shared by Samba or netatalk, then anyone can create a Web page.

> Note: Please use the DHCP Server introduced in Chapter 5 to connect other personal computers to the network. These computers will not connect properly unless they are setup in advance.

Customizing Your Web Server

Changing Settings Files

The Apache settings files are located in the directory /etc/httpd/conf. They are divided into three files: access.conf, httpd.conf, and srm.conf. Apache settings can be changed by editing these files.

This section examines the basic settings of Apache, how they can be changed, and how to verify this operation. Apache must be restarted each time the settings are changed.

Changing Document Roots

1 Create the directory.

Enter the command.

```
[root@server /root]# mkdir /usr/local/www⏎
[root@server /root]# _
```

2 Edit srm.conf.

① Enter the command.

```
[root@server /root]# mkdir /usr/local/www
[root@server /root]# vi /etc/httpd/conf/srm.conf⏎
```

```
# DocumentRoot: The directory out of which you will serve your
# documents. By default, all requests are taken from this directory, but
# symbolic links and aliases may be used to point to other locations.

DocumentRoot /home/httpd/html
```

The directory specified in the DocumentRoot line is assigned as the document root.

② Change to the prepared directory, then save and quit.

```
# DocumentRoot: The directory out of which you will serve your
# documents. By default, all requests are taken from this directory, but
# symbolic links and aliases may be used to point to other locations.

DocumentRoot /usr/local/www
```

3 Edit access.conf.

1 Enter the command.

```
[root@server /root]# vi /etc/httpd/conf/access.conf⏎
```

```
# This should be changed to whatever you set DocumentRoot to.

<Directory /home/httpd/html>
```

With access.conf as well, change the directory
assigned as the document root.

```
# This should be changed to whatever you set DocumentRoot to.

<Directory /usr/local/www>
```

2 Change to the prepared directory, then save and quit.

4 Restart Apache.

1 Change the directory.   2 Enter the command.

```
[root@server /root]# cd /etc/rc.d/init.d⏎
[root@server init.d]# ./httpd restart⏎
Shutting down http: httpd
Starting httpd: httpd
[root@server init.d]# –
```

Assigning Special Directories To Document Root Subdirectories

1 Edit srm.conf.

Enter the command.

```
[root@server /root]# vi /etc/httpd/conf/srm.conf⏎
```

```
# Note that if you include a trailing / on fakename then the server will
# require it to be present in the URL.  So "/icons" isn't aliased in this
# example.

Alias /icons/ /home/httpd/icons/
```

A directory that matches the settings written in
the Alias line is added to the Web directory.

Alias /icons/ /home/httpd/icons

Name assigned following the Web root.   Linux directory.

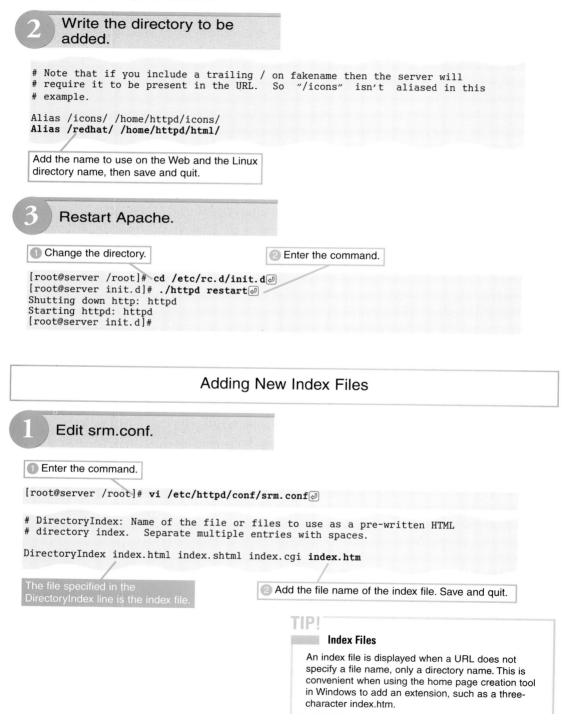

2 Write the directory to be added.

```
# Note that if you include a trailing / on fakename then the server will
# require it to be present in the URL.  So "/icons" isn't  aliased in this
# example.

Alias /icons/ /home/httpd/icons/
Alias /redhat/ /home/httpd/html/
```

Add the name to use on the Web and the Linux directory name, then save and quit.

3 Restart Apache.

① Change the directory.

② Enter the command.

```
[root@server /root]# cd /etc/rc.d/init.d↵
[root@server init.d]# ./httpd restart↵
Shutting down http: httpd
Starting httpd: httpd
[root@server init.d]#
```

Adding New Index Files

1 Edit srm.conf.

① Enter the command.

```
[root@server /root]# vi /etc/httpd/conf/srm.conf↵
```

```
# DirectoryIndex: Name of the file or files to use as a pre-written HTML
# directory index.  Separate multiple entries with spaces.

DirectoryIndex index.html index.shtml index.cgi index.htm
```

The file specified in the DirectoryIndex line is the index file.

② Add the file name of the index file. Save and quit.

TIP!

Index Files

An index file is displayed when a URL does not specify a file name, only a directory name. This is convenient when using the home page creation tool in Windows to add an extension, such as a three-character index.htm.

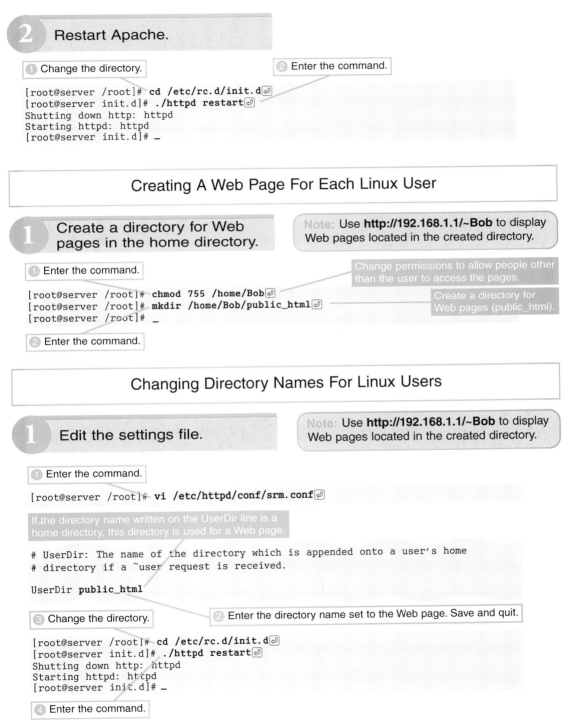

2 Restart Apache.

① Change the directory. ② Enter the command.

```
[root@server /root]# cd /etc/rc.d/init.d⏎
[root@server init.d]# ./httpd restart⏎
Shutting down http: httpd
Starting httpd: httpd
[root@server init.d]# _
```

Creating A Web Page For Each Linux User

1 Create a directory for Web pages in the home directory.

Note: Use **http://192.168.1.1/~Bob** to display Web pages located in the created directory.

① Enter the command.

Change permissions to allow people other than the user to access the pages.

Create a directory for Web pages (public_html).

```
[root@server /root]# chmod 755 /home/Bob⏎
[root@server /root]# mkdir /home/Bob/public_html⏎
[root@server /root]# _
```

② Enter the command.

Changing Directory Names For Linux Users

1 Edit the settings file.

Note: Use **http://192.168.1.1/~Bob** to display Web pages located in the created directory.

① Enter the command.

```
[root@server /root]# vi /etc/httpd/conf/srm.conf⏎
```

If the directory name written on the UserDir line is a home directory, this directory is used for a Web page.

```
# UserDir: The name of the directory which is appended onto a user's home
# directory if a ~user request is received.

UserDir public_html
```

③ Change the directory.   ② Enter the directory name set to the Web page. Save and quit.

```
[root@server /root]# cd /etc/rc.d/init.d⏎
[root@server init.d]# ./httpd restart⏎
Shutting down http: httpd
Starting httpd: httpd
[root@server init.d]# _
```

④ Enter the command.

§TEP UP

Web Server And Apache

Currently, there are a variety of Web servers available, including Microsoft's IIS, Netscape's Enterprise Server, Rapidsite, NCSA httpd, and others. When Red Hat Linux is installed, however, the Apache Web server is automatically installed.

The name Apache is derived from the Apache FAQ, "Why The Name Apache?" (basically, a cute name that stuck: Apache is "A PAtCHy sErver". It was based on some existing code and a series of "patch files".). Apache is based on the National Center for Supercomputing Applications (NCSA) httpd 1.3 Web server, the most widely used server in early 1995. Although Apache was created using code from a number of different programs, it is currently being developed independently. Apache software is distributed at no cost.

It offers powerful functions and is a stable Web server. Apache is easy to operate, making it possible to build a Web server without the use of a high-performance computer. Expanded functions to cope with bugs are being developed one after another.

The freely distributed high-performance Apache is the most widely used Web server in the world today. As of January 1999, Apache's share of Web servers was 54.22% of all Web servers in use on the Internet. The results of this survey, "The Netcraft Web Server Survey," conducted by Netcraft, can be viewed as a graph at **www.netcraft.com/Survey**.

Chapter 10
Creating A Mail Server
For Intranet Use

Setting up a mail server in Linux allows you
to exchange email within the intranet.
Because you can also set up a mail server to
suit your own needs, you can also create email addresses
freely. This chapter explains how to set up a mail server.

Contents Of This Chapter

Understanding How Email Works

sendmail And qpopper

The sendmail program enables Linux to provide email services. The sendmail program sends and stores email addressed to each user in Linux. The email stored in Linux must be retrieved from Linux before it can be read on a Windows or Macintosh system.

The qpopper program provides this retrieval service. Both sendmail and qpopper are used to set up the mail server in this book. You can download qpopper from **ftp.coriolis.com** in the linux_server_vbb folder and the latest version of sendmail from **www.sendmail.org**.

How Email Is Exchanged

With email, the sender specifies a recipient and sends the email. The email is then sent and stored by Linux. When the recipient reads the email, they receive stored email from the mail server. The sending and storing functions, as well as the reading function, are supplied by the mail server.

Role Of The Mail Server

- Receives email.
- Saves email.
- Delivers email.

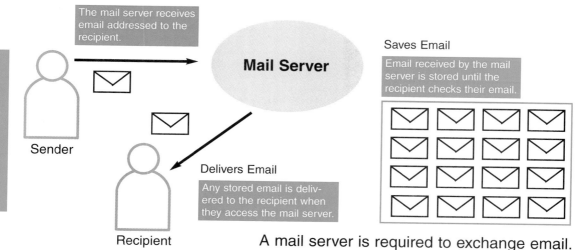

Receives Email

The mail server receives email addressed to the recipient.

Mail Server

Saves Email

Email received by the mail server is stored until the recipient checks their email.

Sender

Delivers Email

Any stored email is delivered to the recipient when they access the mail server.

Recipient

A mail server is required to exchange email.

10.1

Mail Servers Running On Linux

• A mail server is not an independent program.

sendmail - Basic functions include sending and storing email.

qpopper - Supplies functions allowing Windows and Macintosh users to receive email.

Exchanges Between Mail Servers And Mailers

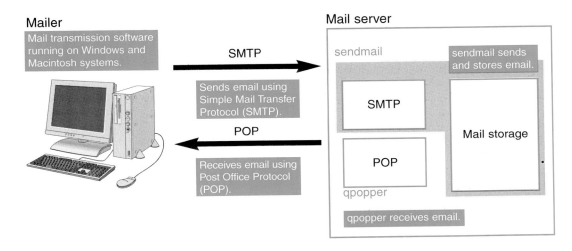

Mailer

Mail transmission software running on Windows and Macintosh systems.

Mail server

sendmail

sendmail sends and stores email.

SMTP

Sends email using Simple Mail Transfer Protocol (SMTP).

SMTP

POP

Receives email using Post Office Protocol (POP).

POP

Mail storage

qpopper

qpopper receives email.

Installation Preparations

1. Install sendmail.
2. Install CF to create the sendmail settings file. (The sendmail settings file is difficult to understand, so this tool is used to create the settings file.)
3. Install qpopper.
4. Change the Linux settings files.

> **Note:** Use the DHCP server introduced in Chapter 5 to connect other personal computers (PC's) to the network. They will not connect properly unless they are set up in advance.

Installing Mail Server Software

Installing sendmail

The sendmail program enables Linux to provide email services. sendmail comes with Red Hat Linux, but it's preferable that you get the latest version and install it. This section explains how to compile and install sendmail. The sendmail home page, **www.sendmail.org**, has the latest version information. If you download it, put the package into the directory /usr/local/src.

Usually, the **make** command is used to compile a program; here, however, the **build** command is used to compile sendmail independently. This allows sendmail to be created to accommodate a variety of environments.

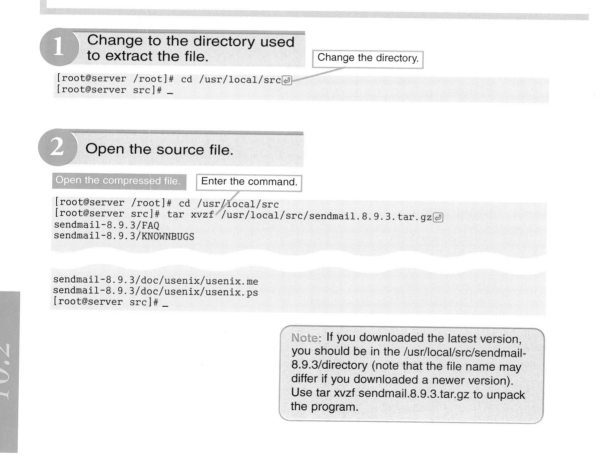

1 Change to the directory used to extract the file.

Change the directory.

```
[root@server /root]# cd /usr/local/src⏎
[root@server src]# _
```

2 Open the source file.

Open the compressed file.   Enter the command.

```
[root@server /root]# cd /usr/local/src
[root@server src]# tar xvzf /usr/local/src/sendmail.8.9.3.tar.gz⏎
sendmail-8.9.3/FAQ
sendmail-8.9.3/KNOWNBUGS
```

```
sendmail-8.9.3/doc/usenix/usenix.me
sendmail-8.9.3/doc/usenix/usenix.ps
[root@server src]# _
```

Note: If you downloaded the latest version, you should be in the /usr/local/src/sendmail-8.9.3/directory (note that the file name may differ if you downloaded a newer version). Use tar xvzf sendmail.8.9.3.tar.gz to unpack the program.

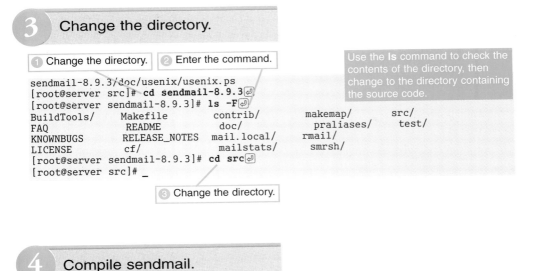

3   Change the directory.

① Change the directory. ② Enter the command.

Use the **ls** command to check the contents of the directory, then change to the directory containing the source code.

```
sendmail-8.9.3/doc/usenix/usenix.ps
[root@server src]# cd sendmail-8.9.3↵
[root@server sendmail-8.9.3]# ls -F↵
BuildTools/     Makefile        contrib/        makemap/        src/
FAQ             README          doc/             praliases/      test/
KNOWNBUGS       RELEASE_NOTES   mail.local/     rmail/
LICENSE         cf/              mailstats/      smrsh/
[root@server sendmail-8.9.3]# cd src↵
[root@server src]# _
```

③ Change the directory.

4   Compile sendmail.

Prepare sendmail for installation.   Enter the command.

```
[root@server sendmail-8.9.3]# cd src
[root@server src]# sh Build↵
Configuration: os=Linux, rel=2.0.36, rbase=2, rroot=2.0, arch=i586, sfx=
Using M4=/usr/bin/m4


groff -Tascii -mandoc newaliases.1 > newaliases.0
groff -Tascii -mandoc sendmail.8 > sendmail.0
[root@server src]# _
```

5   Install sendmail.

Install sendmail.   Enter the command.

```
groff -Tascii -mandoc sendmail.8 > sendmail.0
[root@server src]# sh Build install↵
Configuration: os=Linux, rel=2.0.36, rbase=2, rroot=2.0, arch=i586, sfx=
Making in obj.Linux.2.x.x.ix86


install -c -o bin -g bin -m 444 mailq.0 /usr/man/man1/mailq.1
install -c -o bin -g bin -m 444 newaliases.0 /usr/man/man1/newaliases.1
[root@server src]# _
```

Creating A Mail Server Part 1

Editing sendmail.cf

To use sendmail properly, you must prepare a settings file that is suitable for the installed sendmail program. The sendmail settings file is located in /etc/sendmail.cf, but writing this file yourself is extremely difficult. Consequently, a useful tool called CF that creates the settings file automatically is supplied. This section explains how to use CF to create sendmail.cf. Download CF and sendmail.def from the **ftp.coriolis.com/linux_server_vbb** folder, and copy them to the usr/local/src directory.

---

1 Change to the directory used to extract the file.

Enter the command.

```
[root@server src]# cd /usr/local/src↵
[root@server src]# _
```

2 Open the settings file creation tool.

Open the compressed file.   Enter the command.

```
[root@server src]# cd /usr/local/src
[root@server src]# tar xvzf /usr/local/src/CF-3.7Wp12.tar.gz↵
CF-3.7Wp12/
CF-3.7Wp12/ChangeLog
```

```
CF-3.7Wp12/support/README
CF-3.7Wp12/README
[root@server src]# _
```

10.3

TIP!

vi Commands

i	Inserts characters at the cursor.
x	Deletes characters at the cursor.
r[X]	Replaces the character at the cursor with the entered character [X].
cw	Replaces text from the position of the cursor to the end of the word.
/word↵	Searches for a specified word.
:w↵	Saves the file.
:q↵	Quits the vi editor.

3 Copy the settings file.

Copy the settings file located on the CD-ROM.

Enter the command.

```
CF-3.7Wp12/README
[root@server src]# cp /usr/local/src/sendmail.def /usr/local/src/CF-3.7Wp12 ⏎
[root@server src]# _
```

4 Edit the settings file.

① Enter the command.

```
[root@server src]# cp /usr/local/sendmail.def /usr/local/src/CF-3.7Wp12
[root@server src]# vi /usr/local/src/CF-3.7Wp12/sendmail.def ⏎
```

The vi editor starts.

```
##
CF_TYPE=R8V8

##
DEF_ID=' Linux, March 1999'

##
VERSION=3.7Wp12
VERSION_SEPARATOR=/
LOCAL_VERSION=x0.00

##
OS_TYPE=linux-redhat

##
MY_DOMAIN='coriolis.com'
MY_NAME='mybox.coriolis.com'
OFFICIAL_NAME='$w.$m'

##
FROM_ADDRESS='$m'
RECIPIENT_GENERIC=yes
REWRITE_GENERIC_FROM=lower
REWRITE_GENERIC_TO=lower
"/usr/local/src/CF-3.7Wp12/sendmail.def" 36 lines, 484 characters
```

② Revise applicable locations and save.

```
##
MY_DOMAIN='coriolis.com'
MY_NAME='mybox.coriolis.com'
OFFICIAL_NAME='$w.$m'
```

Change to the domain name set during installation.

Change to the server name set during installation.

Note: Details of sendmail.def files are located at **www.superconnect.or.jp/articles/eng/cfmanual.html**.

5 Create a settings file for sendmail.

Note: Be sure to type the correct file name (sendmail.cf, not sendmail.def).

① Change the directory. ② Enter the command.

```
[root@server src]# cd CF-3.7Wpl2⏎
[root@server CF-3.7Wpl2]# make sendmail.cf⏎
MASTERDIR=./Master TOOLDIR=./Tools
./Tools/Configure sendmail.def > sendmail.cf.tmp
mv -f sendmail.cf.tmp sendmail.cf
[root@server CF-3.7Wpl2]# _
```

The sendmail.cf file used by sendmail is created.

6 Stop sendmail.

Stop sendmail once to verify that the settings file is written correctly.

Enter the command.

```
[root@server CF-3.7Wpl2]# make sendmail.cf
MASTERDIR=./Master TOOLDIR=./Tools
./Tools/Configure sendmail.def > sendmail.cf.tmp
mv -f sendmail.cf.tmp sendmail.cf
[root@server CF-3.7Wpl2]# /etc/rc.d/initd/sendmail stop⏎
Shutting down sendmail: sendmail
[root@server CF-3.7Wpl2]# _
```

7 Start sendmail in test mode.

Switch to the test mode to verify that mail can be sent properly in Linux.

Enter the command.

```
[root@server CF-3.7Wpl2]# /etc/rc.d/init.d/sendmail stop
Shutting down sendmail: sendmail
[root@server CF-3.7Wpl2]# /usr/sbin/sendmail -bt -C./sendmail.cf⏎
ADDRESS TEST MODE (ruleset 3 NOT automatically invoked)
Enter <ruleset> <address>
>
```

8 Carry out a test mailing.

Enter "0" and the email address (the username registered in Linux and the domain name set in sendmail.def).

```
>0 Bob@Coriolis.com⏎
rewrite: ruleset   0   input: Bob @ coriolis . com
rewrite: ruleset  97   input: Bob @ coriolis . com
rewrite: ruleset   3   input: Bob @ coriolis . com
rewrite: ruleset  96   input: < Bob @ coriolis . com  >
rewrite: ruleset  96 returns: < Bob @ coriolis . com  >
rewrite: ruleset   3 returns: < Bob @ coriolis . com  >
rewrite: ruleset   0 returns: < Bob @ coriolis . com  >
rewrite: ruleset  97   input: Bob
rewrite: ruleset   3   input: Bob
rewrite: ruleset   3 returns: Bob
rewrite: ruleset   0   input: Bob
rewrite: ruleset   0 returns: $# local $: Bob
rewrite: ruleset  97 returns: $# local $: Bob
rewrite: ruleset   0 returns: $# local $: Bob
rewrite: ruleset  97 returns: $# local $: Bob
rewrite: ruleset   0 returns: $# local $: Bob
>
```

If the specified email address returns, sendmail is operating properly.

Local represents Linux.

User the email was sent to.

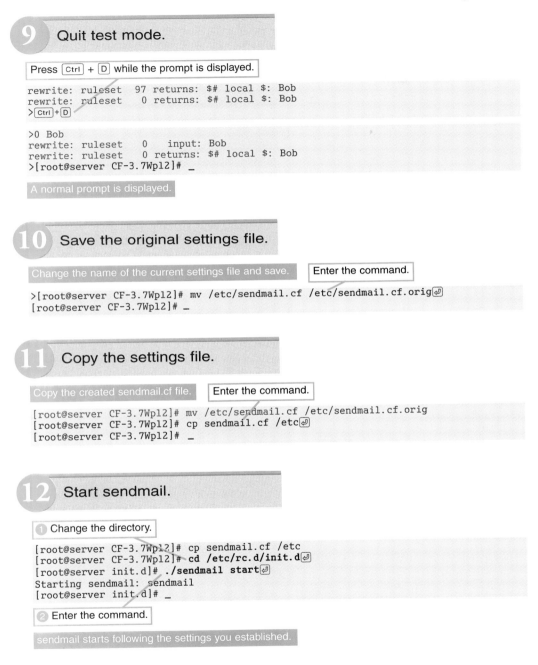

9 Quit test mode.

Press ⌈Ctrl⌋ + ⌈D⌋ while the prompt is displayed.

```
rewrite: ruleset  97 returns: $# local $: Bob
rewrite: ruleset   0 returns: $# local $: Bob
>Ctrl+D

>0 Bob
rewrite: ruleset   0   input: Bob
rewrite: ruleset   0 returns: $# local $: Bob
>[root@server CF-3.7Wp12]# _
```

A normal prompt is displayed.

10 Save the original settings file.

Change the name of the current settings file and save.   Enter the command.

```
>[root@server CF-3.7Wp12]# mv /etc/sendmail.cf /etc/sendmail.cf.orig⏎
[root@server CF-3.7Wp12]# _
```

11 Copy the settings file.

Copy the created sendmail.cf file.   Enter the command.

```
[root@server CF-3.7Wp12]# mv /etc/sendmail.cf /etc/sendmail.cf.orig
[root@server CF-3.7Wp12]# cp sendmail.cf /etc⏎
[root@server CF-3.7Wp12]# _
```

12 Start sendmail.

❶ Change the directory.

```
[root@server CF-3.7Wp12]# cp sendmail.cf /etc
[root@server CF-3.7Wp12]# cd /etc/rc.d/init.d⏎
[root@server init.d]# ./sendmail start⏎
Starting sendmail: sendmail
[root@server init.d]# _
```

❷ Enter the command.

sendmail starts following the settings you established.

Creating A Mail Server Part 2

Installing qpopper

Email sent to users is stored in Linux. To read this email, the user must retrieve the stored email and read it from a Windows or Macintosh system. Mailers in Windows and Macintosh systems use a method called Post Office Protocol (POP) to retrieve email.

To allow use of POP, you must install and start a POP server in Linux. This section explains how to install qpopper as a POP server and establish the settings necessary for it to run. Download the qpopper2.53.tar.gz file from the **ftp.coriolis.com/linux_server_vvb** folder to your /usr/local/src directory.

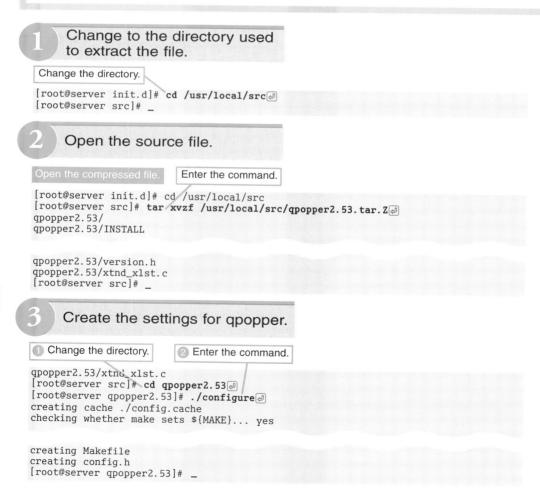

1 Change to the directory used to extract the file.

Change the directory.

```
[root@server init.d]# cd /usr/local/src↵
[root@server src]# _
```

2 Open the source file.

Open the compressed file.   Enter the command.

```
[root@server init.d]# cd /usr/local/src
[root@server src]# tar xvzf /usr/local/src/qpopper2.53.tar.Z↵
qpopper2.53/
qpopper2.53/INSTALL

qpopper2.53/version.h
qpopper2.53/xtnd_xlst.c
[root@server src]# _
```

3 Create the settings for qpopper.

① Change the directory.   ② Enter the command.

```
qpopper2.53/xtnd_xlst.c
[root@server src]# cd qpopper2.53↵
[root@server qpopper2.53]# ./configure↵
creating cache ./config.cache
checking whether make sets ${MAKE}... yes

creating Makefile
creating config.h
[root@server qpopper2.53]# _
```

10.4

4 Compile.

Create an executable qpopper file.   Enter the command.

```
creating config.h
[root@server qpopper2.53]# make⏎
gcc -c -I. -I. -g -O2 -fstrength-reduce -fpcc-struct-return  -DHAVE_CONFIG_H -DL
INUX flock.c -o flock.o


.o pop_xmit.o popper.o pop_bull.o xtnd_xlst.o pop_uidl.o mktemp.o pop_rpop.o pop
_apop.o md5.o pop_auth.o -o popper -lresolv  -lgdbm  -lcrypt
[root@server qpopper2.53]# _
```

5 Install.

Install qpopper.   Enter the command.

```
_apop.o md5.o pop_auth.o -o popper -lresolv  -lgdbm  -lcrypt
[root@server qpopper2.53]# install -s popper /usr/sbin⏎
[root@server qpopper2.53]# _
```

6 Edit the settings file.

Enter the command.

```
[root@server qpopper2.53]# install -s popper /usr/sbin
[root@server qpopper2.53]# vi /etc/inetd.conf⏎


#
# inetd.conf      This file describes the services that will be available
#                 through the INETD TCP/IP super server.  To re-configure
#                 the running INETD process, edit this file, then send the
#                 INETD process a SIGHUP signal.
#
# Version:        @(#)/etc/inetd.conf      3.10      05/27/93
#
# Authors:        Original taken from BSD UNIX 4.3/TAHOE.
#                 Fred N. van Kempen, <waltje@uwalt.nl.mugnet.org>
#
# Modified for Debian Linux by Ian A. Murdock <imurdock@shell.portal.com>
#
# Modified for RHS Linux by Marc Ewing <marc@redhat.com>
#
# <service_name> <sock_type> <proto> <flags> <user> <server_path> <args>
#
# Echo, discard, daytime, and chargen are used primarily for testing.
#
# To re-read this file after changes, just do a 'killall -HUP inetd'
#
#echo    stream  tcp      nowait  root      internal
#echo    dgram   udp      wait    root      internal
#discard         stream  tcp      nowait  root      internal
"/etc/inetd.conf" 91 lines, 3391 characters
```

7 Overwrite the settings file.

Change the POP3 daemon to popper.

```
# Pop and imap mail services et al
#
pop-2    stream   tcp      nowait   root     /usr/sbin/tcpd   ipop2d
pop-3    stream   tcp      nowait   root     /usr/sbin/tcpd   ipop3d
imap     stream   tcp      nowait   root     /usr/sbin/tcpd   imapd
#
```

Change to "popper -s" and save.

```
# Pop and imap mail services et al
#
pop-2    stream   tcp      nowait   root     /usr/sbin/tcpd   ipop2d
pop-3    stream   tcp      nowait   root     /usr/sbin/tcpd   popper -s
imap     stream   tcp      nowait   root     /usr/sbin/tcpd   imapd
#
```

8 Reload the settings.

① Change the directory.

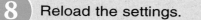

```
[root@server qpopper2.53]# cd /etc/rc.d/init.d⏎
[root@server init.d]# ./inet reload⏎
[root@server init.d]# _
```

② Enter the command.

176

The Role Of inetd.conf

A number of services run in Linux. In a TCP/IP network, IP addresses are used to identify computers connected to the network. Ports are used to distinguish between the numerous services provided on a single computer.

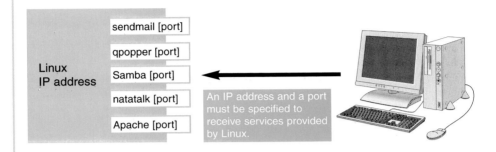

The sendmail and Apache services are daemons that run continuously and monitor access to their ports. Because qpopper does not run continuously, the daemon inetd is used to monitor POP3 access and to start qpopper. inetd monitors services written in /etc/inetd.conf. When accessed, inetd starts the service in accordance with inetd.conf. This section explains how to edit inetd.conf so that popper starts when POP3 is accessed.

```
pop-3    stream  tcp     nowait  root    /usr/sbin/tcpd  popper -s
```

Service name (port specification).   Program name of qpopper.

Preparing To Use Email

Settings On The Client Side

You have completed the settings for the Linux mail server. Now you must set up the Windows and Macintosh mailers to allow the PCs to use email.

In a mailer, you must specify the POP server used to read email and the SMTP server used to send email. For both Windows and Macintosh mailers, use the IP address of the PC on which Linux is set up as a mail server.

Settings For The Mailer Software

POP server	192.168.1.1 (The server IP address set during installation.)
SMTP server	192.168.1.1 (The server IP address set during installation.)
Email address	xxx@coriolis.com (Linux username @ domain name set in sendmail.def)
Account name	xxx (Linux username)
Password	xxxxxx (password of Linux user)

Examples Of Sending Email

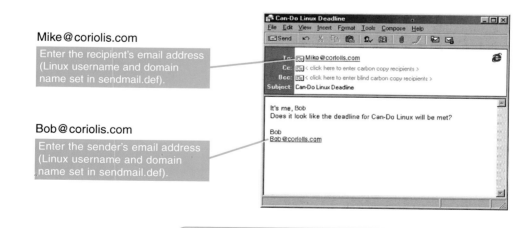

Mike@coriolis.com

Enter the recipient's email address (Linux username and domain name set in sendmail.def).

Bob@coriolis.com

Enter the sender's email address (Linux username and domain name set in sendmail.def).

Note: The mail server created in this book is not connected to the Internet. Provide for Internet email separately.

Examples Of Outlook Express Settings

For the email address, specify a combination of the Linux username and the domain name set in sendmail.

For the POP account and password, specify the Linux username and the Linux password.

For both the POP and SMTP servers, specify the IP address of the Linux server.

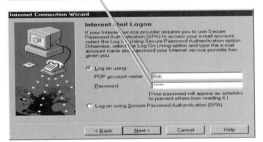

Examples Of PostPet Settings

For the SMTP server, enter the IP address of the Linux server.

For the email address, specify a combination of the Linux username and the domain name set in sendmail.

For the POP account, enter a combination of the Linux user-name and the IP address of the Linux server.

For the name and password, specify the Linux username and the Linux password.

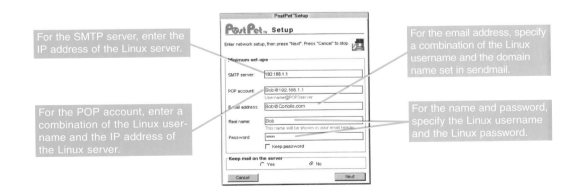

STEP UP

The Road To The Internet

The server set up in this book is for use as an intranet or local area network (LAN). As such, it cannot be used as an Internet server. *Do not* connect the intranet *as is* to another network.

This doesn't mean, of course, that the explanations provided in this book are useless when connecting to the Internet. You can read the basic sections of this book as is, while making the necessary changes to file settings based on an understanding of the Internet.

Physically Connecting To The Internet

To use the Internet, you need a physical connection. If you only want access to the Internet, a telephone line and a modem will do. To use Linux as a server, however, you need a leased line.

Obtaining An IP Address

The addresses used in this book are specifically for an intranet. You must have an IP address assigned to Linux to use it as an Internet server.

Obtaining A Domain Name

The names used in this book were freely chosen. On the Internet, however, domain names are strictly controlled. If you use Linux as an Internet server, you must apply for and obtain your own domain name.

Necessary Considerations For Security

There exists a real danger of attacks from external sources when connected to the Internet. If you experience such an attack, will you not only suffer damage, but other servers connected to the Internet will also experience problems.

Chapter 11
Managing Linux

Administrators must be sensitive to problems regardless of the environment in which they occur. This chapter introduces the knowledge required for administrators to perform routine management and troubleshooting techniques when network problems occur.

Contents Of This Chapter

Trouble On The Network

If your network is not operating properly, first check the settings and operations to try to identify the cause. If the connections don't seem to be functioning properly, use the **ping** command to check the connections. If a single service isn't operating properly, restart the service.

If these actions don't resolve the problem, review the log, a file that saves a record of daemon and kernel operations.

Hardware Troubleshooting

The **ping** command determines whether communication using IP is possible. Executing **ping** to another machine is called *pinging a machine*. Before pinging a machine, try to determine whether it's a client or the server that is exhibiting problems.

Client (Windows, Macintosh)

- A specific PC can receive no services from Linux (cannot send email, share files, or login to Linux using Tera Term Pro or Better Telnet).
- A specific PC can exchange no data with other Windows and Macintosh systems (cannot recognize network PCs).

Server (Linux)

- None of the PCs can receive any services from Linux (e.g. cannot send email, cannot share files, cannot log in to Linux using Tera Term Pro or NCSA Telnet).
- Windows and Macintosh systems can see each other (can see network PCs).

Windows ping

Although the ping command is provided in Linux, here we will ping Linux from the MS-DOS prompt of Windows. The MS-DOS prompt is located in Start|Programs.

```
C:/WINDOWS>ping 192.168.1.1⏎

Pinging 192.168.1.1 with 32 bytes of data:

Reply from 192.168.1.1: bytes=32 time<10ms TTL=64
Reply from 192.168.1.1: bytes=32 time=1ms TTL=64
Reply from 192.168.1.1: bytes=32 time<10ms TTL=64
Reply from 192.168.1.1: bytes=32 time<10ms TTL=64

Ping statistics for 192.168.1.1:
    Packets: Sent = 4, Received = 4, Lost = 0 (0% loss),
Approximate round trip times in milli-seconds:
    Minimum = 0ms, Maximum =  1ms, Average =  0ms

C:/WINDOWS>
```

While a **ping** command is executing, the hub LEDs that correspond to the PC executing **ping** and the PC of the specified address will flash for a fixed period. If the communication is accomplished, then communication itself between Windows and Linux isn't the problem. If Linux doesn't respond to a ping, check a different Windows PC address by pinging it. Find the IP address of a Windows PC by using winipcfg, Select Start|Run, and then type "winipcfg" in the Open box.

When You Get No Response To **ping**

When operations do not function properly from the start, the cause is almost always a mistake made in the initial settings. A problem that suddenly occurs in a running PC, however, is probably due to a recently developed hardware problem.

Problems With Settings

• The IP address settings are incorrect (duplicated settings, wrong network address, and so on). To resolve this problem for devices other than servers and printers, assign an IP address from the DHCP server.

Hardware Problems

• A cable is disconnected.
• The hub power supply is off.
• A PC is connected to the cascading port of a hub with a straight cable.
• A port is in use in the hub that cannot be employed simultaneously with the cascading port.

Service Troubleshooting

If network connections are functioning normally but active services are not operating properly, restart each service. Services (shown in the following list) must also be restarted when changing settings.

Service Name	Troubleshooting Measure
dhcpd	/etc/rc.d/init.d/dhcpd restart
samba	/etc/rc.d/init.d/smb restart
netatalk	/etc/rc.d/init.d/rc.atalkd restart
Apache	/etc/rc.d/init.d/httpd restart
sendmail	/etc/rc.d/init.d/sendmail restart
	/usr/lib/sendmail -q
qpopper	/etc/rc.d/init.d/inet restart
Printer	/etc/rc.d/init.d/lpd restart
	Clear spool /var/spool/lpd/printer name/
	Turn printer off and then on again

Clearing The Spool

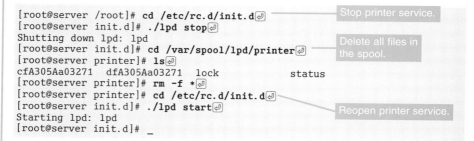

```
[root@server /root]# cd /etc/rc.d/init.d⏎          Stop printer service.
[root@server init.d]# ./lpd stop⏎
Shutting down lpd: lpd
[root@server init.d]# cd /var/spool/lpd/printer⏎   Delete all files in
[root@server printer]# ls⏎                          the spool.
cfA305Aa03271   dfA305Aa03271   lock        status
[root@server printer]# rm -f *⏎
[root@server printer]# cd /etc/rc.d/init.d⏎
[root@server init.d]# ./lpd start⏎                 Reopen printer service.
Starting lpd: lpd
[root@server init.d]# _
```

When the printer is sent data that it cannot process, canceling the print job may be difficult. In this case, clear the spool directory. Stop the printer service. Delete all files in the spool. Reopen the printer service. You may be able to recover by toggling the printer off and then on again.

Gathering Information From Log Files And Web Pages

The log is a record of daemon and kernel operations. When a problem occurs, clues about how to resolve the problem may be found in the log. At first glance, log messages may make little sense. But even if you don't understand the full meaning of the log messages, look for keywords to help you identify an answer.

Search the Web using common search sites and search phrases such as the keywords in the log; the name of the daemon having problems; and words such as "Linux," "Unix," and other program names. You can search documents on the Web and documents in mailing lists.

Service Name	Log File
dhcpd	/var/log/messages
samba	/var/log/samba/log.smb
	/var/log/samba/log.nmb
	/var/log/samba/log."computer name"
netatalk	/var/log/messages
Apache	/var/log/httpd/access_log
	/var/log/httpd/error_log
sendmail	/var/log/maillog
Printer	/var/log/spooler

When you look at the log, you will probably not completely understand the messages it contains. You will, however, find keywords in the text of the log to assist your Web search.

Links To Linux-Related Search Sites:
www.linux.org -Has all kinds of information and also links to Linux-related search sites.
www.freebsd.org -Web site for FreeBSD, another PC-Unix operating system(OS). Although this is a different OS from Unix, much of the software is the same, and a wide variety of pertinent information is available.

Using Your Hard Drive Efficiently

The capacity of your hard disk decreases as you use it. Use the **df** command to check hard disk capacity. If your remaining hard disk capacity is insufficient, consider the following actions (in the order listed):

1. Delete unnecessary files.
2. Move directories to different locations.
3. Expand your hard disk capacity.

Checking Disk Capacity

Use the **df** command to check the remaining hard disk capacity of mounted file systems.

```
[root@server /root]# df⏎
Filesystem          1024-blocks    Used  Available  Capacity  Mounted on
/dev/hdb2                 66365   28664      34274       46%   /
/dev/hdb3               2343607  246907    1975539       11%   /usr
```

| Device name. | Disk capacity. | Capacity in use. | Available capacity. | Usage rate. | Mount point. |

Adjust hard disk capacity if the following condition occurs while using Linux:

```
[root@server /root]# df⏎
Filesystem          1024-blocks    Used  Available  Capacity  Mounted on
/dev/hdb2                 66365   66365          0      100%   /
/dev/hdb3               2343607  246907    1975539       11%   /usr
```

Over-capacity.

Cleaning Up Unwanted Files

Use the **du** command to check the disk capacity being used by each directory.

Start directory (indicates a file system that is over-capacity).

Displays directories in numeric order (large directories are displayed last).

```
[root@server /root]# du -xS / | sort -n⏎
1       /



13476   /home/Bob
20789   /home/Mike
[root@server /root]# _
```

The largest directory is displayed last. In large directories, determine which files you need and which you do not, and then delete unnecessary files. If you cannot make a determination, it's safer not to delete a file.

Move To A Less-Used File System

If the disk is still over-capacity even after files are deleted, move the directory to a different file system and create a symbolic link. Although this is a makeshift solution, it's effective if you are unable to add a new hard disk.

Example 1: When Printer And Email Usage Exceed The Capacity Of /var/spool

1. Stop services that use /var/spool.

Stop to prevent data from entering the printer spool.

```
[root@server /root]# cd /etc/rc.d/init.d↵
[root@server init.d]# ./lpd stop↵
Shutting down lpd: lpd
[root@server init.d]# ./sendmail stop↵
Shutting down sendmail: sendmail
[root@server init.d]# _
```

Stop to prevent email storage.

2. Move the directory and create a symbolic link.

Copy the contents of /var/spool to /usr/spool and back up the original directory.

```
[root@server init.d]# cd /var↵
[root@server /var]# cp -a spool /usr↵
[root@server /var]# mv spool spool.bak↵
[root@server /var]# ln -s /usr/spool /var↵
[root@server /var]# ls /var/spool↵
at          lpd         mqueue      samba       uucppublic
cron        mail        rwho        uucp
[root@server /var]# _
```

If the link is correct, you'll see the contents of the directory.

Create a /var/spool linked to /usr/spool.

3. Restart services.

```
[root@server /root]# cd /etc/rc.d/init.d⏎
[root@server init.d]# ./lpd start⏎
Starting lpd: lpd
[root@server init.d]# ./sendmail start⏎
Starting sendmail: sendmail
[root@server init.d]# _
```

Use the services for a short time. If no problems appear, delete /var/spool.bak.

```
[root@server /root]# cd /var⏎
[root@server /var]# rm -rf spool.bak⏎
[root@server /var]# _
```

Example 2: When User Usage Exceeds The Capacity Of /home

1. Stop services that use /home.

```
[root@server /root]# cd /etc/rc.d/init.d⏎
[root@server init.d]# ./smb stop⏎           Stop to prevent access
Shutting down SMB services: smbd nmbd       from Windows.
[root@server init.d]# ./rc.atalk stop⏎
Shutting down appletalk:papd afpd atalkd    Stop to prevent access
[root@server init.d]# _                      from Macintosh.
```

2. Move the directory and create a symbolic link.

```
                                            Copy the contents of /home
[root@server init.d]# cp -a /home /usr⏎     to /usr/home and back up the
[root@server init.d]# mv /home /home.bak⏎   original directory.
[root@server init.d]# ln -s /usr/home /⏎
[root@server init.d]# ls /home⏎
ftp    Bob      httpd    Dave    Tim        samba     Mike
[root@server init.d]# _
```

Create a /home linked   If the link is correct, you'll see
to /usr/home.   contents of the directory.

3. Restart services.

```
[root@server init.d]# ./smb start⏎
Starting SMB services: smbd nmbd
[root@server init.d]# ./rc.atalk start⏎
Starting appletalk: atalkd nbprgstr papd afpd
[root@server init.d]# _
```

Use the services for a short time. If no problems appear, delete /home.bak.

```
[root@server /root]# rm -rf /home.bak⏎
[root@server /root]# _
```

Directories That Should Not Be Moved

Never move the directories /bin, /sbin, /root, /lib, /dev, /etc and /boot. These directories contain the minimum required files to boot the system used before other file systems are mounted.

Expanding Hard Disk Capacity

If your total remaining hard disk capacity is limited, you cannot resolve the problem by moving directories. You need to purchase a new hard disk. You'll need to make many preparations before using the new hard disk.

Adding A SCSI Card

If you purchase and install a new SCSI card, drivers must also be included. The drivers are installed when the installer detects the SCSI card and performs an update installation.

Adding A Hard Disk

Not limited to SCSI cards and IDE drives, follow these procedures to add a hard disk:
- Set the partitions of the expanded hard disk (fdisk).
- Create a file system (**mke2fs**).
- Mount the disk (**mount**).
- Set up the system to mount the disk during the boot sequence (/etc/fstab) automatically.

For details, see page 196.

Backing Up Data

Back Up Methods

If Linux stops operating and your environment settings are backed up, you can use the same settings files to recover the environment after you re-install Linux.

The settings files should fit on one floppy disk. If you also back up shared data, consider using a different type of storage media.

Backing Up Settings Files And Shared Files

After installing Linux, the following files are required to recover the environment that has been set up to this point. If you have back ups of these files, you can recover the current environment simply by copying the settings files.

/etc/passwd	User information
/etc/group	Group information
/etc/printcap	Printer settings
/etc/sendmail.cf	sendmail settings
/etc/hosts	Chart of host names and corresponding IP addresses
/etc/inetd.conf	inetd settings (such as qpopper)
/etc/dhcpd.conf	DHCP settings
/etc/smb.conf	Samba settings
/etc/smbpasswd	Samba password settings
/etc/httpd/conf/access.conf	Apache settings
/etc/httpd.conf	Apache settings
/etc/srm.conf	Apache settings
/usr/local/atalk/etc/AppleVolumes.default	netatalk settings
/usr/local/atalk/etc/AppleVolumes.system	netatalk settings
/usr/local/atalk/etc/papd.conf	netatalk settings
/usr/local/src/CF-3.7Wp12/sendmail.def	sendmail settings

In addition, back up /home and other shared folders.

Backing Up Settings Files

1. Create a temporary directory and copy the files.

```
[root@server /root]# mkdir /tmp/etc⏎
[root@server /root]# cp /etc/passwd /tmp/etc⏎
                   :
```

Repeat this operation to copy all settings files.

2. Create an archive file.

```
[root@server /root]# cd /tmp⏎
[root@server /tmp]# tar cvfz etc.tar.gz etc⏎
```

Use the tar command to compress /tmp/etc as is.

Save the etc.tar.gz file to a floppy disk or another external storage device.

Recovering Settings Files

```
[root@server /root]# cd /tmp⏎
[root@server /tmp]# tar xvfpz etc.tar.gz etc⏎
[root@server /tmp]# cp etc/passwd /etc⏎
                   :
```

Repeat this operation to copy all settings files.

Moving The Linux Environment To Another PC

This section introduces how to move the settings files from the PC currently being used to another PC.

1. Install Linux.

2. Install each daemon. (It isn't necessary to write the settings files.)

dhcpd	Install using rpm.
netetalk	Compile, install, setup boot script.
sendmail	Compile, install.
qpopper	Compile, install.

3. Copy the backed up settings files to the original directories.

4. Create the necessary directories.

/var/spool/lpd/printer name

5. Restore all backed up shared files.

6. Restart each daemon.

/etc/rc.d/init.d/dhcpd restart
/etc/rc.d/init.d/smb restart
/etc/rc.d/init.d/rc.atalkd restart
/etc/rc.d/init.d/sendmail restart
/etc/rc.d/init.d/httpd restart
/etc/rc.d/init.d/inet restart
/etc/rc.d/init.d/lpd restart

Back Up Methods By Media

Using The Hard Disk Of Another Computer On The Network

In this method, create back up files, then copy them to another computer on the network. This method is the easiest and most reasonable because the client PCs are likely to have larger hard disks.

To recover the settings before sharing (Samba and netatalk) is set up, use a service such as FTP to transfer the backed up files.

Precautions When Backing Up Shared Folders

In a mixed Macintosh and Windows environment, copying shared folders *as is* to another PC may damage the data. Using tar (archive) in Linux to collect the files in a shared folder into a single file and then copying them to another location is a safer method. If you have large folders and append the **z** option to **tar** to compress the folder, note that this process requires some time to execute.

Backing Up /home

```
[root@server /tmp]# tar cvf backup.tar /home⏎
```

Recover

```
[root@server /tmp]# cd /⏎
[root@server /]# tar xvfp backup.tar⏎
```

Using A Floppy Disk

If you are only backing up the settings files, a floppy disk usually will be sufficient. Although there are a number of ways to use floppy disks in Linux, a method to mount the floppy disk is introduced in this section.

Warning! You must exercise caution when mounting and using floppy disks. Do not remove the floppy disk from the disk drive before unmounting it. Unlike a CD-ROM, a log of the disk being removed is not kept for a floppy disk, so it can be removed while still mounted. This is dangerous and can result in a loss of data.

Format	mkdosfs /dev/fd0
Mount	mount −t vfat −o sync /dev/fd0 /mnt/floppy
Unmount	sync
	umount /mnt/floppy

Using A CD-R (**mkisofs**)

Use the **mkisofs** command to create an image file for a CD-R. This command creates a file system in accordance with names. Because it creates a file system used by the CD-ROM, if you specify this for the image file and *burn* (record data on) the CD-R, you will be able to view the CD-R from Windows and Macintosh (and Linux) like you would from a standard CD-ROM.

```
[root@server /tmp]# rpm -i /mnt/cdrom/RedHat/RPMS/mkisofs-1.12b5-2.i386.rpm⏎
[root@server /tmp]# mkisofs -adDNRTV "home" -o backup.img /home⏎
```

Options

a	Include all files.
d	Do not append "." to the end of file names that do not have a "."
D	Do not use deep directory relocation.
N	Do not append version numbers to file names.
R	Create SUSP and PR records.
T	Create TRANS.TBL.
V	Set volume ID.
o	Specify the file name of the image file.

Because the CD-R image file can be mounted before burning the CD-R, you can verify the contents before actually burning the CD-R.

Image file.

```
[root@server /tmp]# mount -t iso9660 -o loop bakup.img /mnt/tmp⏎
```

Mount point.

A CD-R can be connected to Linux and then burned, but, because many types of corresponding devices exist, it's better to create the image file in Linux and then use writing software in a Windows or Macintosh system.

Shutting Down Linux Safely

Checking For Users

Abruptly disconnecting the power when turning off an expanded hard disk, SCSI card, or other device may cause damage to the file system. When shutting down Linux, you must stop the system safely.

Linux users must be notified in advance of the shutdown. Use the **smbstatus** command to determine which users are currently using Samba. Netatalk doesn't have a command like **smbstatus**, but the following section covers how to determine which users are using netatalk.

Checking Each Service For Linux Users

Samba

Use the **smbstatus** command supplied with Samba to view information about users who are currently logged in.

```
[root@server /root]# smbstatus⏎

Samba version 1.9.18p10
Service      uid      gid      pid      machine
------------------------------------------------------
Mike      Mike users      1702      pc-Mike (192.168.1.1) Fri Feb 12
20:37:02 1999

No locked files

Share mode memory usage (bytes):
   102232(99%) free + 112(0%) used + 56(0%) overhead = 102400(100%)
total
[root@server /root]#
```

netatalk

To determine which users are currently using netatalk, view the operating status of afpd, a program related to netatalk.

Enter the data in the following order to view the operating status of afpd;

Display programs that are running.

Display only the lines that contain afpd.

```
[root@server /root]# ps axcu | grep afpd⏎
root        305  0.0  1.4  1040  400  ?  S      17:36   0:00 afpd
[root@server /root]# _
```

If a line displays a username other than root, then that user is using netatalk.

telnet

Use the **w** command to determine which users are using telnet to log into Linux.

```
[root@server /root]# w⏎
 5:45am  up   7:00,   2 users,   load average: 0.06, 0.03, 0.00
USER     TTY      FROM             LOGIN@   IDLE   JCPU   PCPU  WHAT
Bob      tty1                      5:44pm   0.00s  0.73s  0.73s  w
Mike     ttyp0    192.168.1.1      8:41pm   3.00s  0.36s  0.06s  -bash
```

Users Bob and Mike are logged in.

Shutdown Methods

Use the **shutdown** command to quit Linux.

Reboot

```
[root@server /root]# shutdown -r now⏎

Broadcast message from root (ttyp0) Mon Feb  8 04:39:36 1999...

The system is going down for reboot NOW !!
```

Stop

```
[root@server /root]# shutdown -h now⏎
```

The shutdown timer can be configured.

Stop after five minutes

```
[root@server /root]# shutdown -h +5⏎
```

Reboot at 3:00 A.M.

```
[root@server /root]# shutdown -r 03:00⏎
```

Expanding The File Sharing Hard Disk

fstab

In this section, the entire expanded hard disk is assigned to /home.
To use the hard disk, you must ensure that the partitions are correct, and then format them for Linux. Use the **fdisk** command to set up partitions and the **mke2fs** command to format the partitions.

Move the current data in /home to the new hard disk, and mount the disk. The settings used to mount the hard disk during the boot are in the file /etc/fstab.

Partitioning The Hard Disk

There are restrictions on how to partition a hard disk. A disk can be divided into a maximum of four primary partitions. One of these four partitions is an extended partition, which can be divided into logical partitions (logical partitions can only exist in an extended partition). Linux can use a maximum of 63 partitions for each IDE hard disk and 15 partitions for each SCSI hard disk.

Within these restrictions, you can divide the partitions as you like, although you must format (create a file system) and mount each region before you can use it.

In Linux, a number that represents regions on the hard disk is appended to the end of hard disk device names. The primary partitions are numbered from 1 to 4, and logical partitions start at 5. If a number isn't appended, it represents the entire hard disk.

Hard Disk Device Names

IDE Hard Disk

/dev/hda Primary master
/dev/hdb Primary slave
/dev/hdc Secondary master
/dev/hdd Secondary slave

SCSI Hard Disk

/dev/sda 1st SCSI hard disk
/dev/sdb 2nd SCSI hard disk
/dev/sdc 3rd SCSI hard disk
:

(The numbers are in lowest SCSI ID order.)

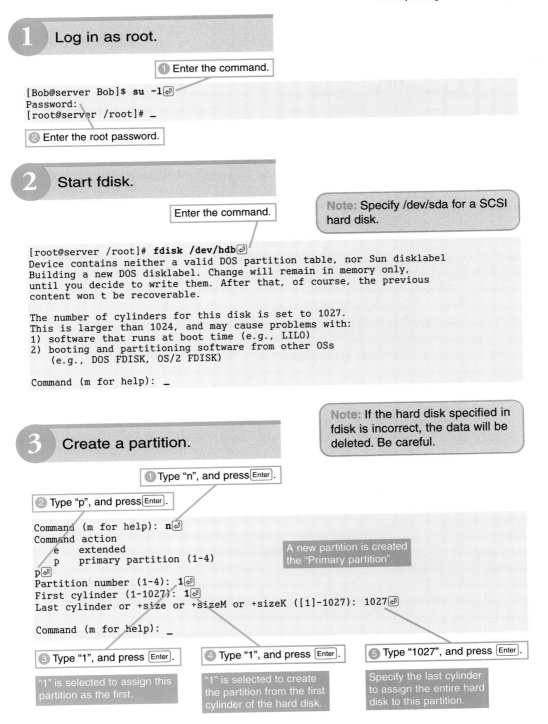

1 Log in as root.

① Enter the command.

```
[Bob@server Bob]$ su -l↵
Password:
[root@server /root]# _
```

② Enter the root password.

2 Start fdisk.

Enter the command.

Note: Specify /dev/sda for a SCSI hard disk.

```
[root@server /root]# fdisk /dev/hdb↵
Device contains neither a valid DOS partition table, nor Sun disklabel
Building a new DOS disklabel. Change will remain in memory only,
until you decide to write them. After that, of course, the previous
content won t be recoverable.

The number of cylinders for this disk is set to 1027.
This is larger than 1024, and may cause problems with:
1) software that runs at boot time (e.g., LILO)
2) booting and partitioning software from other OSs
   (e.g., DOS FDISK, OS/2 FDISK)

Command (m for help): _
```

Note: If the hard disk specified in fdisk is incorrect, the data will be deleted. Be careful.

3 Create a partition.

① Type "n", and press Enter.

② Type "p", and press Enter.

```
Command (m for help): n↵
Command action
   e   extended
   p   primary partition (1-4)
p↵
Partition number (1-4): 1↵
First cylinder (1-1027): 1↵
Last cylinder or +size or +sizeM or +sizeK ([1]-1027): 1027↵

Command (m for help): _
```

A new partition is created the "Primary partition".

③ Type "1", and press Enter.

"1" is selected to assign this partition as the first.

④ Type "1", and press Enter.

"1" is selected to create the partition from the first cylinder of the hard disk.

⑤ Type "1027", and press Enter.

Specify the last cylinder to assign the entire hard disk to this partition.

4 Verify the partition.

Type "p", and press Enter.

```
Command (m for help): p⏎

Disk /dev/hdb: 255 heads, 63 sectors, 1027 cylinders
Units = cylinders of 16065 * 512 bytes

   Device Boot    Start    End    Blocks    Id    System
/dev/hdb1                1    1027  8249346    83    Linux native

Command (m for help):
```

The partition /dev/hdb1 is created
in the expanded hard disk.

5 Register the partition.

Type "w", and press Enter.

```
Command (m for help): w⏎
The partition table has been altered!

Calling ioctl() to re-read partition table.
 hdb: hdb1
 hdb: hdb1
Syncing disks.

WARNING: If you have created or modified any DOS 6.x
partitions, please see the fdisk manual page for additional
information.
[root@server /root]# _
```

The contents of the set partition have been registered.

6 Create a file system.

Create a file system to allow
the created partition to be used.

Enter the command.

```
[root@server /root]# mke2fs /dev/hdb1⏎
mke2fs 1.12, 9-Jul-98 for EXT2 FS 0.5b, 95/08/09
warning: 1 blocks unused.
```

```
        8208385, 8216577, 8224769, 8232961, 8241153

Writing inode tables: done
Writing superblocks and filesystem accounting information: done
[root@server /root]# _
```

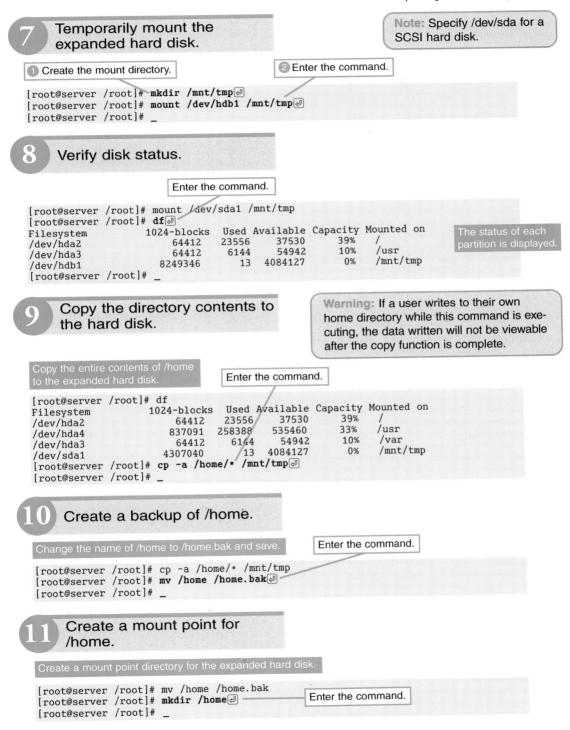

7 Temporarily mount the expanded hard disk.

Note: Specify /dev/sda for a SCSI hard disk.

❶ Create the mount directory.

❷ Enter the command.

```
[root@server /root]# mkdir /mnt/tmp⏎
[root@server /root]# mount /dev/hdb1 /mnt/tmp⏎
[root@server /root]# _
```

8 Verify disk status.

Enter the command.

```
[root@server /root]# mount /dev/sda1 /mnt/tmp
[root@server /root]# df⏎
Filesystem         1024-blocks   Used  Available  Capacity  Mounted on
/dev/hda2               64412    23556     37530      39%     /
/dev/hda3               64412     6144     54942      10%     /usr
/dev/hdb1             8249346       13   4084127       0%     /mnt/tmp
[root@server /root]# _
```

The status of each partition is displayed.

9 Copy the directory contents to the hard disk.

Warning: If a user writes to their own home directory while this command is executing, the data written will not be viewable after the copy function is complete.

Copy the entire contents of /home to the expanded hard disk.

Enter the command.

```
[root@server /root]# df
Filesystem         1024-blocks   Used  Available  Capacity  Mounted on
/dev/hda2               64412    23556     37530      39%     /
/dev/hda4              837091   258388    535460      33%     /usr
/dev/hda3               64412     6144     54942      10%     /var
/dev/sda1             4307040       13   4084127       0%     /mnt/tmp
[root@server /root]# cp -a /home/* /mnt/tmp⏎
[root@server /root]# _
```

10 Create a backup of /home.

Change the name of /home to /home.bak and save.

Enter the command.

```
[root@server /root]# cp -a /home/* /mnt/tmp
[root@server /root]# mv /home /home.bak⏎
[root@server /root]# _
```

11 Create a mount point for /home.

Create a mount point directory for the expanded hard disk.

```
[root@server /root]# mv /home /home.bak
[root@server /root]# mkdir /home⏎
[root@server /root]# _
```

Enter the command.

199

12 Change the boot settings.

❶ Enter the command.

```
[root@server /root]# mkdir /home
[root@server /root]# vi /etc/fstab⏎
```

Change the settings so that expanded hard disk
is mounted in the /home directory at bootup.

❷ Add this line.

```
/dev/hda2          /                ext2    defaults       1 1
/dev/hda4          /usr             ext2    defaults       1 2
/dev/hda3          /var             ext2    defaults       1 2
/dev/hda1          swap             swap    defaults       0 0
/dev/hdb1          /home            ext2    defaults       1 2
/dev/fd0           /mnt/floppy      ext2    noauto         0 0
/dev/cdrom         /mnt/cdrom       iso9660 noauto,ro      0 0
none               /proc            proc    defaults       0 0
```

❸ Save and quit after changing the settings.

13 Restart Linux.

Enter the command.

```
[root@server /root]# shutdown -r now⏎
```

14 Verify disk status.

❶ Log in.

❷ Enter the command.

```
server login: Bob⏎
Password:
Last login: Wed Jan  6 12:14:51 on tty1
[Bob@server /Bob]$ df⏎
Filesystem        1024-blocks   Used  Available Capacity Mounted on
/dev/hda2              64412    23767     37319     39%    /
/dev/hda3             837091   258388    535460     33%    /usr
/dev/hdb1            8249346    19584   7836936      0%    /home
[Bob@server /Bob]$  _
```

The expanded hard disk is mounted
in the /home directory.

Precautions When Using IDE Hard Disks Larger Than 8GB

Linux can handle IDE hard disks with a capacity over 8.4GB, but if the PCs is an older version, you can use only 8.4GB of the disk. In this situation, access the Web site of the hard disk manufacturer and try to find information related to BIOS updates. Depending on the manufacturer, the BIOS update information may be publicly available on the Web. Updating the BIOS should allow you to work with hard disks larger than 8.4GB.

There is a chance that if the BIOS update fails, the PC may not boot. Be sure to read the documentation from the manufacturer carefully and follow the instructions provided.

Using Linux More Efficiently

Linux Hints

This section introduces techniques to manage Linux more efficiently. The shell (bash) used to enter commands in Linux has a function called an alias. Using an alias allows you to enter often-used commands with even greater ease.

By making the most of keyboard functions, you can switch between multiple screens and terminate running commands.

Command Line Alias

The standard shell used to enter commands in Linux (called *bash*) has a function called an *alias*. An alias defines a different name for a command, which lets you more easily enter frequently-used commands. For example, because the **ls** command is an often used command, enter the following instructions to create an alias that execute **ls** by just typing.

```
[root@server /root]# alias l='ls'↵
[root@server /root]# l↵
data  mbox
[root@server /root]# _
```

If an alias were simply a different name for a command, it would not be very useful. An alias, however, can include options, as follows:

```
[root@server /root]# alias l='ls -F'↵
[root@server /root]# l↵
data/  mbox
[root@server /root]# _
```

Use **unalias l** to remove this alias.

Settings At Login
Because an alias must be set each time you login, it can be a little troublesome. To ensure that the alias is valid, edit the bashrc file, located in the home directory. If you add the line alias l = 'ls –F' to the end of the bashrc file, the alias will be valid the next time (and every time) you log in.

```
alias mv='mv -i'
alias l='ls -F'
```

Add New Alias

Forcibly Terminating Running Commands

If you execute the **ls** command in a directory containing a large number of files, or if you execute a command that seems to be taking a long time to complete, you can press ⌈Ctrl⌉+ ⌈C⌉ to forcibly terminate the running command.

```
[root@server /root]# ls -l /usr/doc/↵
    ⋮
⌈Ctrl⌉+⌈C⌉
[root@server /root]#
```
The **ls** command is terminated, and the prompt is displayed.

Useful Operations In Linux

When you log in to Linux from a Windows or Macintosh system, and if you log in from multiple workstations running windows, multiple operations can be executed simultaneously in Linux. Although it may appear that only one operation can be executed from the Linux screen, press ⌈Alt⌉ + the appropriate function key(s) to switch to a different window.

When you are logged in from a Windows or Macintosh system, you can scroll to view previous Linux screens by pressing ⌈Shift⌉+ ⌈Page Up⌉ to scroll up or ⌈Shift⌉+ ⌈Page Down⌉ to scroll down. You cannot use the ⌈Alt⌉ + function keys to switch and scroll through multiple windows.

When Commands Cannot Be Entered

If the screen is scrolling too quickly to view the contents, press ⌈Ctrl⌉+ ⌈S⌉ to stop the display. Press ⌈Ctrl⌉+ ⌈Q⌉ to restart the display.

If you make a mistake and press ⌈Ctrl⌉ + ⌈S⌉, you must press ⌈Ctrl⌉ + ⌈Q⌉ to recover. Pressing other keys generates no response. The actions of keys pressed during this no-response pause are reflected on screen the instant you press ⌈Ctrl⌉+ ⌈Q⌉.

If The Linux Screen Goes Blank

If the keyboard isn't touched for a fixed period in Linux, the screen darkens and goes blank. This is Linux's screen saver; it doesn't mean that Linux has stopped operating. Press [Shift] or [Ctrl] to return to the original screen.

Displaying File Contents

The **less** command is useful when you want to view a file's contents. Execute the following command to display a file:

[root@server /root]# **less** "file name"

Using key operations, the less command can search, move up and down, and perform other functions. The key operations of the less command imitate the vi editor but are specifically intended for viewing files.

The Main Key Functions Of The less Command

f	Move forward one screen [spacebar].
b	Move backward one screen.
d	Move forward half a screen.
u	Move backward half a screen.
j	Move forward one line ([↓]).
k	Move backward one line ([↑]).
/	Search forward.
?	Search backward.
-i	Search is/is not case sensitive (toggle).
n	Search forward again.
N	Search backward again.
F	Read from the end of the file. (If added to a file, the file is quickly displayed. Press [Ctrl] + [C] to return.
v	Start the vi editor to edit a file.
:n	View the next file when specifying multiple files.
:p	View the previous file when specifying multiple files.
:q	Exit less.

Combining Commands

When a command is executed, because of the large amount of data being displayed on screen, you probably will not see the result of the execution. To view the data, use the less command in addition to scrolling backward. The tool used to combine commands is called a pipe. A pipe interprets the command following it as input and displays the results on the current screen. For example, entering the commands as follows will allow you to view the results of ls using the **less** command.

```
[root@server /root]# ls -laF | less
```

Because the **ls** command itself determines whether something is displayed on the screen, entering the commands as follows will display one file per line.

```
[root@server /root]# ls | less
```

Sending Displayed Command Results To A File

Some programs are not files, so they cannot be handled with an editor like vi, as in the following example:

```
[root@server /root]# ls -laF | vi ———— Not executed properly.
```

If you want to edit the results of ls by using vi, you must write to a file and then edit it.

A pipe enters the display into other commands. Use redirection to write the display to a file. Redirection uses [>], [>>], and [<], as shown in this section.

Write the display to a file:

```
[root@server /root]# ls -laF > lslaF
```

Add the display to the end of a file:

```
[root@server /root]# ls -laF >> lslaF
```

Read from file and use as input:

```
[root@server /root]# less < lslaF
```

STEP UP

In Case Of Emergency

Generally, special attention isn't needed, but you should be aware of the following things when managing your system.

If You Forget The Root Password

When an ordinary user forgets their password, the administrator can become root and change the password. If you, as administrator, forget the root password, however, it cannot be changed. In this case, restart and boot Linux in a different mode. If you cannot enter the shutdown command, press the [Ctrl] + [Alt] + [Delete] on the keyboard of the PC where Linux is installed to forcibly restart Linux.

When the PC restarts and the LILO: prompt appears on the screen, type [linux single] and press [Enter]. The command prompt will appear. From here, change the root password using the password command. In this state, Linux operates differently than when in normal mode. Restart Linux to return to the normal mode.

Endlessly Increasing Logs

In Red Hat Linux, each type of log is sorted periodically. Processing is set to occur at approximately 4:00A.M. each day; consequently, if you turn off the power at night, the logs will gradually accumulate and increase in size.

The periodic processing time is set in /etc/crontab. To change the time for the log adjustments, change the line numbers located in cron.daily.

For example: to change from 4:02A.M. to 12:50P.M. (afternoon), take these steps:

```
2  4 * * * root run-parts /etc/cron.daily
 ↓
50 12 * * * root run-parts /etc/cron.daily
```

How To Set Up A Windows Client PC

Adding Network Cards To Desktop PCs

1 Insert the network card into the Windows PC.

Insert the network card into the client PC.

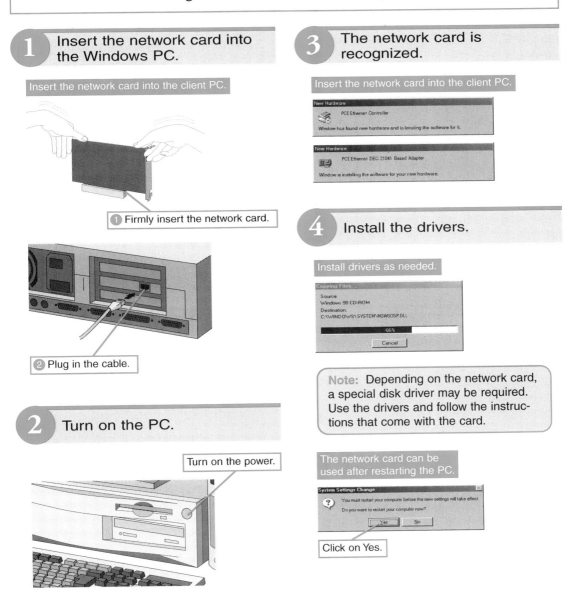

① Firmly insert the network card.

② Plug in the cable.

2 Turn on the PC.

Turn on the power.

3 The network card is recognized.

Insert the network card into the client PC.

New Hardware
PCI Ethernet Controller
Window has found new hardware and is locating the software for it.

New Hardware
PCI Ethernet DEC 21041 Based Adapter
Window is installing the software for your new hardware.

4 Install the drivers.

Install drivers as needed.

Copying Files
Source:
Windows 98 CD-ROM
Destination:
C:\WINDOWS\SYSTEM\MSW60SP.DLL
66%
Cancel

Note: Depending on the network card, a special disk driver may be required. Use the drivers and follow the instructions that come with the card.

The network card can be used after restarting the PC.

System Settings Change
? You must restart your computer before the new settings will take effect.
Do you want to restart your computer now?
Yes   No

Click on Yes.

Adding Network Cards To Laptop PCs

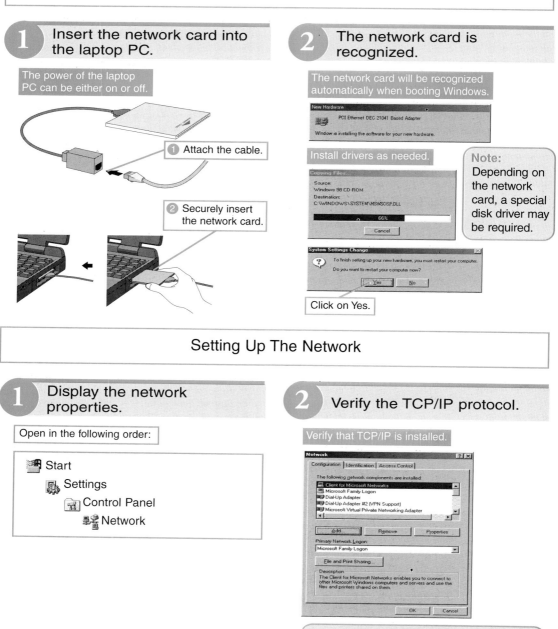

1 Insert the network card into the laptop PC.

The power of the laptop PC can be either on or off.

① Attach the cable.

② Securely insert the network card.

2 The network card is recognized.

The network card will be recognized automatically when booting Windows.

New Hardware

PCI Ethernet DEC 21041 Based Adapter

Window is installing the software for your new hardware.

Install drivers as needed.

Copying Files...

Source:
Windows 98 CD-ROM
Destination:
C:\WINDOWS\SYSTEM\MSWSOSP.DLL

66%

Cancel

System Settings Change

To finish setting up your new hardware, you must restart your computer.

Do you want to restart your computer now?

Yes   No

Click on Yes.

Note: Depending on the network card, a special disk driver may be required.

Setting Up The Network

1 Display the network properties.

Open in the following order:

Start
  Settings
    Control Panel
      Network

2 Verify the TCP/IP protocol.

Verify that TCP/IP is installed.

Network   ? X

Configuration | Identification | Access Control

The following network components are installed:

Client for Microsoft Networks
Microsoft Family Logon
Dial-Up Adapter
Dial-Up Adapter #2 (VPN Support)
Microsoft Virtual Private Networking Adapter

Add   Remove   Properties

Primary Network Logon:

Microsoft Family Logon

File and Print Sharing...

Description
The Client for Microsoft Networks enables you to connect to other Microsoft Windows computers and servers and use the files and printers shared on them.

OK   Cancel

Note: If the TCP/IP protocol is not installed, see page 210 for information on the procedures to be followed.

3 Set up the Windows NT domain.

❶ Select Client for Microsoft Networks.

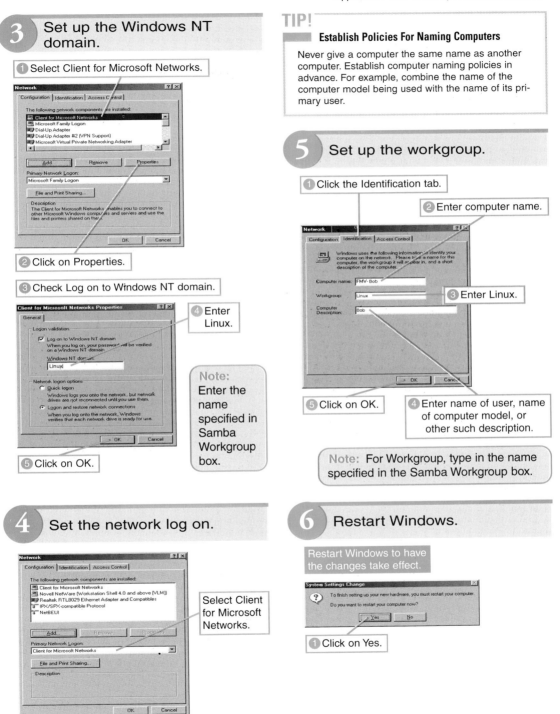

❷ Click on Properties.

❸ Check Log on to Windows NT domain.

❹ Enter Linux.

❺ Click on OK.

Note: Enter the name specified in Samba Workgroup box.

4 Set the network log on.

Select Client for Microsoft Networks.

TIP!

Establish Policies For Naming Computers

Never give a computer the same name as another computer. Establish computer naming policies in advance. For example, combine the name of the computer model being used with the name of its primary user.

5 Set up the workgroup.

❶ Click the Identification tab.

❷ Enter computer name.

❸ Enter Linux.

❹ Enter name of user, name of computer model, or other such description.

❺ Click on OK.

Note: For Workgroup, type in the name specified in the Samba Workgroup box.

6 Restart Windows.

Restart Windows to have the changes take effect.

❶ Click on Yes.

7 **Restart Windows.**

Log in using the username and password set in Samba.

① Enter username, password, and domain.

② Click on OK.

③ Enter password again.

④ Click on OK.

Adding The TCP/IP Protocol

1 Add the TCP/IP.

TCP/IP is not installed, so it needs to be added.

Click on Add...

2 Select the file to be installed.

① Select Protocol.

② Click on Add...

3 Select the protocol to be added.

① Select Microsoft.

② Select TCP/IP.

③ Click on OK.

How To Use Shared Folders

1 Open network computer.

① Double-click on the Network Neighborhood icon on your desktop.

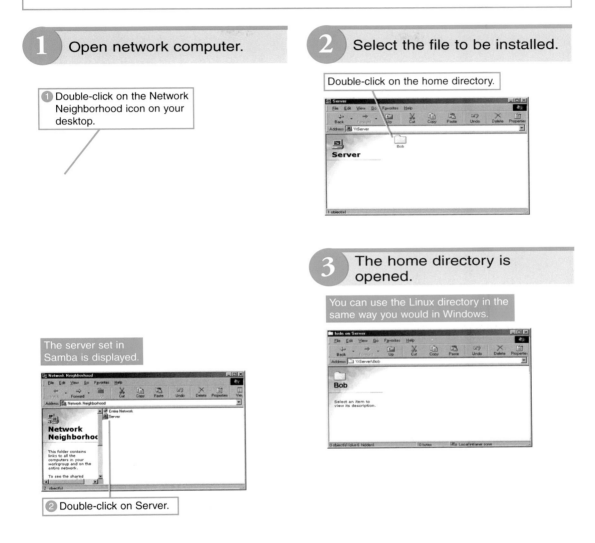

The server set in Samba is displayed.

② Double-click on Server.

2 Select the file to be installed.

Double-click on the home directory.

3 The home directory is opened.

You can use the Linux directory in the same way you would in Windows.

How To Change Passwords

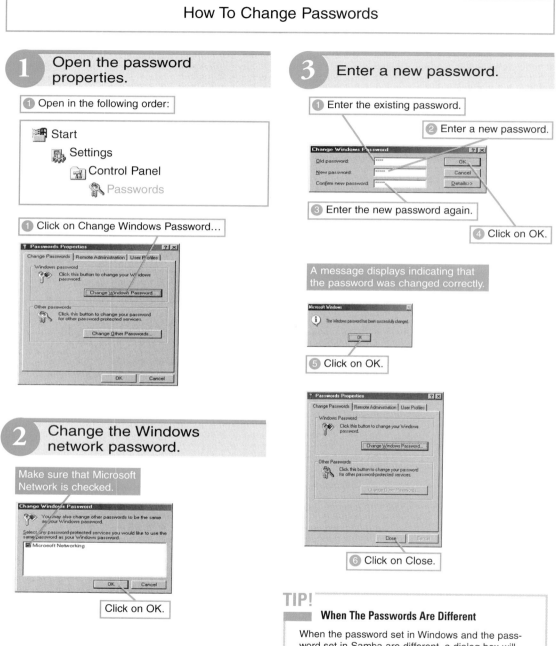

1 Open the password properties.

1 Open in the following order:

🗃 Start
　　🗃 Settings
　　　　🗃 Control Panel
　　　　　　🔑 Passwords

1 Click on Change Windows Password...

2 Change the Windows network password.

Make sure that Microsoft Network is checked.

Click on OK.

3 Enter a new password.

1 Enter the existing password.

2 Enter a new password.

3 Enter the new password again.

4 Click on OK.

A message displays indicating that the password was changed correctly.

5 Click on OK.

6 Click on Close.

TIP!

When The Passwords Are Different

When the password set in Windows and the password set in Samba are different, a dialog box will display asking you to enter one of the two passwords again. If this occurs, make the change by entering either the Windows or Samba password.

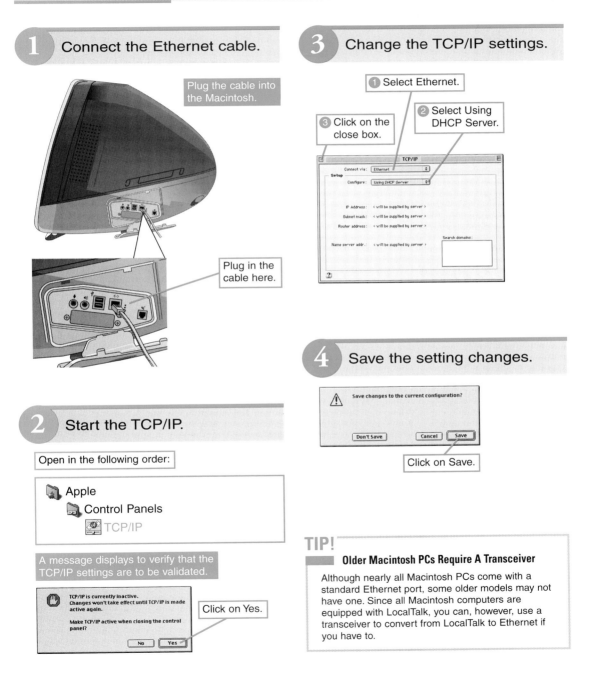

How To Set Up A Macintosh Client

1 Connect the Ethernet cable.

Plug the cable into the Macintosh.

Plug in the cable here.

2 Start the TCP/IP.

Open in the following order:

- Apple
  - Control Panels
    - TCP/IP

A message displays to verify that the TCP/IP settings are to be validated.

TCP/IP is currently inactive.
Changes won't take effect until TCP/IP is made active again.

Make TCP/IP active when closing the control panel?

No   Yes

Click on Yes.

3 Change the TCP/IP settings.

1 Select Ethernet.

2 Select Using DHCP Server.

3 Click on the close box.

TCP/IP

Connect via: Ethernet

Setup
Configure: Using DHCP Server

IP Address: < will be supplied by server >
Subnet mask: < will be supplied by server >
Router address: < will be supplied by server >

Name server addr.: < will be supplied by server >

Search domains:

4 Save the setting changes.

Save changes to the current configuration?

Don't Save   Cancel   Save

Click on Save.

TIP!

Older Macintosh PCs Require A Transceiver

Although nearly all Macintosh PCs come with a standard Ethernet port, some older models may not have one. Since all Macintosh computers are equipped with LocalTalk, you can, however, use a transceiver to convert from LocalTalk to Ethernet if you have to.

213

How To Use A File Server

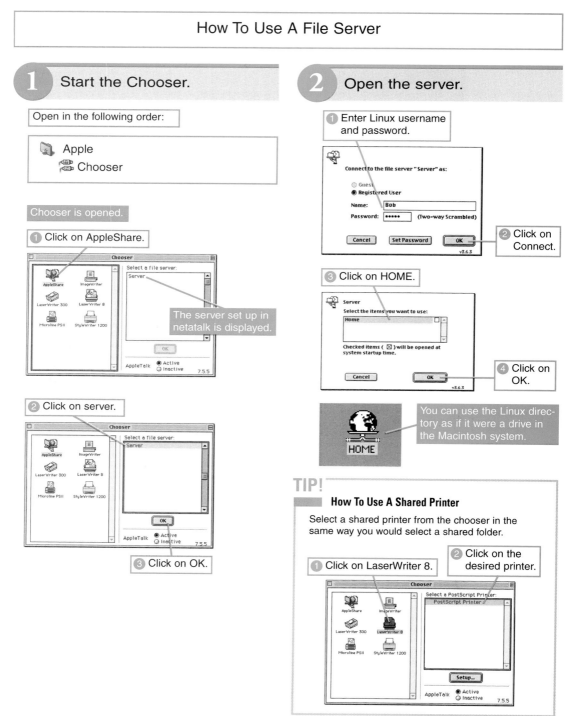

1 Start the Chooser.

Open in the following order:

📁 Apple
   🖥 Chooser

Chooser is opened.

❶ Click on AppleShare.

❷ Click on server.

❸ Click on OK.

2 Open the server.

❶ Enter Linux username and password.

❷ Click on Connect.

❸ Click on HOME.

❹ Click on OK.

You can use the Linux directory as if it were a drive in the Macintosh system.

HOME

TIP!

How To Use A Shared Printer

Select a shared printer from the chooser in the same way you would select a shared folder.

❶ Click on LaserWriter 8.

❷ Click on the desired printer.

How To Install A SCSI Card

1 Exit Linux.

```
[root@server /root]# shutdown -h now⏎
```
Enter the command.

```
The system is halted
System halted
```
Turn off the PC when this message is displayed.

2 Install the SCSI card into the PC.

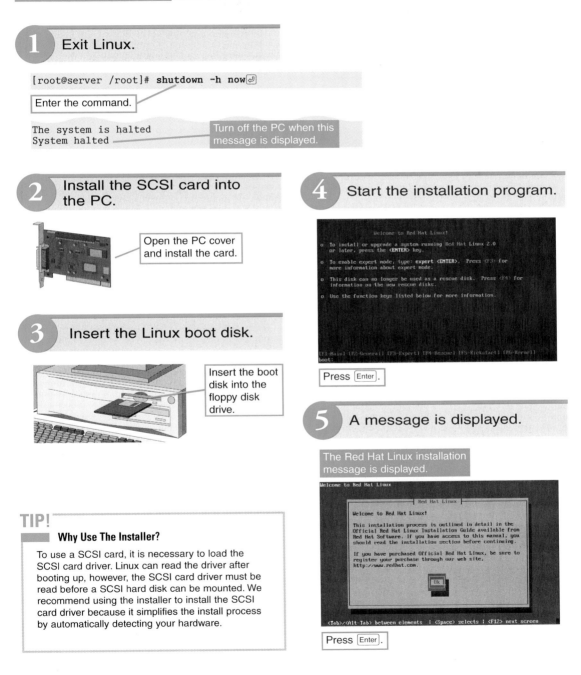

Open the PC cover and install the card.

3 Insert the Linux boot disk.

Insert the boot disk into the floppy disk drive.

4 Start the installation program.

```
                    Welcome to Red Hat Linux!

o  To install or upgrade a system running Red Hat Linux 2.0
   or later, press the <ENTER> key.

o  To enable expert mode, type: expert <ENTER>. Press <F3> for
   more information about expert mode.

o  This disk can no longer be used as a rescue disk. Press <F4> for
   information on the new rescue disks.

o  Use the function keys listed below for more information.



[F1-Main] [F2-General] [F3-Expert] [F4-Rescue] [F5-Kickstart] [F6-Kernel]
boot:
```

Press Enter .

5 A message is displayed.

The Red Hat Linux installation message is displayed.

```
Welcome to Red Hat Linux

                  ┤ Red Hat Linux ├

   Welcome to Red Hat Linux!

   This installation process is outlined in detail in the
   Official Red Hat Linux Installation Guide available from
   Red Hat Software. If you have access to this manual, you
   should read the installation section before continuing.

   If you have purchased Official Red Hat Linux, be sure to
   register your purchase through our web site,
   http://www.redhat.com.

                      ┌──────┐
                      │  Ok  │
                      └──────┘


<Tab>/<Alt-Tab> between elements  |  <Space> selects  |  <F12> next screen
```

Press Enter .

TIP!

Why Use The Installer?

To use a SCSI card, it is necessary to load the SCSI card driver. Linux can read the driver after booting up, however, the SCSI card driver must be read before a SCSI hard disk can be mounted. We recommend using the installer to install the SCSI card driver because it simplifies the install process by automatically detecting your hardware.

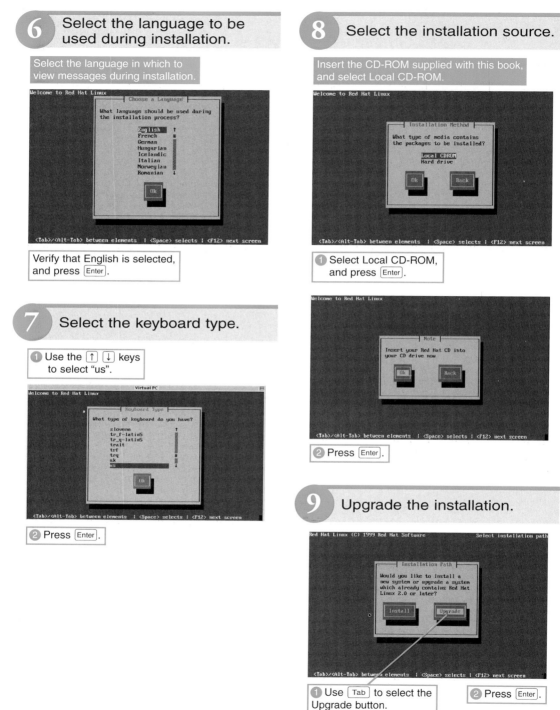

6 Select the language to be used during installation.

Select the language in which to view messages during installation.

Verify that English is selected, and press Enter.

7 Select the keyboard type.

1 Use the ↑ ↓ keys to select "us".

2 Press Enter.

8 Select the installation source.

Insert the CD-ROM supplied with this book, and select Local CD-ROM.

1 Select Local CD-ROM, and press Enter.

2 Press Enter.

9 Upgrade the installation.

1 Use Tab to select the Upgrade button.

2 Press Enter.

10 The system is searched for SCSI cards.

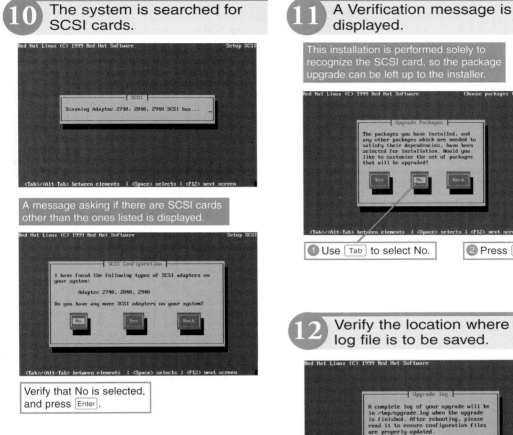

A message asking if there are SCSI cards other than the ones listed is displayed.

Verify that No is selected, and press Enter.

TIP!

If No SCSI Cards Are Recognized

If your SCSI card is not recognized automatically select the card you are using. When a list of corresponding SCSI cards appears; select the current card's driver you are using.

11 A Verification message is displayed.

This installation is performed solely to recognize the SCSI card, so the package upgrade can be left up to the installer.

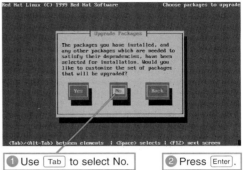

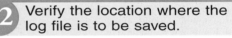

1 Use Tab to select No.   2 Press Enter.

12 Verify the location where the log file is to be saved.

Press Enter.

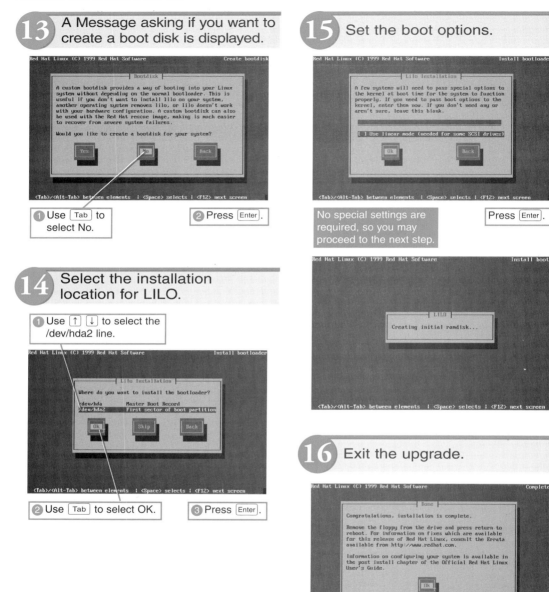

13 A Message asking if you want to create a boot disk is displayed.

Red Hat Linux (C) 1999 Red Hat Software   Create bootdisk

┤ Bootdisk ├

A custom bootdisk provides a way of booting into your Linux system without depending on the normal bootloader. This is useful if you don't want to install lilo on your system, another operating system removes lilo, or lilo doesn't work with your hardware configuration. A custom bootdisk can also be used with the Red Hat rescue image, making is much easier to recover from severe system failures.

Would you like to create a bootdisk for your system?

    Yes   No   Back

<Tab>/<Alt-Tab> between elements | <Space> selects | <F12> next screen

1 Use `Tab` to select No.

2 Press `Enter`.

14 Select the installation location for LILO.

1 Use `↑` `↓` to select the /dev/hda2 line.

Red Hat Linux (C) 1999 Red Hat Software   Install bootloader

┤ Lilo Installation ├

Where do you want to install the bootloader?

/dev/hda   Master Boot Record
/dev/hda2   First sector of boot partition

    Ok   Skip   Back

<Tab>/<Alt-Tab> between elements | <Space> selects | <F12> next screen

2 Use `Tab` to select OK.

3 Press `Enter`.

15 Set the boot options.

Red Hat Linux (C) 1999 Red Hat Software   Install bootloader

┤ Lilo Installation ├

A few systems will need to pass special options to the kernel at boot time for the system to function properly. If you need to pass boot options to the kernel, enter them now. If you don't need any or aren't sure, leave this blank.

[ ] Use linear mode (needed for some SCSI drives)

    Ok   Back

<Tab>/<Alt-Tab> between elements | <Space> selects | <F12> next screen

No special settings are required, so you may proceed to the next step.

Press `Enter`.

Red Hat Linux (C) 1999 Red Hat Software   Install bootl

┤ LILO ├

Creating initial ramdisk...

<Tab>/<Alt-Tab> between elements | <Space> selects | <F12> next screen

16 Exit the upgrade.

Red Hat Linux (C) 1999 Red Hat Software   Complete

┤ Done ├

Congratulations, installation is complete.

Remove the floppy from the drive and press return to reboot. For information on fixes which are available for this release of Red Hat Linux, consult the Errata available from http://www.redhat.com.

Information on configuring your system is available in the post install chapter of the Official Red Hat Linux User's Guide.

    Ok

<Tab>/<Alt-Tab> between elements | <Space> selects | <F12> next screen

Press `Enter`.

Appendix D Command Reference

* Brackets [ ] around a command argument in the syntax sections indicate that the argument is optional and can be omitted.

cd

Changes the current directory.
- Syntax
  cd [*directory name*]
- Commonly used option
  - (hyphen) Change to previous directory.
- Related commands: ls, pwd
- Examples
  cd /etc   Change to /etc.
  cd   Change to home directory.

chgrp

Changes the group owner of a file.
- Syntax
  chgrp *group name   file/directory name*
- Commonly used option
  -R   Changes all files and directories in the specified directory.
- Related commands: chown, chmod, ls

chmod

Changes file permissions.
- Syntax
  chmod *permission setting   file/directory name* ...
- Commonly used option
  -R   Changes all files and directo ries in the specified directory.
- Related commands: chown, chgrp, ls

chown

Changes the owner of a file.
- Syntax
  chown *username[.group name]   file/directory name* ...
- Commonly used option
  -R   Changes all files and directories in the specified directory.
- Related commands: chgrp, chmod, ls

clear

Clears the screen and places the command prompt at the top of the screen.
- Syntax
  clear
- Note
  Pressing Ctrl + L achieves the same results.

cp

Copies files.
- Commonly used options
  -a   Maintains original file permissions as much as possible.
  -i   Asks for confirmation to copy each file.
  -f   If the file already exists at the destination, the copied file overwrites the existing file.
  - Related commands: mv, rm, ls, ln

date

Displays and sets the current time and date.
- Syntax
  date *[string representing date]*
- Related command: rdate
- Note
  Only root can set the date. If no argument is specified, the current time and date displays. If an argument is specified, the time and date is set.

df

Displays the disk capacity used by a file system.
- Syntax
  df *[directory name]*
- Commonly used options
  -k   Displays amounts in kilobytes.
  -h   Displays in an easy-to-understand format.
- Related commands: du, mount, umount, fdisk
- Note
  Executing the df command without specifying a directory displays the disk capacity used by all mounted file systems.

diff

Displays differences in files.
- Syntax
  diff *file1   file2*
- Commonly used options
  -c   Displays the results in a *context output format*.
  -u   Displays the results in a *unified output format*.
  -d   Makes the set of changes as minimal as possible.
  -b   Ignores differences in the number of blank spaces.
  -B   Ignores differences in the number of blank lines.
  -r   If a directory is specified with this option, all files in that directory are compared.
- Note
  The results of diff can be used as a batch file.

dmesg

Displays the kernel log.
- Syntax
  dmesg

du

Displays the disk capacity used by each directory.
- Syntax
  du *[directory name]*
- Commonly used options
  -k   Displays amounts in kilobytes.
  -x   Stays in one file system.
  -s   Displays totals only.
  -S   Displays only the disk capacity used within each directory.
  -h   Displays in an easy-to-understand format.
  -a   Displays all files as well.
- Related command: **df**

find

Searches files.
- Syntax
  find *starting directory conditions*
- Commonly used options
  -name - *file name*   Searches for the file name.
  -size - *number*   Searches for files this size.
  -type - *character*   Searches for or finds matches only with files of this type.
- Note
  When specifying a number (n), [+n] indicates a value greater than n, [n] indicates a value equal to n, and [-n] indicates a value less than n. For the size, appending [c] after the character displays the result in bytes, [k] in kilobytes, and [b] (or nothing at all) will display the result in blocks of 512 bytes. After -type, appending [d] displays directories, [f] displays normal files, and [l] displays symbolic links.

fsck

Checks and repairs file systems.
- Syntax
  fsck *[device name]*
- Commonly used option
  -y   Answers yes to all questions.
- Related commands: **mount, umount, df**
- Note
  When Linux boots, the **fsck** command executes automatically if the drive has been mounted more than 20 times since the last check. Additionally, **fsck** executes automatically if the shutdown command did not execute properly or if a file system error occurs.

fuser

Displays the processes that are using files and file systems and sends a signal.
- Syntax
  fuser *file/directory name*
- Commonly used options
  -l   Displays a list of signals that can be sent.
  -v   Displays details.
  -m   Displays the processes that are using file systems containing specified files and directories.
  -HUP   Sends hang-up signal. Often used when re-reading settings in a daemon.
  -kill   Sends a signal to forcibly quit. Use sparingly, such as when a program refuses to quit.
- Related commands: **mount, umount, kill**
- Note
  If processes are using files within a file system, you cannot unmount the file system. Using the **fuser** command allows you to search for these types of processes and quit them.

grep

Searches within files and displays the results in line units.
- Syntax
  grep character string filename ...
- Commonly used options
  -n   Outputs line numbers.
  -i   Does not distinguish case.
  -v   Displays non-matching lines.
  -w   Searches words.
  -number Displays the specified number of lines both before and after a match.
- Related command: **less**

gzip

Compresses files.
- Syntax
  gzip *file*
  gunzip *file*
- Commonly used option
  -d   Extracts compressed files.
- Note
  The **gzip** command compresses files and then saves them with the extension .gz appended. A function to collect files is not included in **gzip** itself. In Linux, use the **tar** command to collect files. Generally, **tar** will call on **gzip** to compress files.

id

Displays user ID and group ID information.
- Syntax
  id *[username]*
- Related commands: **su, useradd, userdel**
- Note
  If a username is not specified, the user who executes the **id** command will be specified.

kill

Sends a signal to a process.

- Syntax
  kill *process ID*
- Commonly used options
-l	Displays a list of signals that can be sent.
-HUP	Sends hang-up signal. Often used when re-reading settings in a daemon.
-KILL	Sends a signal to forcibly quit. Use sparingly, such as when a program refuses to quit.
-TERM	Sends a signal to quit (default).
- Related commands: **top, ps, pstree, killall**

killall

Sends a signal to a process.

- Syntax
  killall *command name*
- Commonly used options
-l	Displays a list of signals that can be sent.
-HUP	Sends hang-up signal. Often used when re-reading settings in a daemon.
-KILL	Sends a signal to forcibly quit. Use sparingly, such as when a program refuses to quit.
-TERM	Sends a signal to quit (default).
- Related Commands: **top, ps, pstree, kill**
- Note
  The difference between the **killall** command and the **kill** command is that **killall** specifies processes using the command name, while **kill** specifies processes using the process ID (number to specify the process). Each process has a unique ID number, but multiple processes can have the same command name. **killall** sends a signal to all processes having the same command name.

last/lastlog

Displays user login sessions.

- Syntax
  last *[username]*
  lastlog
- Related command: **w**
- Note
  If a username is not specified, the **last** command displays the entire log. If a username is specified, the **last** command displays only the login records for that user. The **lastlog** command displays the time and date of the last login for each user.

less

Displays the contents of a file.

- Syntax
  less *filename* ...
- Key Operations
f, b	Moves up/down one screen.
d, u	Moves up/down half screen.
/, ?	Searches forward/backward.
-i	Search is/is not case-sensitive (toggle).
n, N	Search forward/backward again.
F	Read from the end of the file. (If appended to a file, the file will quickly display.)
v	Starts the vi editor and edits a file.
- Related command: **more**

ln

Creates a link.

- Syntax
  ln *file/directory file/directory*
  ln *file/directory _c. directory*
- Commonly used option
-s	Creates a symbolic link.
- Related commands: **cp, mv, rm, ls**
- Note
  If the -s option is not specified, a hard link is created. Hard links, however, are seldom used.

locate

Searches for files.

- Syntax
  locate *filename*
- Related commands: **find, updatedb**
- Note
  In contrast to the **find** command, which searches all directories, the **locate** command first makes a database of file names, and then searches for file names in the database. Consequently, the **locate** command can search significantly faster than the **find** command.

ls

Displays file names.

- Syntax
  ls *file/directory*
- Commonly used options
-l	Displays in long format.
-F	Displays with the file type appended to the end of the file name.
-a	Displays all files including those starting with a dot (.).
-R	Displays all files and directories in the specified directory.
- Related command: **find**

man

Displays a manual.
- Syntax
  man *[section] name*
- Commonly used option
  -k   Searches titles of manuals.

mount/umount

Mounts and unmounts file systems.
- Syntax
  mount *device name mount point*
  umount *device name or mount point*
- Commonly used option
  -o   Mount option.
  -t   File system type.
- Related commands: **df, fuser, fstab**
- Note
  If you execute the **mount** command without specifying a device name or mount point, the file system currently mounted displays.

mv

Moves files and directories.
- Syntax
  mv *file file/directory*
  mv *file _c directory*
- Commonly used options
  -f   If the file already exists at the destination, the moved file overwrites the existing file.
  -i   Requests user confirmation for each move.
- Note
  The **mv** command can also be used to change file names.

passwd

Changes passwords.
- Syntax
  passwd *[user name]*
- Related commands: **chfn, chsh**
- Note
  Only root can specify usernames. Ordinary users can only change their own passwords.

patch

Applies a patch.
- Syntax
  patch < *file*
- Commonly used option
  -p   Specifies a description of a file name within the patch file.
- Related command: **diff**

ping

Verifies whether a network is connected.
- Syntax
  ping *host name/IP number*
- Note
  When ping is executed, data is sent to the host with a request to return that data as is. The ping display is related to the returned data.

ps

Displays processes.
- Syntax
  ps *[process ID]*
- Commonly used options
  a   Displays processes of all users.
  x   Displays processes not controlled by a terminal.
  u   Displays in username format.
  w   Expands the display width for each line.
  c   Displays only executable file names in the command name column.
- Related commands: **top, pstree, kill, killall**
- Note
  If you execute the **ps** command without specifying a process ID, only the processes of the user who executed the command will display. If a process ID is specified, only the process of the specified process ID will display. You must enter an option after the process ID.

pwd

Displays the current directory.
- Syntax
  pwd
- Related commands: **cd, ls**

reset/resize

Carries out terminal settings.
- Syntax
  eval 'resize'
  reset
- Related commands: **stty**
- Note
  The **resize** command is used to change the size of a window. The **reset** command is used when unintelligible characters are encountered, as when a binary file displays on screen.

rm

Deletes files.
- Commonly used options
  -r   Deletes all files in the current directory.
  -f   Deletes read-only files as well without confirmation.
  -i   Requests user confirmation to delete each file (Red Hat default).
- Related commands: **cp, mv, ln**
- Note
  Deleted files cannot be recovered, so exercise caution when using this command.

shutdown

Quits the system.
- Syntax
  shutdown *[-h:-r] time [message]*
- Commonly used options
  -h   Quit.
  -r   Reboot.
  -c   Cancels a scheduled shutdown.
- Related command: **sync**
- Note
  If you specify "now" in the time option, the shutdown operation begins immediately. A shutdown that has already begun cannot be canceled. If -h or -r are not specified, the system switches to single-user mode. In single-user mode, all services are stopped. Use this command when necessary during administrative tasks.

smbpasswd

Changes passwords in Samba.
- Syntax
  smbpasswd *[username]*
- Commonly used option
  -a   Adds a new user rather than changing the password of an existing user.
- Related commands: **smbstatus, testparm, testprns**
- Note
  Users added by using **smbpasswd -a** must already be registered Linux users.

smbstatus

Display the status of Samba.
- Syntax
  smbstatus
- Related commands: **smbpasswd, testparm, testprns**

sort

Sorts files by line.
- Commonly used options
  -n   Sorts arithmetically.
        (The default is alphabetically.)
  -r   Sorts in reverse order.
  -u   Lines having identical content display only once.
  -b   Ignores leading blank characters.

su

Changes the user ID.
- Syntax
  su *[username]*
- Commonly used options
  -l   Matches environment settings to the user being changed to.
  -m   Matches environment settings to the current user.
  -c *command*   Executes a command.
- Related command: **id**

sync

Writes the cache to the disk.
- Syntax
  sync
- Related commands: **shutdown, df**
- Note
  The **sync** command executes automatically when you remove a mount or shut down the system. Use the **sync** command as often as you want: this can help avoid situations where data remaining in the cache cannot be written to a file.

tar

Collects files (archive).
- Syntax
  tar *option directory*
- Commonly used options
  c   Creates an archive.
  t   Displays a list of files in the archive.
  x   Opens an archive.
  v   Displays the progress of the command.
  f file   Specifies a file.
  z   Uses compression.
- Examples
  tar cvfz bakup-home.tar.gz /home
  tar tvfz aaa.tar.gz
  tar xvfz aaa.tar.gz
- Note
  The **tar** command was originally a tape archive. Consequently, if you do not specify a file name by using the f option, Linux will attempt to send the data to a tape archive.

testparm/testprns

Samba related utilities.
- Syntax
  testparm [smb.conf file]
  testprns *printer name* [printcap *filename*]
- Note
  These utilities are for checking Samba settings. The **testparm** command displays all shared settings. The **testprns** command checks whether a printer has been validated by the Samba printer service.

top

Monitors the status of processes.
- Primary Key Operations

  Space bar   Rewrites the new status.

  u   Displays only specific users
  (enter *username*).

  k   Sends signals
  (enter the process ID and type of signal).

  ?   Displays Help.
- Related commands: **ps, pstree, kill, killall**
- Note

  This command is like repeating the **ps** acux command over and over again with the results displayed continuously on screen. With **ps**, only the current status is displayed. With **top**, however, you can use key operations to send a signal.

touch

Changes the time stamp of a file. If the file does not exist, this command creates a file with a size of 0.
- Syntax

  touch *file*

umask

Specifies the permissions given to a new file or directory when it is created.
- Syntax

  umask   *[umask value]*
- Commonly used umask values

  022   Other users are read-only.

  077   Other users cannot read or write.
- Related commands: **ls, chmod**
- Note

  A umask value sets the initial permissions of a file or directory when it is created. All permissions are open before umask values are set. If a umask value is not specified, the current umask value will display.

useradd/userdel

Creates/deletes users.
- Syntax

  useradd *username*

  useradd -D

  userdel *username*
- Commonly used options

  -g *group*   (useradd) Sets the primary group.

  -p *password*   (useradd) Sets the password.

  -r   (userdel) Deletes the home directory as well.
- Related command: **id**
- Note

  useradd -D sets the default values.

vi

Edits text files.
- Syntax

  vi *file*

w

Displays users who are logged in.
- Syntax

  w

watch

Executes and displays commands at fixed intervals.
- Syntax

  watch *command*
- Commonly used option

  -n *number*   Sets the interval in seconds.
  (The default is two seconds.)
- Related command: **top**
- Note

  Quit by pressing Ctrl + C.

wc

Displays the number of lines, words, and characters in a file.
- Syntax

  wc *file*
- Commonly Used Options

  -l   Displays the number of lines.

  -w   Displays the number of words.

  -c   Displays the number of characters.
- Note

  The default display is: lines, words, characters, and file name.

which

Displays which file will be executed when a command is entered.
- Syntax

  which *command*
- Related commands: **whereis, find, locate**
- Note

  In Linux, if a command does not contain a slash (/) to specify a directory, the default directory path is searched for the executable file. The **which** command displays the location of the file to be executed.

Finding Out Which Commands Are Available

When you want to know which commands are available, enter the first characters of the command and then press [Tab] [Tab] to display the command names that begin with those characters. Pressing only [Tab] [Tab] displays all the commands.

To learn how to use a command, use the man command to view the command's manual. Enter "man *command name*" to display the manual for the command.

We have included the GNU General Public License (GPL) for your reference as it applies to the software this book was about. However, the GPL does not apply to the text of this book.

Version 2, June 1991

Copyright ©1989, 1991 Free Software Foundation, Inc.

59 Temple Place, Suite 330, Boston, MA 02111-1307 USA

Everyone is permitted to copy and distribute verbatim copies of this license document, but changing it is not allowed.

Preamble

The licenses for most software are designed to take away your freedom to share and change it. By contrast, the GNU General Public License is intended to guarantee your freedom to share and change free software--to make sure the software is free for all its users. This General Public License applies to most of the Free Software Foundation's software and to any other program whose authors commit to using it. (Some other Free Software Foundation software is covered by the GNU Library General Public License instead.) You can apply it to your programs, too.

When we speak of free software, we are referring to freedom, not price. Our General Public Licenses are designed to make sure that you have the freedom to distribute copies of free software (and charge for this service if you wish), that you receive source code or can get it if you want it, that you can change the software or use pieces of it in new free programs; and that you know you can do these things.

To protect your rights, we need to make restrictions that forbid anyone to deny you these rights or to ask you to surrender the rights. These restrictions translate to certain responsibilities for you if you distribute copies of the software, or if you modify it.

For example, if you distribute copies of such a program, whether gratis or for a fee, you must give the recipients all the rights that you have. You must make sure that they, too, receive or can get the source code. And you must show them these terms so they know their rights.

We protect your rights with two steps: (1) copyright the software, and (2) offer you this license which gives you legal permission to copy, distribute and/or modify the software.

Also, for each author's protection and ours, we want to make certain that everyone understands that there is no warranty for this free software. If the software is modified by someone else and passed on, we want its recipients to know that what they have is not the original, so that any problems introduced by others will not reflect on the original authors' reputations.

Finally, any free program is threatened constantly by software patents. We wish to avoid the danger that redistributors of a free program will individually obtain patent licenses, in effect making the program proprietary. To prevent this, we have made it clear that any patent must be licensed for everyone's free use or not licensed at all.

The precise terms and conditions for copying, distribution and modification follow.

Terms And Conditions For Copying, Distribution, And Modification

This License applies to any program or other work which contains a notice placed by the copyright holder saying it may be distributed under the terms of this General Public License. The "Program", below, refers to any such program or work, and a "work based on the Program" means either the Program or any derivative work under copyright law: that is to say, a work containing the Program or a portion of it, either verbatim or with modifications and/or translated into another language. (Hereinafter, translation is included without limitation in the term "modification".) Each licensee is addressed as "you".

Activities other than copying, distribution and modification are not covered by this License; they are outside its scope. The act of running the Program is not restricted, and the output from the Program is covered only if its contents constitute a work based on the Program (independent of having been made by running the Program). Whether that is true depends on what the Program does.

1. You may copy and distribute verbatim copies of the Program's source code as you receive it, in any medium, provided that you conspicuously and appropriately publish on each copy an appropriate copyright notice and disclaimer of warranty; keep intact all the notices that refer to this License and to the absence of any warranty; and give any other recipients of the Program a copy of this License along with the Program.
    You may charge a fee for the physical act of transferring a copy, and you may at your option offer warranty protection in exchange for a fee.

2. You may modify your copy or copies of the Program or any portion of it, thus forming a work based on the Program, and copy and distribute such modifications or work under the terms of Section 1 above, provided that you also meet all of these conditions:

a) You must cause the modified files to carry prominent notices stating that you changed the files and the date of any change.

b) You must cause any work that you distribute or publish, that in whole or in part contains or is derived from the Program or any part thereof, to be licensed as a whole at no charge to all third parties under the terms of this License.

c) If the modified program normally reads commands interactively when run, you must cause it, when started running for such interactive use in the most ordinary way, to print or display an announcement including an appropriate copyright notice and a   notice that there is no warranty (or else, saying that you provide a warranty) and that users may redistribute the program under these conditions, and telling the user how to view a copy of this License. (Exception: if the Program itself is interactive but does not normally print such an announcement, your work based on the Program is not required to print an announcement.)

These requirements apply to the modified work as a whole. If identifiable sections of that work are not derived from the Program, and can be reasonably considered independent and separate works in themselves, then this License, and its terms, do not apply to those sections when you distribute them as separate works. But when you distribute the same sections as part of a whole which is a work based on the Program, the distribution of the whole must be on the terms of this License, whose permissions for other licensees extend to the entire whole, and thus to each and every part regard less of who wrote it.

Thus, it is not the intent of this section to claim rights or contest your rights to work written entirely by you; rather, the intent is to exercise the right to control the distribution of derivative or collective works based on the Program.

In addition, mere aggregation of another work not based on the Program with the Program (or with a work based on the Program) on a volume of a storage or distribution medium does not bring the other work under the scope of this License.

3. You may copy and distribute the Program (or a work based on it, under Section 2) in object code or executable form under the terms of Sections 1 and 2 above provided that you also do one of the following:

a) Accompany it with the complete corresponding machine-readable source code, which must be distributed under the terms of Sections 1 and 2 above on a medium customarily used for software interchange; or,

b) Accompany it with a written offer, valid for at least three years, to give any third party, for a charge no more than your cost of physically performing source distribution, a complete machine-readable copy of the corresponding source code, to be distributed under the terms of Sections 1 and 2 above on a medium customarily used for software interchange; or,

c) Accompany it with the information you received as to the offer to distribute corresponding source code. (This alternative is allowed only for noncom mercial distribution and only if you received the program in object code or executable form with such an offer, in accord with Subsection b above.)

The source code for a work means the preferred form of the work for making modifications to it. For an executable work, complete source code means all the source code for all modules it contains, plus any associated interface definition files, plus the scripts used to control compilation and installation of the executable.

However, as a special exception, the source code distributed need not include any thing that is normally distributed (in either source or binary form) with the major components (compiler, kernel, and so on) of the operating system on which the executable runs, unless that component itself accompanies the executable.

If distribution of executable or object code is made by offering access to copy from a designated place, then offering equivalent access to copy the source code from the same place counts as distribution of the source code, even though third parties are not compelled to copy the source along with the object code.

4. You may not copy, modify, sublicense, or distribute the Program except as expressly provided under this License. Any attempt otherwise to copy, modify, sublicense or distribute the Program is void, and will automatically terminate your rights under this License. However, parties who have received copies, or rights, from you under this License will not have their licenses terminated so long as such parties remain in full compliance.

5. You are not required to accept this License, since you have not signed it. However, nothing else grants you permission to modify or distribute the Program or its derivative works. These actions are prohibited by law if you do not accept this License. Therefore, by modifying or distributing the Program (or any work based on the Program), you indicate your acceptance of this License to do so, and all its terms and conditions for copying, distributing or modifying the Program or works based on it.

6. Each time you redistribute the Program (or any work based on the Program), the recipient automatically receives a license from the original licensor to copy, distribute or modify the Program subject to these terms and conditions. You may not impose any further restrictions on the recipients' exercise of the rights granted herein. You are not responsible for enforcing compliance by third parties to this License.

7. If, as a consequence of a court judgment or allegation of patent infringement or for any other reason (not limited to patent issues), conditions are imposed on you (whether by court order, agreement or otherwise) that contradict the conditions of this License, they do not excuse you from the conditions of this License. If you cannot distribute so as to satisfy simultaneously your obligations under this License and any other pertinent obligations, then as a consequence you may not distribute the Program at all. For example, if a patent license would not permit royalty-free redistribution of the Program by all those who receive copies directly or indirectly through you, then the only way you could satisfy both it and this License would be to refrain entirely from distribution of the Program.

    If any portion of this section is held invalid or unenforceable under any particular circumstance, the balance of the section is intended to apply and the section as a whole is intended to apply in other circumstances.
    It is not the purpose of this section to induce you to infringe any patents or other property right claims or to contest validity of any such claims; this section has the sole purpose of protecting the integrity of the free software distribution system, which is implemented by public license practices. Many people have made generous contributions to the wide range of software distributed through that system in reliance on consistent application of that system; it is up to the author/donor to decide if he or she is willing to distribute software through any other system and a licensee cannot impose that choice.

    This section is intended to make thoroughly clear what is believed to be a consequence of the rest of this License.

8. If the distribution and/or use of the Program is restricted in certain countries either by patents or by copyrighted interfaces, the original copyright holder who places the Program under this License may add an explicit geographical distribution limitation excluding those countries, so that distribution is permitted only in or among countries not thus excluded. In such case, this License incorporates the limitation as if written in the body of this License.

9. The Free Software Foundation may publish revised and/or new versions of the General Public License from time to time. Such new versions will be similar in spirit to the present version, but may differ in detail to address new problems or concerns.

   Each version is given a distinguishing version number. If the Program specifies a version number of this License which applies to it and "any later version", you have the option of following the terms and conditions either of that version or of any later version published by the Free Software Foundation. If the Program does not specify a version number of this License, you may choose any version ever published by the Free Software Foundation.

10. If you wish to incorporate parts of the Program into other free programs whose distribution conditions are different, write to the author to ask for permission. For software which is copyrighted by the Free Software Foundation, write to the Free Software Foundation; we sometimes make exceptions for this. Our decision will be guided by the two goals of preserving the free status of all derivatives of our free software and of promoting the sharing and reuse of software generally.

No Warranty

11. BECAUSE THE PROGRAM IS LICENSED FREE OF CHARGE, THERE IS NO WARRANTY FOR THE PROGRAM, TO THE EXTENT PERMITTED BY APPLICABLE LAW. EXCEPT WHEN OTHERWISE STATED IN WRITING THE COPYRIGHT HOLDERS AND/OR OTHER PARTIES PROVIDE THE PROGRAM "AS IS" WITHOUT WARRANTY OF ANY KIND, EITHER EXPRESSED OR IMPLIED, INCLUDING, BUT NOT LIMITED TO, THE IMPLIED WARRANTIES OF MERCHANTABILITY AND FITNESS FOR A PARTICULAR PURPOSE. THE ENTIRE RISK AS TO THE QUALITY AND PERFORMANCE OF THE PROGRAM IS WITH YOU. SHOULD THE PROGRAM PROVE DEFECTIVE, YOU ASSUME THE COST OF ALL NECESSARY SERVICING, REPAIR OR CORRECTION.

12. IN NO EVENT UNLESS REQUIRED BY APPLICABLE LAW OR AGREED TO IN WRITING WILL ANY COPYRIGHT HOLDER, OR ANY OTHER PARTY WHO MAY MODIFY AND/OR REDISTRIBUTE THE PROGRAM AS PERMITTED ABOVE, BE LIABLE TO YOU FOR DAMAGES, INCLUDING ANY GENERAL, SPECIAL, INCIDENTAL OR CONSEQUENTIAL DAMAGES ARISING OUT OF THE USE OR INABILITY TO USE THE PROGRAM (INCLUDING BUT NOT LIMITED TO LOSS OF DATA OR DATA BEING RENDERED INACCURATE OR LOSSES SUSTAINED BY YOU OR THIRD PARTIES OR A FAILURE OF THE PROGRAM TO OPERATE WITH ANY OTHER PROGRAMS), EVEN IF SUCH HOLDER OR OTHER PARTY HAS BEEN ADVISED OF THE POSSIBILITY OF SUCH DAMAGES.

How To Apply These Terms To Your New Programs

If you develop a new program, and you want it to be of the greatest possible use to the public, the best way to achieve this is to make it free software which everyone can redistribute and change under these terms.

To do so, attach the following notices to the program. It is safest to attach them to the start of each source file to most effectively convey the exclusion of warranty; and each file should have at least the "copyright" line and a pointer to where the full notice is found.

```
<one line to give the program's name and a brief idea of what it
does.>
Copyright © 20yy   <name of author>

This program is free software; you can redistribute it and/or
modify it under the terms of the GNU General Public License as
published by the Free Software Foundation; either version 2 of
the License, or (at your option) any later version.

This program is distributed in the hope that it will be useful,
but WITHOUT ANY WARRANTY; without even the implied warranty of
MERCHANTABILITY or FITNESS FOR A PARTICULAR PURPOSE.  See the GNU
General Public License for more details.

You should have received a copy of the GNU General Public License
along with this program; if not, write to the Free Software
Foundation, Inc., 59 Temple Place, Suite 330, Boston, MA
02111-1307   USA
```

Also add information on how to contact you by electronic and paper mail.
If the program is interactive, make it output a short notice like this when it starts in an interactive mode:

```
Gnomovision version 69, Copyright © 20yy name of author
Gnomovision comes with ABSOLUTELY NO WARRANTY; for details type
'show w'. This is free software, and you are welcome to redis-
tribute it under certain conditions; type `show c' for details.
```

The hypothetical commands 'show w' and 'show c' should show the appropriate parts of the General Public License. Of course, the commands you use may be called something other than 'show w' and 'show c'; they could even be mouse-clicks or menu items--whatever suits your program.

You should also get your employer (if you work as a programmer) or your school, if any, to sign a "copyright disclaimer" for the program, if necessary. Here is a sample; alter the names:

```
Yoyodyne, Inc., hereby disclaims all copyright interest in the
program 'Gnomovision' (which makes passes at compilers) written
by James Hacker.

<signature of Ty Coon>, 1 April 1989
Ty Coon, President of Vice
```

This General Public License does not permit incorporating your program into proprietary programs. If your program is a subroutine library, you may consider it more useful to permit linking proprietary applications with the library. If this is what you want to do, use the GNU Library General Public License instead of this License.

■ Glossary

Number

10Base-T
100Base-TX
See Ethernet.

A

Absolute path
See path.

Access rights
See permissions.

Address
Number or name for specifying another device location. On the Internet, an address is a number called an IP address used to specify a computer or device. An email address is a character string that specifies a destination for email.
See also email and IP address.

Administrator, admin
See also root and user.

Alias
Refers to defining another name for a command in Linux. On a Macintosh system, a symbolic link to a file is called an alias.
See also symbolic link and command.

Apache
Name of the most widely used Web server in the world.
URL: **www.apache.org**
See also Web.

AppleTalk
Set of information exchange rules used when a Macintosh system communicates via, for example, Ethernet or LocalTalk.
See also netatalk.

Archiver / archive
An archiver refers to a program that collects numerous files and places them in one file and a file created by an archiver is called an archive. The archiver most often used in Linux is tar. Archivers often used in Windows are WinZip and lha, and Stuffit in Macintosh. All these programs have a compression utility. In Linux the archiver and compression software are considered to be separate programs and in many cases an archive file is compressed separately.
See also compress.

Argument
See command.

B

Back up
Saving and storage of data at a separate location to prevent catastrophic data loss due to software and/or hardware failure.

Boot disk
A floppy disk used when loading a PC OS.

Boot manager
A program that allows you to select a bootable OS during a system boot.

Broadcast address
An IP address that is used for communication between all devices in a network.
See also IP address, and network address.

Bug
An error in a program.

C

Cascade
See hub.

CF
Program to create a settings file (sendmail.cf) for sendmail.
See also sendmail.

Command
Called a command line in Linux, the command line forms the core interface where character strings (commands) are input and results returned. Using spaces after commands on the command line allows character strings called arguments to be passed to commands. From among the arguments, an option is the device that influences the way a command operates. When using many options for a Linux command, specify the options by continuing one character after a hyphen (-) or continuing the character string after a double hyphen (--). However, an exception is the ps command (a (-) is not prepended) and the tar command (a (-) need not be prepended).

Compile / compiler

Compiling is the operation to convert source code into an executable file. A compiler is a program that translates source code into an executable file. In Linux the compiler command is make.
See also source, make, GNU.

Compress

Refers to reducing the size of data. Returning the data to its original state is called *extraction*. In Linux, the compression program mainly used is gzip.

Cross cable

A cable for directly connecting two PCs.
See also straight cable and Ethernet.

Current directory

Refers to the present location within the file hierarchy. The current directory is indicated by a period and a slash (./). The directory just after logging in is the home directory. The home directory is the directory from which user operations initially start.
See also directory and path.

D

Daemon

A program executed during the boot of Linux and that continues to run and control/process services.
See also server / service.

Default

A fixed value that is assumed if nothing is specified. The default value can also be changed.

Development environment

A set of files and programs needed to create programs. Even if you don't create programs, it will be necessary to compile programs from source in order to install software. The main development environment used in Linux is GNU.
See also compiler, source, make, and GNU.

Device

A piece of peripheral equipment. Hard drives, keyboards and mice are peripheral equipment devices. Device names are attached to each device. In Linux, files exist that correspond to devices, and access to the devices is made through these files. The file name of the file that corresponds to a device is the device name, and these files are always placed in the /dev directory.

Device name

See device.

DHCP (Dynamic Host Configuration Protocol)

Method to automatically handle the network settings of an operating PC (such as IP address or netmask).
See also IP address and netmask.

Directory

A location where files are placed, equivalent to a folder in Macintosh and Windows systems. In Linux, there is one large directory structure and the root of that structure is called the root directory and is represented by a slash (/). Files and other directories are placed within a directory. To represent that directory B is contained within directory A, directory B is called a subdirectory of A or, in contrast, A is called the parent directory of B. A parent directory is represented by two periods and a slash (../).
See also user, current directory, and path.

Distribution

See kernel and Linux.

Driver

A driver is a piece of software necessary to use hardware (device driver).

Domain name

See host name.

Dual speed hub

See hub.

E

Email

A method to transfer messages across a network.
See also sendmail, SMTP, qpopper, and POP.

Ethernet

Communications protocol and hardware that enable two or more computers to share information. Divided into two types: 10Base with a maximum data transfer speed of 10Mbits/sec and 100Base with a maximum data transfer speed of 10Mbits/sec. There are many cables and connection methods but 10Base-T and 100Base-TX are mainly used, which utilize a modular type telephone jack for the connections. *See also* LAN.

Extended partition

See partition.

F

fdisk

Name of a program to set disk partitions.
See also partition.

File server

A server that manages files. *See also* share / sharing.

File sharing
See share / sharing.

File system
A structure that defines access to files. Linux uses many different file systems. ext2 is mainly used for Linux, iso9660 is used for CD-ROMs, and vfat is used for Windows. When mounting a disk using the mount command, append a -t option to specify a file system or specify a file system by using the fstab command.
See also mount.

Folder
See directory.

FSF (Free Software Foundation)
See GNU.

fstab
Settings file in which information is written about file systems to be loaded automatically during the boot procedure.
See mount and file system.

FTP (File Transfer Protocol)
Communication conventions used when transferring files in a TCP/IP network.
See also HTTP.

G

GNU
A freely distributed and changeable software development project. GNU (short for GNU's Not Unix) software is distributed by the FSF (Free Software Foundation). All distributions of Linux make use of many GNU software packages such as compilers, basic commands and editors. A GPL (General Public License) is a software license that defines the GNU software, which protects the freedom to re-distribute and change the code. The Linux kernel is also distributed based on GPL.
URL: **www.gnu.org**

GPL (General Public License)
See GNU and source.

Group
A unit used when collecting and managing rights of numerous users. There are groups for files and directories and access rights of users belonging to these groups can be set. Moreover, users must belong to one or more groups, and the grouping to which they initially belong is called the primary group. All users are set to belong to the primary group.
See also permissions.

Group owners
Used to manage permissions of files and directories of group owners. Group owner file permissions are set in the file to group owners belonging to the primary user group. The group owner settings of a file can be changed using the chown or chgrp command.
See also group and permissions.

H

Hidden files
A file whose file name begins with a period (.). Hidden files are mainly placed in the home directory as settings files of individual users. Hidden files will not be displayed if an -a option is not appended to the ls command. Because these hidden files are not displayed by the ls command, they will not be a nuisance.

Home directory
See current directory.

Host name
A character string that represents the name of a computer. A host name is expressed by using a combination of alphanumeric characters and hyphens (-). A domain name is a character string that represents the system to which the address belongs. Alphanumeric characters and hyphens are used for domain names and separated by dots (.). Even larger names can be made by appending characters to the end of a string. You can also express domain and host names by appending a dot.
See also IP address.

HTTP (Hypertext Transfer Protocol)
Communication conventions used when transferring Web pages in a TCP/IP network.
See also FTP and Web.

Hub
A device for connecting PCs by Ethernet. There are different types of hubs, including: hubs that transmit only a given speed in a network, dual speed hubs that correspond to both 10BaseT / 100BaseTX, and switching hubs that regulate the transmission of information to increase network efficiency. A special port is sometimes attached to a hub, allowing the network to be expanded by connecting this port to another hub. This is known as cascading.
See also Ethernet.

I

ID (identifier)
Used to distinguish between various similarities. In Linux, ID is managed by using numbers. This includes process Ids, user Ids and group IDs.
See also process, user, and group.

IDE (Integrated Drive Electronics)
A standard for connecting peripheral devices such as hard disks and CD-ROMs to PCs.
See also SCSI.

Index file
A file displayed when specifying a directory in a URL on the Web. Many of these files include index.html, index.htm or default.htm. These file names can be freely set on a Web server.
See also Apache and Web.

Internet
A worldwide network of networks. A network connects computers and devices, and the Internet connects networks. The communication protocol used on the Internet is TCP/IP.
See intranet.

IP address
An address for detecting computers in a network. Uses numbers from 0 to 255 organized in four groups, separated by a period (.), which is called dotted quad notation. In this book, for example, the IP address 192.168.1.1 was set to the Linux server.
See also netmask and broadcast address.

ISA (Industry Standard Architecture)
A standard for connecting peripheral devices such as network cards and SCSI cards to a PC.
See also PCI and PCMCIA.

iso9660
See file system.

K

Kernel
The portion of code that forms the core of an OS. As introduced in this book, Linux is the name of a kernel. Additionally, it is also used with systems that utilize a Linux kernel. When installing Linux, you install what is known as distribution. Here, "distribution" is a system comprising a set of a kernel, basic commands, and applications. In this book, a method is introduced to set up a server using a distribution called Red Hat Linux.
See also Linux.

L

LAN (Local Area Network)
Two or more computers in relatively close proximity to each other (same building), connected in such a way that they can share information.
See also Ethernet.

Library
A file consisting of various collected program parts.

LILO (Linux Loader)
See also boot manager.

Link
See symbolic link.

Linux
A Unix-based OS. This book describes how to set up a server by using Linux. Linux is actually the name of the kernel that forms the core of the OS. Note that in many cases, Linux is used to refer to systems that use the Linux kernel.
See also kernel.

LocalTalk
Name of a port in a Macintosh system that connects printers and other peripherals.
See also AppleTalk.

Log
The log is a record of daemon and kernel operations.
See also daemon and kernel.

Log in
Refers to a situation when the user begins work. In Windows, logging in is called logging on.
See also log out.

Log out
Refers to a situation when the user completes work. In Windows, logging out is called logging off.
See also log in.

Logical partition
See partition.

M

Mail address
A character string that represents the sender and recipient of mail. If a mail address is broken down, the right side of the at symbol (@) represents the address of the system to which the address belongs and the left side of the (@) represents the address within the system (name of user that corresponds to the mail address).
See also address.

make

The make command executes a procedure to write to a file named "Makefile". The make command is often used to compile programs so many people say "make" when referring to the compiling of a program.
See also compile and development environment.

Mode

The word "mode" has many meanings. For example, the "mode of a file" indicates permissions. A "vi mode" indicates the state of the vi editor (input mode / edit mode).
See also vi and permissions.

Mount

Linking a file system to a specified directory. In Linux, one large directory structure is used. When a hard drive or CD-ROM is initially used, it will link to one portion of this large structure.
See also file system.

N

NE2000 compatible

An NE2000 compatible card is a network card that can be used by Linux. NE2000 compatibility is defined as having functions compatible with the standards of a network card named NE2000.
See also Ethernet and network card.

netatalk

The name of a server that provides sharing services with a Macintosh system.
URL: **www.umich.edu/~rsug/netatalk**
See also AppleTalk.

NetBIOS

A protocol to allow Windows systems to communicate in a TCP/IP network. A name used by NetBIOS to distinguish PCs and peripherals is a "NetBIOS name."
See also TCP/IP.

Netmask

A figure for dividing addresses of an entire network and addresses within a network.
See also network address, broadcast address, and IP address.

Network

A network connects computers and allows communication.

Network address

An address that indicates the entire network.
See also network address, broadcast address, and IP address.

Network card

An expansion card for connecting a network. Also called an Ethernet card, LAN card and a NIC (network interface card).
See also Ethernet and LAN.

nobody

A system defined user name. Although it is possible to su nobody, this user doesn't actually exist as such, and it isn't generally possible to log on with the user name "nobody". The name nobody is used in Linux when it's necessary to have a user with the lowest possible access rights.
See also user.

NT domain (Windows NT Domain)

Range in which users who Login to a network in Windows are managed. *See also* workgroup.

O

Open source

URL: **www.opensource.org**
See source.

Option

See command.

OS (Operating System)

Fundamental software program for using a computer. An OS allocates resources of the computer to users and processes.

Owner

A user that corresponds to a file used to manage permissions of files and directories. Usually, the user who created the file becomes the owner of the file. The owner of a file can be changed by using the "chown" command.
See also user and permissions.

P

Package

In Linux, a package is a format that allows software to be quickly and easily installed.

Parent directory

See directory.

Partition

A region on a hard drive. On PC/AT compatible machines the following restrictions exist when creating partitions due to limitations of MS-DOS. There can be a maximum of four primary partitions. When setting more than four primary partitions, from among the primary partitions, one partition will be set to an extended partition, and the extended partition will be divided into a several logical partitions.

Password

A key to access a computer. During log in on Linux, the user name and password typed verify the user.
See also user and log in.

Path

A route followed to a file. Directories in a path are separated by (/). The path that starts from the root directory (/) is called an absolute path, and paths that start from current directories other than the root directory are called relative paths.
See also directory.

Patch

A revision for text files. Often used to revise source files. Moreover, "patch" is also a name of a program to apply a patch.
See also text file.

PCI (Peripheral Component Interconnect)

A standard for connecting peripheral devices such as network cards and SCSI cards to a PC.
See also ISA and PCMCIA.

PCMCIA

A standard for connecting peripheral devices such as network cards and SCSI cards, to a PC. Used mainly for notebook PCs. Originally, the name of an organization (Personal Computer Memory Card International Association) that managed standards but now, it mostly concerns the use of slots or cards.
See also ISA and PCI.

Permissions

Access rights to files and directories. In Linux, you can set whether or not to allow reading, writing, and executing for three types of users; owners, groups, and other users. Also called file attributes and file modes.
See also user and group.

POP (Post Office Protocol)

Communication method for sending your email located on a mail server to another address in a TCP/IP network.
See also qpopper and SMTP.

Port

A port of a hub is an inlet for connecting cable connectors. Moreover, in TCP/IP, another location is specified by an IP address, and a service is specified by a port number.
See also hub, IP address, and server / service.

PostScript

Name of a programming language for printing using a printer. Printers that correspond to the PostScript language are called PostScript printers.

Primary group

See group.

Primary partition

See partition.

Printer sharing

See share / sharing.

Private address

An IP address that cannot be used on the Internet. It is recommended to use private addresses on an intranet. The range of private addresses can be: 10.0.0.0 – 10.255.255.255 (a network that has 16,277,216 addresses X 1), 172.16.0.0 – 172.31.255.255 (65,536 X 16), and 192.168.0.0 – 192.168.255.255 (256 X 256). The instructions introduced in this book on how to set up a network used addresses of 192.168.1.0 – 192.168.1.255.
See also IP address, Internet, and intranet.

Process

An executed program running on an OS. Each process is managed by an integer value called a process ID. When a program is executed, a process is created and a process ID assigned. At this time, processes that have identical process IDs cannot exist simultaneously. When the execution completes, the process is deleted.
See also program.

Program

Computer code that can be executed (run) on a computer. Almost all programs are saved in files.
See also process.

Prompt

A character string displayed on screen, such as a command line for eliciting input. In addition to the command line prompt displayed by the shell, there is also a login prompt and a LILO prompt during the boot sequence.
See also command.

Pseudo tty (virtual terminal)

A virtual terminal allows identical operations from another networked PC as if you were using a PC with Linux directly installed on it. A Linux screen emulated by an application such as telnet is called a virtual terminal (pseudo tty).

Q

qpopper

Name of a POP server introduced in this book.
URL: **www.eudora.com/freeware**
See POP.

R

Red Hat
Company that produces a Linux distribution and is also the name of the distribution. Red Hat Linux CD-ROM is available for purchase.
URL: **www.redhat.com**
See also Linux and distribution.

Relative path
See path.

root
User who administers a Linux system. Also called a super user. Root is a user who is not restricted by Linux security. For example, permissions attached to files and directories are not valid for root. The root user can read and write all files and directories.
See also user.

Root directory
See directory.

rpm (Red Hat Package Manager)
Name and file format of a Red Hat Linux package (a software format that allows quick installations). Also the name command for operating rpm files.
See also Red Hat.

S

Samba
Name of a server that provides sharing services with a Windows system in Linux.
URL: **www.samba.org**
See also share / sharing.

SCSI
Small Computer System Interface. A standard for connecting peripheral devices such as hard drives and CD-ROMs to a PC. Pronounced "scuzzy."
See also IDE.

sendmail
Name of an e-mail delivery server introduced in this book.
URL: **www.sendmail.org**
See also SMTP and server / service.

Server / service
A service provides some type of useful service or utility to other computers, and a server is a program that provides these services. In this book a dhcpd server that provides DHCP services and a Samba server that provides sharing services with Windows were introduced.
See also daemon and network.

Share / sharing
Sharing refers to the ability to access to files and directories from separate computers on a network. In this book, software called Samba and netatalk are used to share files and printers located on a Linux server from Windows and Macintosh systems.
See also Samba and netatalk.

Short cut
See symbolic link.

shutdown
Stopping the system. When exiting Linux, rebooting or turning OFF the power, a correct shutdown procedure must be executed. This happens because there is a chance that data may be lost before being written to the disk if the power is suddenly turned OFF.

SMTP
Simple Mail Transfer Protocol. Set of communication rules for delivering email under TCP/IP.
See also email and sendmail.

Source
A text file written by a person when creating a program. The execution procedure of a program is written in source. Compiling a source file produces an executable file. It was often the case that source was the property of developers only. Due to the success of Linux and (to a greater degree) GNU/FSF, however, great interest developed in the idea of making source publicly available and allowing all interested people to develop programs (open source).
See also Linux and Apache.

Source file
See source.

Source list
See source.

Spool
A location where data is temporarily stored when sending data to another device or program. In Linux, the data is often placed in the /var/spool and /usr/spool directories. The spool is used to store mail not yet received and data sent to a printer.

Straight cable
A cable for connecting a PC and a hub by Ethernet.
See also cross cable and Ethernet.

su (substitute user / switch user)
Command to change user IDs. The default reverts to root.
See also user and root.

Subdirectory
See directory.

Super user
See root and user.

Symbolic link
A file that indicates a file located at another separate location. When a symbolic link is accessed, the file indicated by the symbolic link will be accessed. In Macintosh and Windows these same types of links are called an "alias" and a "shortcut," respectively.

Swap
A file or disk partition used by the operationg system to give the impression of having more memory than is physically present. A hard drive partition is often used as swap space.
See also partition.

Switching hub
See hub.

T

TCP/IP (Transmission Control Protocol / Internet Protocol
A communication method widely used on the Internet.
See also Internet and intranet.

Text file
The simplest document file format in which only character information is written. Text files do not depend on specific applications and have many uses, such as settings files and program source. Text files in Linux are handled in the same manner as Windows and Macintosh, although the Return/Enter key codes are different.
See also source.

U

Uncompress (extract)
See compress.

Unix family OS
Unix was initially developed in the Bell laboratories of AT&T in 1971. Since then, it has developed into various forms and presently many varieties of Unix-based systems are being developed. These systems are part of the Unix family OS. The Linux program was written from scratch, but was modeled after the Unix family OS.
See also Linux and OS.

User
An individual registered to use Linux. A user is the basic unit in Linux when managing permissions.
See also root, permissions, and group.

V

vfat
See file system.

vi
Name of a screen editor. Used to edit text files.
See also text file.

W

Web
Refers to the World Wide Web, also called WWW. It is called a Web because pages located in the Internet are joined by links like a spider web. Presently, the Web is the name used to refer to the Internet as a whole and currently an approximate 70% of the data flowing through the Internet is said to be related to the Web.

Windows NT
Name of a network OS produced by Microsoft.
See also Samba.

Workgroup
A unit that manages a computer on a network in Windows.
See also NT domain.

WWW (World Wide Web)
See Web.
See also IP address and network address.

Index